Creating an Effective Public Sector

This book offers an in-depth look at developing effectiveness in the public sector and how to achieve the best possible outcomes for people rather than just good or efficient outputs.

In 15 comprehensive chapters, the authors present structured ideas and practical approaches for achieving a more effective public sector. The book sets out a framework for visualising success in complex situations with multiple stakeholders. Topics include how you stimulate change and influence people to adopt changes, how you manage politics, set targets and standards, and measure them, and how you create a culture of high performance with a focus on getting the right things done. Effectiveness does not arise from excellence in one area alone and the book weaves together ideas on leadership, managing expectations, and keeping focus on the longer term.

Creating an Effective Public Sector will be of interest to decision makers in the public sector, project managers working on central and local government projects, and senior civil servants. It will also be invaluable for advanced undergraduate and post-graduate students studying in the fields of government, project management, and public-sector management.

Mike Bourne is Professor of Business Performance at Cranfield University where he is Director of the Centre for Business Performance. He chairs the Performance Measurement Association and is Director of the Infrastructure and Project Authority's (Cabinet Office and Treasury) Performance Leadership Programme (PLP) that has engaged more than 1,200 senior public servants. He is a lead on the subject of governance for Project X (the collaboration between academia and government, working towards better project delivery). He has a PhD from the University of Cambridge and speaks internationally on the theme of organisational performance.

Pippa Bourne is a Visiting Fellow at Cranfield School of Management and Director of Bourne Performance, a consultancy helping organisations to achieve higher levels of performance. Her particular interest is the relationship between the culture of the organisation and its performance. She has many years of practical experience working in Higher Education and professional organisations managing the relationships between different groups of people to create effective organisations. Most recently, she has been involved in research with a group of universities interviewing those involved in major government projects in the US and the UK. She has an MBA and has completed a certificate in Coaching at the University of Cambridge's Institute for Continuing Education.

Creating an Effective Public Sector

Mike Bourne and Pippa Bourne

Routledge
Taylor & Francis Group

LONDON AND NEW YORK

Cover image: © Getty Images

First published 2022
by Routledge
4 Park Square, Milton Park, Abingdon, Oxon OX14 4RN

and by Routledge
605 Third Avenue, New York, NY 10158

Routledge is an imprint of the Taylor & Francis Group, an informa business

© 2022 Mike Bourne and Pippa Bourne

British Library Cataloguing-in-Publication Data
A catalogue record for this book is available from the British Library

Library of Congress Cataloging-in-Publication Data
Names: Bourne, Pippa, author. | Bourne, Mike, author.
Title: Creating an effective public sector / Mike Bourne & Pippa Bourne.
Description: New York : Routledge, 2022. | Includes bibliographical references and index. |
Identifiers: LCCN 2021046529 | ISBN 9780367566609 (Hardback) |
ISBN 9780367569174 (Paperback) | ISBN 9781003099895 (eBook)
Subjects: LCSH: Public administration. | Performance—Management. |
Employee motivation. | Organizational effectiveness.
Classification: LCC JF1338.A2 B638 2022 | DDC 351—dc23/
eng/20220112
LC record available at https://lccn.loc.gov/2021046529

ISBN: 9780367566609 (hbk)
ISBN: 9780367569174 (pbk)
ISBN: 9781003099895 (ebk)

DOI: 10.4324/9781003099895

Typeset in Adobe Garamond Pro
by codeMantra

Contents

Illustrations

Figures

Tables

Preface

The Covid-19 pandemic has brought the public sector into sharp focus in countries around the world. Within weeks, days even, government- and public-sector bodies had to work together to protect citizens from the virus, whether that was health services ramping up their capability to deal with unprecedented numbers of highly infectious patients, police forces implementing lockdowns, or local councils finding new ways to deal with essential business such as education and social care, whilst respecting social distancing rules.

For many citizens, the public sector has been an entity, probably not well understood, that operates in the background quietly providing the infrastructure for everyday living, such as the emptying of bins, the education of children, and the lighting of roads. Within a very short period of time that has changed. The power of the government and the public sector to affect the way we live and to protect us has become clear. That makes it even more apparent how important it is that the public sector is as effective as it can be.

Creating an effective public sector is an enormous subject. The public sector itself is complex. According to the UK's Office for National Statistics' figures for December 2019 (even before the Covid pandemic), some 5.6 m people were employed in the public sector. This represents over 16% of people in paid employment. It comprises many disparate groups, from civil servants working centrally to the military, from emergency services to social care, and many more. Each is different and has its own characteristics. Added to this, the public sector has complex relationships with the private sector, with charities (who often provide much needed services) and, not least, with citizens who pay for everything. Then, of course, there is the structure of elected representatives who lead policy and paid employees who provide advice and carry out the work. How can it be possible to establish any guidance on achieving effectiveness in such a complex situation?

We believe there are some key constructs that shine a light on how effectiveness can be achieved. There are tools that can be used and adapted to suit different circumstances. There are ways of working which create an environment that is conducive to promoting successful outcomes. In this book we set out what these approaches are, the visible and tangible tools such as performance management systems, and the less visible and perhaps even more important, such as communication, leadership, and management of change.

This is not a book about Politics, although the relationship and communication between politicians and paid employees cannot be ignored. It is a book which we hope will help provide not only food for thought but also practical guidance to those working in the public sector, a number of whom we know and admire.

References

ONS Report (2019) "Public Sector Employment," *ONS*, December, https://www.ons.gov.uk/employmentandlabourmarket/peopleinwork/publicsectorpersonnel/bulletins/publicsectoremployment/latest

Acknowledgements

We are most grateful to people who supported us in the writing of this book, and who agreed to be interviewed, not all of whom wanted to be named.

Nick Alston, former Police and Crime Commissioner for Essex
Patricia Atkins, Former Teacher
Ed Balls, former Cabinet Minister and now Professor of Political Economy at King's College, London
Jamie Banks, Director, Anglia Business Resources
Anthony Browne MP
Rt Hon Liam Byrne MP
Tom Carter, Headteacher, King Edward VI Grammar School, Chelmsford
Graeme Hawkins-Dady, Former Teacher
Mark Hawkins-Dady, Editor and Author
Katie Davis, Speaker on the Project Leadership Programme at Cranfield University
Mark Evans, former Chief Inspector
Graham Farrant, Chief Executive, BCP Council
Barbara Follet, Former Member of Parliament for Stevenage
Elayne Grimes, Senior Consultant, Stantec
John Healey MP
Sir Bernard Jenkin MP, formerly the Commons Chair of the Public Administration Select Committee
Javed Khan, former Chief Executive Barnardo's
Chris Manners, song maker, Singer and Guitarist and formerly Regional Director, ICAEW
Andy Reed OBE, former MP and now Director, Saje Impact
Pat Smith, Company Director, former Director of EEIDB, provider of Business Link Services,
Canon Dr John Spence CBE DL, Councillor, Essex County Council
Chief Superintendent Mick Stamper
Sharon Taylor OBE, Leader, Stevenage Borough Council
Marcus Warnes, Accountable Officer, Staffordshire and Stoke-on-Trent CCG

Tom Wheatley, Governor, HM Prison, Wakefield

Rob Whiteman, Chief Executive, The Chartered Institute of Public Finance & Accountancy, formerly Chief Executive of UK Border Agency

Paul Winter, Deputy Director of Corporate Governance, Compliance and Data Protection, NHS Staffordshire, and Stoke-on-Trent CCGs

Our friends and colleagues from the Centre for Business Performance at Cranfield School of management, Abdelkader Aoufi, Rick Forster, Monica Franco-Santos, Andrey Pavlov, and our support Team Michell Steele, Emma Shrimpton, and Sue Wilson; former friends and colleagues, Andy Neely, Pietro Micheli, Jutta Tobias Mortlock, Veronica Martinez, Mike Kennerley, Mark Wilcox, Laszlo Torjai.

Mike's past and current doctoral candidates, Mark Baker, Mike Lauder, Ingo Fortenliecher, Khalid Al Akwa, Daniele Tumidei, Richard Allen, Abdulah Aldhafer, Jack Chivers, Hassan Deria, Ishwinder Singh, Akin Soname, Dan Stull, Fritz Wiegle, and our visitors, Martin Parr. Patrick Hoverstadt, David Anker, Sarah Coleman, Dina Gray, Amadeo Watkins, Andre de Waal, Glenn Chambers Terry Cooke-Davis, and our other colleagues from Cranfield University Peter Allen, Mark Jenkins.

Friends and colleagues from the AEI Group and the Project leadership Programme, John Algar, Peter Thornton, Kim Turnbull-James, Steve Carver, Elmar Kutsch, Neil Turner, David Denyer, Keith Goffin, Sherry Davison, Val Bickerton, Tracy O'Neil, including those currently and formerly with PA Consulting Tony Wood, Tom Smith, Barbara Bradley, and The Project Academy, Paul Erricker, Laura Tailorson.

Mike's former friends and colleagues from Cambridge IfM John Mills, Ken Platts, Huw Richards, Mike Gregory, Gerry Frizell.

Our close collaborators on Project X (Better Government projects)

Richard Kirkham, Terry Williams, Hang Vo, Terri Harrington, Jo Bradshaw, and Mike's friends and colleagues from the wider academic community Umit Bititci, Nigel Slack, Jill MacBryde, Andre Bellisario, Paul Van veen-Dirks, Mike Lewis, David Otley, Steve Melnick, Matteo Mura, Lorenzo Lucianetti, and Oliver Krauser.

Introduction

Being effective sounds as if it should be common sense, but in reality, it is hard to achieve and one person's effectiveness may not necessarily be the same as another's, depending on their perception of the world.

We will describe what we mean by effectiveness in more detail in the next section, but in essence it is about achieving the best possible outcome through a series of actions and through efficient use of resources.

In this introduction, we give an overview of how we see the various ingredients that comprise the recipe for effectiveness and how they blend together. As any good cook knows, there is more to creating a truly delicious cake than simply following the recipe. Ingredients differ slightly, depending on their source, every oven is a little different and the way the mixture is beaten will govern how much air is retained and how light the cake will be. When the cake is eventually eaten, some people will adore it, some will think it is too sweet, and others will think there is not enough sugar. And before you start making the cake everyone will have a different view on the best way of achieving results. Even the simple process of making a cake from a written set of instructions is less straightforward than it looks. So, the first point to make is that there is no failsafe recipe. But there are guidelines and pointers to how you can achieve a good outcome.

We begin the book by looking at what effectiveness is and why it is important, and we will examine some of the internal and external challenges that emerge when trying to achieve it. Encouraging people to concentrate on longer term effectiveness when for decades there has been pressure to deliver results in the short term inevitably involves change. For that change to take root and bear fruit you will have to ensure your actions and initiatives fall on good ground, so the next section deals with how you create an environment that is fertile for change. We will examine the less-tangible but highly important ingredients for effectiveness such as leadership and how you handle internal and external pressures. We will also discuss one of the most important elements in this blend: how you communicate. How do you gain consensus? In the complex world of the public sector where there are many stakeholders and accountability is highly visible, this is tough. On top of that, people have differing views on what the facts are, if they are even available, and situations can change rapidly as we have seen from the Coronavirus pandemic. These are the skills necessary for making progress, creating change, and ensuring everyone is working towards the same aim.

In the following chapters, we describe some of the most useful tools and explain how they can best be deployed. These are the tangible mechanisms that are known to be helpful such as success maps, decision-making tools, and Key Performance Indicators (KPIs). Many of these are widely used in both the public and private sectors with varying levels of success. Used in the right way and in the right context, they are enormously helpful in tracking and communicating progress, providing evidence from which to learn, and in throwing light on the path ahead. However, tools on their own are not sufficient. We have seen organisations where there is so much emphasis on using the tools and so much time and resource put into making them work that the point of having them in the first place has long since been forgotten. People spend hours, days even, compiling Key Performance Indicators (KPIs) and associated reports but do not know why. They never see what has changed as a result of their work. They carry on churning them out because that is what is required of them. So, having the tools is not enough. They can simply become time wasters without being used in the right setting. They can drain resources and sap energy from key activities almost without it being noticed.

In order to be effective, you need not only skills and tools but also wisdom and judgement. It is not easy to explain wisdom or the exercise of judgement so we have tried to think of ways of imparting that knowledge. We decided to interview people who have the experience of dealing with complex situations and to pick their brains about the approaches they took. We are grateful to the people who took time to give us their insights which we have used throughout the book.

Any organisation is only as good as the people working within it. Effective organisations comprise individuals who operate and think effectively. To be an effective individual you need to be self-aware and willing to learn at any age or level of seniority. We are all affected by our view of the world, formed by our upbringing and our own experience, and everyone will have a slightly different perspective on the same issue. To reach an outcome that is as beneficial as it can be you must understand where you are coming from and have an appreciation of how others may be seeing the world.

Think about different political philosophies. Most politicians would agree that alleviating poverty would be an admirable goal. Simple. Except, of course it is not. To start with, there will be disagreements about the definition of poverty and many different opinions about how it should be alleviated. Everyone will have their own picture of what success will look like. Then of course, as society evolves, so will perceptions of poverty. So, the whole process is constantly in flux. That of course is not a reason to avoid any attempt at alleviating poverty, it is just to say big and complex problems are to a large extent unstructured. They do not have a defined beginning, middle and end, which most of us feel more comfortable dealing with. They are messy. There is no certainty that x will result if y action is implemented. You cannot put them into a neat box and try to categorise everything. Trying to pin things down and to measure them too early sometimes backfires, as we will describe later on in the book. But this should be seen against a background where stakeholders expect a level of certainty and want to see progress, and you must create a balance between meeting reasonable expectations and delivering what is right for the longer term. You can only do your best, accept, and work with some lack of structure and certainty but understand that others look for it.

Creating effectiveness is not just about *what* to do. *How* something is done really matters when it comes to effectiveness, especially in complex and uncertain situations. Leaders must be trustworthy so people have confidence in the decisions they make and understand that sometimes mistakes will occur, and actions taken in good faith will not necessarily lead to the outcomes they want. To instil trust, they must respect others, including those who hold different views from themselves. They must communicate with transparency and attempt to create a common understanding, and they must accept responsibility and behave with integrity. If you are able to build trust, over time you can work together with your stakeholders to deliver beneficial outcomes that are sustainable. Acting otherwise may appear to be effective in the short term but is unlikely to be so in the longer term and effectiveness is ultimately about the long-term outcome.

Part 1

Creating the environment for change

> If the ladder is not leaning against the right wall, every step we take just gets us to the wrong place faster.
>
> ~ Stephen Covey

The change needed to embed a culture of achieving effective outcomes is profound. It requires a major shift in thinking, the managing of expectations and changes in the way people operate. Unless new ways of working and thinking become embedded habits, we tend to go back to our old ways of dealing with matters when we are under pressure (Markman, 2013). We search for the comfort of certainty in the measurements and numbers that show we are doing what is required of us. Those to whom we report do the same. Often, we know what should be done. We read books, go on courses, and talk to people, and yet when it comes down to doing the right thing, we are side-tracked and the end result is satisfactory but not as good as it might have been.

In this section, we will look at why effectiveness is so important and examine some of the pressures that force people into shorter term thinking which mitigates against achieving an effective outcome. We will highlight the skills needed to create an environment for change, starting with aspects of leadership which support the creation of an effective organisation. In the following chapters, we will present some tools to help you embed that change and explain how they can be used to best effect.

DOI: 10.4324/9781003099895-2

Reference

Markman, A. (2013), "Both good and bad habits are boosted in times of stress," *Psychology Today*, June, https://www.psychologytoday.com/us/blog/ulterior-motives/201306/both-good-and-bad-habits-are-boosted-in-times-stress

Chapter 1

What are the challenges?

To make improvements one must understand where the weaknesses lie and have an idea of how they have arisen. In this chapter, we will highlight some of the challenges, tensions, and contradictions encountered when aiming for effectiveness. Most people will recognise at least some of these because they are woven into the fabric of our daily lives, whether as readers of the news, policy makers or as employees trying to fulfil our objectives. To some extent, we accept them as "just how things are" and work with or round them, but if changes are to be made, we need to put a spotlight on them and see them for what they are. But first, let's start by explaining why effectiveness matters.

Why is effectiveness so important?

Business guru Peter Drucker once said: "Efficiency is doing things right: effectiveness is doing the right things." Consider the building of a road. It may have been completed within time and within budget, but if people do not use it and it fails to deliver the expected benefits the fact it has been constructed in an efficient way will be entirely irrelevant. The money spent on it will have been wasted.

It is easy to see the importance of concentrating on effectiveness rather than just efficiency in this simple example of a visible construction project, but the principle holds true for all projects and actions. A case study of projects in NHS Digital (provider of information, data, and IT systems for those involved the National Health Service) showed that even when an application had been well designed and efficiently created and there was a good rationale for its implementation, benefits were not always fully realised within the expected time scale because users were slow or unwilling to change the way they worked (Williams et al. 2019). Without buy-in from stakeholders, systems will not work, no matter how obvious the benefits appear

DOI: 10.4324/9781003099895-3

to the designer of the system, or how efficiently they have been created. This was well understood in NHS Digital and they took steps to consult and involve stakeholders from the outset and throughout the lifecycle of the project in order to ensure the outcomes were effective, rather than focussing primarily on efficiency in the way they created the new system, even if this did take some time.

In most situations there is still a strong focus on efficiency and, we would argue, this is often at the expense of effectiveness. In the case of projects, the same study found that the realisation of benefits (which could be equated to the effectiveness of a project) was in focus at the beginning of a project (used in order to justify the business case) but waned considerably as the project progressed and emphasis switched away from benefits and outcomes towards ensuring there was no overspend and timescales were on track. This was true of public sector projects in all the countries studied. (And, incidentally, it is true in the private sector, too.) You would expect there to be a focus on completing a project on time and within budget, especially as public money is involved. Of course that's important, but the reduction of focus on the effectiveness of the end result is of concern. Having spent money and resources and put a great deal of emotion, effort, and expectation into the running of the project, it is important to establish whether it is finally delivering benefits and to learn from what actually happened, and to do this in a transparent manner which is not overly time consuming. This is not to say reviews don't happen. They do, but we question whether enough is learnt from them in terms of establishing effectiveness (Bourne et al. 2020).

So, why is there such a focus on efficiency? There are many reasons, but it is essentially the result of a mixture of internal and external pressures. Efficiency is relatively easy to understand and measure. Money spent, progress made, and time taken can be calculated and reported with comparative ease. Effectiveness is less easy to define and measure.

The percentage of patients treated within emergency departments within four hours has been a long-standing target in the NHS, although at the time of writing it is currently under review. On the face of it, it is clear and easy to understand, and it can be measured and reported on. The public can relate to waiting times because they experience them personally, as anyone who has been to a large A & E department on a Saturday night can testify. There is no doubt that waiting times affect people and make them unhappy. However, important though they are, what is the purpose of A&E? It is not to ensure patients have the shortest possible waiting times, but to ensure people receive the best possible timely treatment and recover from accidents and illnesses as soon as they can. In practical terms, this will mean people with less serious injuries will wait longer than others and that when there is a major incident with many grave injuries, or a particularly virulent flu season, waiting time targets will be broken. So, on one hand, A&E waiting times are a good measure. Everyone wants them to be as short as possible and having a target should help motivate hospitals to improve their processes to make this happen. On the other hand, do they encourage the wrong behaviour? There have been reports of people being kept in ambulances to delay the ticking of the waiting time clock, and people being admitted to wards to stop the clock ticking. Perhaps the point here is that everyone knows it is sensible to have a target for waiting times, but we also need to recognise that it should not be cast in stone. Sometimes it will be broken for very good reason. That reason is to ensure the ultimate aim is achieved: so that people receive timely treatment and make the quickest possible recovery.

Another reason for measurement is the need to provide good news, to show progress. "Crime rate down 20%" is an attention-grabbing headline. But as one interviewee from the police service related to us, media headlines are only sound bites without the full context. One would have to consider the relative seriousness of a crime. Is the theft of a mobile phone the same as a serious sexual assault? Clearly not. So, to understand whether the police force in an area was being more effective or not is a far more complex issue than simply looking at headline figures.

Developing an effective police force should indeed result in lowering the crime rate. We know that one means of creating a sustainable reduction in crime rate is for the police and other agencies to work with troubled families to improve peoples' lives and tackle the underlying causes of crime. However, this takes a long time, and it is hard to measure. In the meantime, the media and the public want to see progress. Senior police officers want to be able to provide evidence of their success and want it to be recognised to support promotion in their own careers and for the benefit of those reporting to them. Politicians want the public to see they are being tough on crime so they can be re-elected. Naturally, this is not confined to the police force and all these motivations are entirely understandable, but whether we like it or not, they feed the desire to concentrate on shorter-term measures of efficiency.

Then you have the issue of different agencies competing for funding. Governments are more likely to provide funds to organisations which have a good track record of success as judged by their performance metrics, so it is in the interests of the leaders of that organisation or department to ensure they meet or exceed their targets.

As you can see, one of the big challenges to creating an effective public sector is the tension between the culture of society expecting measures of efficiency for reasons we have highlighted above and focussing on what really matters – a beneficial final outcome.

In summary, what we are saying is that it is important to keep the ultimate aim in mind at all times and find ways of measuring and tracking progress that also encourage thinking about longer term outcomes. Whilst most of us may believe we are doing that, in practice there are various tensions and pressures that can blow us off course and force us into shorter-term thinking.

The relationship between efficiency and effectiveness

There is a strong focus on performance in the public sector – not just in the United Kingdom but worldwide. Resources are always tight because the number of possible outputs from the public sector is virtually endless and users of services, in developed countries at least, have come to expect they will receive whatever they need as a matter of course. [Incidentally, we are using the term "output" to mean an immediate product or service created from an activity whereas an "outcome" is the medium or longer-term result of the activity – the benefit arising from it.] With healthcare, for example, there is ever more that can be done to improve the well-being of the population and support those who fall ill. So, there is always a pressure to do more with less. Paul Winter, Deputy Director of Corporate Governance, Compliance and Data Protection, NHS Staffordshire, and Stoke-on-Trent CCGs had a lovely expression: "If the culture demands a Rolls Royce level of effectiveness and you have a Trabant level of investment. There is a problem."

Whilst you cannot always afford to increase the level of resources, you can make better use of what you have by being more efficient. However, there is a limit to how efficient you can be. Over time, the gains become smaller and smaller whilst the pressure on employees grows until it begins to have an adverse effect on performance. Nobody can work at full stretch with limited resources over a long period of time and deliver the same high-level results. Effectiveness on the other hand provides a different perspective by examining the actions that will provide the greatest impact.

Being effective is paramount but that doesn't mean to say that efficiency doesn't matter at all. It's obvious that it does matter to an extent, and you could argue that efficiency is part of effectiveness. You can be efficient without being effective, but you probably can't be effective without considering efficiency, too. Throwing seemingly endless resources at a problem, as has happened in some countries whilst combatting the effects of the coronavirus pandemic, is a judgement call and the pandemic was potentially such a catastrophic event that extreme measures were justified. However, efficient use of resources is also important because they are not infinite and what you spend in one place you cannot spend in another. There was certainly a debate to be had about whether normal processes to ensure efficiency (such as value for money in procurement, for example) would be appropriate in the emergency situation, and there is a line under which they probably wouldn't be appropriate. Planning in advance should result in establishing a mechanism for what happens in an emergency so people having to make decisions at least have a guide, but ultimately the test is whether resources are being spent on something that will be effective in solving the problem. Let us take an example. The idea of having a track and trace system to reduce the number of people infected with the virus circulating in the population and infecting others would appear to be an effective approach to limiting the spread of the virus. Ultimately, money spent on a track and trace system that is run efficiently should result in an outcome of fewer cases of illness, fewer hospitalisations, and fewer deaths. But the system must be efficient at identifying infected individuals within a given time period and encouraging them to self-isolate, otherwise the desired outcomes will not be realised.

Here is an example from the private sector. Clive Jeans, former Chief Executive of Milliken in Europe told the story of their "samples" operation. Milliken were manufacturers of carpets for hotels, conference centres, and large venues. Previously they had taken the approach of responding to enquiries and despatching samples by courier from their central warehouse. However, when they analysed their customer base and their customer needs, they discovered that a very large percentage of the product specifiers were architects based in central London. Having realised this, they decided to substantially improve their customer response time. They fitted out a van with a wide selection of samples and every day the van toured the centre of London receiving requests for samples and delivering them directly to the architects' offices. So, a specifier could request a sample in the morning and be happily surprised to receive that sample when they returned from lunch. Cost wise this may not have been the cheapest operation, but it was extremely effective in getting their products specified.

So, efficiency and effectiveness go hand in hand. You need to be clear about the ultimate outcomes you want but, rather like a chain, there are links of individual decisions and actions each of which has an element of effectiveness and efficiency within it. John Spence CBE, formerly director of retail distribution for Lloyds Bank and now a County Councillor (amongst many other things) has a wonderful expression. "Keep your eyes focussed on the horizon, but don't fall over the steppingstones or you won't reach your Nirvana." Bear in mind, you also need to ensure you don't follow the steppingstones without checking they are going in the right direction. You may inadvertently be heading for hell.

Clarifying the pressures

We have pointed out some of the pressures that lead people to concentrate on setting goals and measurements that focus on the shorter term and to concentrate on individual aspects of performance rather than on the whole, both of which work against the idea of achieving the most effective outcome. Efficiency is easy to measure as you go along, whereas effectiveness can only be seen at the end. Efficiency is easy to see in individual elements of a project or initiative, whereas effectiveness is achieved in bringing those elements together in the best possible way.

But the pressures are real and cannot be ignored. Stakeholders want and need to see progress and success. Individuals and teams need to be motivated. You need shorter-term measurements of performance to know what is working and to check you are on track. If you are measured against progress towards a goal, that is where your efforts will be focused. Yet in working towards these shorter-term goals, you may be overlooking the bigger picture. As the saying goes: "You can't see the wood for the trees."

This prompts a number of questions. How can these two seemingly opposing forces be reconciled? How can you focus both on the longer-term outcome and also on the efficiency of the process used to achieve it? How can you manage stakeholder expectations when stakeholders are not in possession of all the evidence? How can you avoid being blown off course by unexpected events to which stakeholders will expect a response?

There is no simple answer to these questions. Understanding the conflict between pressure for efficient working and effectiveness and between long- and short-term focus is a good start, but working effectively, holding up a picture of the successful outcome and keeping eyes focussed on that, requires a change in culture and expectations which takes time to achieve.

Producing plans and charts showing the actions needed to achieve a successful outcome is common practice, but producing an honest analysis of the pressures, internal, and external, which will need to be managed is less common. For example: what objections are stakeholders likely to have? What performance measures will *they* expect to see? What *behaviour* will those measures encourage? What will the consequences be? These issues may be raised in a risk analysis, but it is important that they are considered thoroughly, not in a formulaic way, and that there is an open and honest debate about them (Figures 1.1 and 1.2).

What is a successful outcome?

There is a further challenge in creating effectiveness, one of trying to gain consensus on what it will look like. It is almost impossible to make everyone happy as the perception and definition of success will depend on the views and perspectives of different groups of stakeholders.

Let us take the simple example of a project to extend a railway further out of the city to enable more commuters to travel in to work without using their cars. On the face of it, that sounds an excellent idea. Success for the local authority will be less road congestion, perhaps, and cleaner air. City residents will probably share the same view. Businesses in the city will be pleased because they will be able to attract candidates from a wider area and fewer people will be late for work. Some people will

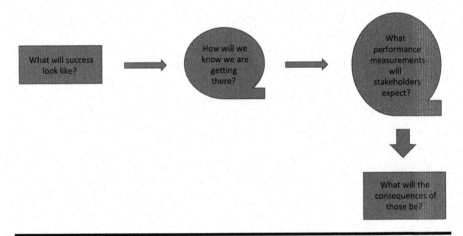

Figure 1.1 Questions to ask when examining the pressures.

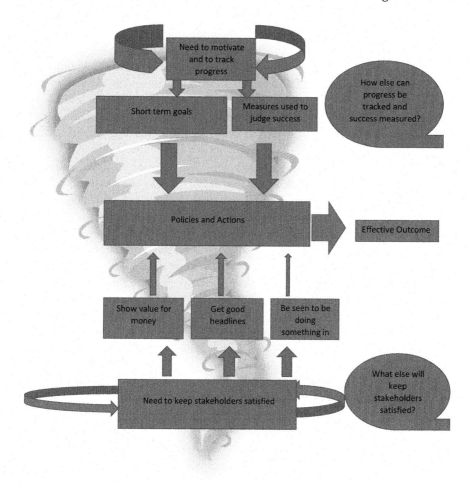

Figure 1.2 Forces affecting achievement of effective outcomes.

be happy because the railway extension will increase the value of their properties. There will be detractors, though, including people whose houses will be compulsorily purchased for the development, those whose lives will be affected by noise, and newcomers who will have to pay more to live closer to work. Some taxpayers will be unhappy because their taxes are being spent on a project from which they can see no benefit.

At the beginning of any project, it is standard practice to conduct an analysis of potential stakeholder benefits for the purposes of justifying the business case and a decision is made on the relative weights of cost matched against those benefits. However, particularly with large projects, benefits will change over time. In the railway example above, a major employer may move out of the area, or there may be a rapid transition to homeworking as can be seen during the pandemic, meaning fewer people would be traveling into the city. In that situation, the case for extending the railway would be much weaker and when it is completed even those who promoted the idea in the first place would not deem it a success because passenger levels would be lower than expected. The point here is that perceptions of success will change as the environment changes and measures of success that were calculated based on information available at the time may no longer be appropriate.

Understanding perceptions of success applies not only to discrete projects but also to ongoing work to improve everyday lives. We talked to a former police and crime commissioner who, before taking on the role, made it his business to go around and talk to members of the public exhaustively to hear their views, so he could understand what mattered to them. In doing this he gained a much clearer picture of what local people would perceive as success and he was also able to refine his own thinking. A prison governor told us about former Justice Minister, Rory Stewart, who took time to visit prisons and talk and listen to prison staff in order to gain a deeper understanding of how the prison system functioned and what those within it considered to be important for a successful outcome. As that governor told us, most people have a view about prisons, but few elected representatives who have a responsibility for them, have any deep understanding when they take on the role, because they have not worked in the prison sector or been prisoners themselves. It is through talking to people who do have that understanding that they can gain more than a superficial knowledge.

It is not only important to consider what success looks like from different perspectives but also to consider how it is measured and what the implications of that measurement are. Some people will believe success has been achieved when a target has been reached, whereas others will believe success lies in having created a benefit that is appreciated by people. Several people we interviewed talked with frustration about the focus on evaluating correct use of process and procedures to measure success and the emphasis on achieving short term targets, rather than concentrating on the longer-term outcomes which they believed to be their ultimate purpose.

Take the example of achieving sustained levels of crime reduction. Reducing the number of crimes committed can be done by arresting prolific burglars. However, it is much harder to sustain that reduction over a longer period of time. Rather like a marketplace where one business moves out and another moves in to take its place, without longer term measures to address root causes, new burglars will just come in to fill the void. Being "tough on crime" may result in deterring some would-be criminals (and it does fulfil the desire to see punishment imposed) but is it the most effective approach?

Crime prevention is a complex issue that can take decades to achieve and is often best done in conjunction with other agencies, such as social services, tackling issues faced by problem families. But these measures take many years to bear fruit and it is difficult to establish direct cause and effect. If measures of success concentrate on short term results and process and who did what and when they did it and what it cost, rather than including success in achieving milestones towards a longer-term goal and cross-agency working, then it is clear where people will put their efforts. This is the unhelpful side of KPIs which we will discuss in Chapter 10.

We have already mentioned the importance of being self-aware. Whether an initiative is deemed a success will also depend on the personal view of each individual, whether it chimes with their beliefs, values, and opinions on how things should be done. As we are human beings and not robots, we are all subject to this bias although we may not always be aware of it. All we can do is to attempt some form of analysis of our own opinions and judgements to understand how they are formed and to ensure there is diversity of background amongst those whose role it is to evaluate success.

You may be asking why it matters how we perceive success. The reason is that how we perceive it will govern how we measure it and the milestones we put in place to measure progress. In turn, the way in which we measure it and the goals we put in place will govern what people do and where they direct their efforts.

To complete this section on what is a successful outcome, let us consider one of the UK's most challenging infrastructure projects of the late 20th century – the Channel Tunnel. This is the 50.5 km-long railway tunnel under the English Channel linking Folkestone with Coquelles in France, financed and built by a private sector consortium. Increasing construction costs and underestimates of the competitive response by the ferry companies contributed towards near financial collapse and the need for major restructuring. Viewed from the perspective of an early investor, the project could be seen as a disaster. However, nearly 30 years later, it is difficult to view it as anything but a success. The construction was innovative and led to learning which was employed in future projects. The tunnel eventually offered an alternative to taking the ferry and thus kept a lid on prices. And, finally, shareholders are receiving dividends.

What does all this mean for creating effectiveness? There are a number of simple conclusions. To decide what success should look like and how it can be achieved, you must understand the perspectives of all major stakeholders. That means being prepared to listen to them, being open minded and being prepared to adapt your own thinking. As you cannot make every stakeholder happy (take the railway extension example above) you must be prepared to deal with the consequences of that. Having created the picture of a successful outcome, you then need to make it happen and find ways of knowing when you are achieving it, putting measurements and milestones in place to provide some structure and signals to others that all is on course. That is the difficult part which we will tackle next.

References

Bourne, M., Anker, D., Chambers, G., & Torjai, L. (2020), "How to measure and manage the UK Government's major project portfolio," *Measuring Business Excellence*, Vol. 24, No. 4, 461–474.

Williams, T., Vo, H., Bourne, M., Bourne, P., Cooke-Davies, T., Kirkham, R., Masterton, G., Quattrone, P., & Valette, J. (2019), "A cross-national comparison of public project benefits management practices – the effectiveness of benefits management frameworks in application," *Production Planning and Control*, Vol. 31, No. 8, 644–659.

Chapter 2

Leadership and creating a culture of effectiveness

Everyone thinks of changing the world, but nobody thinks of changing himself.

Leo Tolstoy

What is leadership?

Leaders are the people who shape the organisation and who create the environment in which others can perform well in their work. They bring people and resources together to make the organisation more than the sum of its individual parts. A good leader will be a role model who inspires everyone, employees, and stakeholders alike, to co-operate in achieving common aims. However, on a rather sobering note, a UK-wide Workforce Development Survey conducted in 2019 by the Workforce Development Trust in partnership with Edinburgh Napier University (Parry et al., 2019) revealed that more than 80% of respondents from the public sector said there needed to be improvement in leadership and management capability and action (Grant & Williams, 2019). Leadership is a very important aspect of the development and maintenance of an effective organisation that is sometimes lost in a plethora of rules, processes, and standards.

You can think of an organisation as being like a garden where you must create the right environment for it to flourish. Firstly, you need to choose the right plants for your location and type of soil. Then you must make sure they are planted in the right place and that they have adequate supplies of nutrients, water, and sunlight. A leader is like the head gardener, creating a vision of what the garden will look like, selecting the plants and ensuring the team of gardeners provides what the plants

DOI: 10.4324/9781003099895-4

need to grow and thrive, despite the vagaries of pests (expected and unexpected) and extreme weather.

What does that involve in practice?

The changing role of leaders

Scholars have been reflecting on leadership for more than 100 years. Frederick Taylor (1856–1915), one of the earliest, created the scientific management theory which set out to find the best way of fulfilling a task by studying how work was performed and the effect it had on productivity. The aim was to prescribe a specific approach and standards so that tasks could be performed more efficiently. It seems he was not a great fan of common sense or the individual approach and was not always trusting of workers. (He is quoted as saying: "Hardly a competent workman has been found who does not devote a considerable amount of time to studying just how slowly he can work and still convince his employer that he is going at a good pace.") Although perhaps we should not be too hard on him because is also quoted as saying: "The principal object of management should be to create the maximum prosperity for the employer coupled with the maximum prosperity for each employee."

The sociologist, Max Weber, whose ideas became prominent in the middle of the last century considered there to be three types of leaders: Charismatic, Traditional and Bureaucratic. Charismatic leaders exercised soft power. Their authority came through their influence over followers and the ability to maintain their prosperity. The downsides of this, of course, are that the leader must exercise *moral* influence and the focussing of power in one area can lead to the "cult of personality" and the absence of checks and balances. The traditional leader, on the other hand, gained their power from what had happened in the past. They maintained a hold on information and issued orders with little attention to teams and consultation. One of the clear drawbacks here is that they are slow to change, and they also fail to gain the best from those working for them. Bureaucratic leadership, as seen by Weber, involved a hierarchical structure with clearly laid out roles, processes, and rules and unlike the charismatic type, bureaucratic leadership was impersonal. Many people will recognise the downsides here – red tape and inflexibility.

More recently, there have been thinkers such as Psychologist, Daniel Goleman (1996) who popularised the idea of emotional intelligence in his bestselling book of the same name. Having a high IQ (in the traditional meaning of having a good brain) is not enough to guarantee success because you also need to be able to understand emotions and connect in a positive way with other people. Daniel Goleman's ideas are about relating to and communicating with others, and about the importance of tuning into feelings. He talks about empathy and self-awareness and the ability to cope with setbacks and to manage stress.

Stephen Covey (2020) was also a best-selling author of *The 7 Habits of Highly Effective People* in which he crystallised his study of what makes people successful into seven principles: be proactive; begin with the end in mind (highly appropriate for the subject of this book); put first things first; think "win/win"; seek first to understand and then to be understood; synergise (remember the whole is greater than the sum of the parts); sharpen the saw (take time to invest in yourself, to keep yourself sharp – physically, emotionally, and mentally). Stephen Covey and Daniel Goleman both discuss the idea of values and importance of the individual and their relationship with other people in order to achieve success.

What is interesting in this quick race through the thinking about leadership over the last 100 years or so is that older ideas still exist and are practised in the workplace. Some readers will recognise the type of leader described by Taylor – the person who prescribes exactly how a task should be done, without allowing any room for autonomy – or the charismatic leader depicted by Weber who relies on the power of their own personality and influence to implement their ideas. The bureaucrat most certainly exists, with structured hierarchies and formal and rigid processes. But the working environment has changed and what may have worked in the relatively stable situations of the past is no longer appropriate in a world where there is flux, 24-hour communications and in which everyone feels entitled to have an opinion on anything. That is not to say there is nothing useful in the ideas of earlier thinkers. In certain circumstances, it is a good idea to have standardisation of processes and in emergencies issuing orders which are instantly obeyed can save lives, but the ideas of Covey and Goleman work well in times of uncertainty where values, relationships, and trust come to the fore.

The practice of leadership has changed in recent years for a number of reasons. The first is complexity. In almost any reasonable-sized organisation, the operating environment has become more complex and specialised. It is impossible for a leader to know everything, to understand how all the technology works, or to understand the intricate web of relationships upon which the organisation relies. So, a leader must listen to the advice of people who do understand.

The second reason is employee expectations. The relationship between employees and employers has changed. The workforce is more educated, and employees expect a greater say in what they are doing; they are looking for job satisfaction and few people now expect to work with the same employer for the whole of their lives. New technologies mean that more people than ever are working from home, with enormous implications for leadership and trust placed in employees. (Although it is interesting to note that the demand for so-called "spy-software," capturing keystrokes and the websites visited by employees working from home has increased substantially during the period of the coronavirus pandemic.)

Another factor is the availability of information. Stakeholders have access to more information – accurate and inaccurate – than before. This means they feel better informed and able to express their views about something whether it affects them directly or not and whether they understand it or not. People have far fewer inhibitions about expressing their opinions, as you can see from social media.

What does all this mean for leadership? In essence, the working environment is less structured, more complex, and faster moving than in previous years. This makes the more traditional command and control model of leadership difficult to employ. A leader of today cannot possibly know and do everything themselves. The leader's role is now about creating a believable vision of the future and working with others to achieve it. This means knowing where to go for reliable advice and exercising judgement in taking that advice. It is also about creating a fertile environment for success and ensuring the capability is there to take advantage of it.

At the time of writing, we are in the midst of the coronavirus pandemic and there is much comment about the leadership style of women heads of state who appear to have been particularly skilful in navigating their nations through choppy waters to more successful outcomes. Commentators have drawn attention to their compassion and empathy, to "reasoning rather than rousing" (Zoe Marks, PhD, lecturer in public policy at Harvard Kennedy School, speaking about Angela Merkel) and their willingness to collaborate. If you compare these traits to those of the Traditional Leader, described by Max Weber in 1947, but espoused by many leaders since, you can see an enormous difference. Max Weber's traditional leader believed it was up to him (it usually was a "him" in those days) to provide the solution. The traditional leader believed that resources should only be allocated when proven necessary, that people should adhere to roles and responsibilities, and that staff performance should be reviewed annually in line with company policy. There was little room for feelings, empathy, and compassion. It would be good to think that times have changed but from our observations and experience there a still many leaders who operate in this way.

Creating the vision

One of the most important tasks of a leader is to communicate vision and purpose. The vision is the picture of the outcome and the purpose is the reasoning behind it which illuminates why people are there and what they need to do. Several of the people we interviewed stressed how important it was to get this right. One senior police officer (Chief Superintendent Mick Stamper) was able to encapsulate purpose to his team in a few simple words:

> "What are you doing today to prevent crime, detect crime and keep people safe?"

This phrase is memorable, understandable and provides a focus on what is needed without the clutter of detail. In effect it says: "This is why you are here and everything you do should focus on those aims."

There is much debate on just how reasonable a vision should be. (The same debate surrounds the setting of goals.) Some people believe that a vision should be unreasonable, arguing that this is the only way to motivate people to action, to stretch them to achieve more that anyone might expect. This is not a view to which we subscribe. Our view is that it may achieve short-term results, but it is not sustainable in the longer term, which is what matters. In fact, we believe creating an unreasonable vision (and goals) works against the idea of effectiveness. By "unreasonable" we mean "not fully reasoned with some evidence that it is the right thing to do and it can be achieved." Here are our arguments for this stance.

1. It is like treating your employees as if they were children. Your employees are adults and will know full well what you are doing, and it will undermine your credibility.
2. It encourages people to "game the system," to resort to practices such as choosing figures that show only good progress (and statistics can always be presented to show the desired picture). That means you will not be able to see a true picture.
3. Instead of being motivational, people will become disillusioned and fatigued and you may lose your best people.
4. Trying to reach the unattainable will take focus away from the business of achieving a more reasonable vision.

That is not to say that a vision should not be stretching or exciting. Building a tunnel under the sea between England and France was a stretching vision, but it was not unreasonable. There was logic and purpose behind it, which people could see and buy in to.

President Kennedy's ambition of sending a manned spaceship to the moon was probably the most audacious goal of the 20th century but it involved much consideration before making it public and it was achieved at a time when there was trust between the government and the people. Kennedy was under pressure politically as a result of the Bay of Pigs debacle and the feeling that the United States was behind in the space race after the success of Yuri Gagarin's first orbit of the earth. According to NASA History, Kennedy (1961) wanted to announce a program that the United States had a strong chance of achieving before the Soviet Union.

> After consulting with Vice President Johnson, NASA Administrator James Webb, and other officials, he concluded that landing an American on the Moon would be a very challenging technological feat, but an area of space exploration in which the U.S. actually had a potential lead.

There is another point to add here and that is about consistency. If you set an unreasonable vision, over time it will become apparent, and you will have to back pedal or water it down. If you do it too often you will lose credibility and trust. We both have to confess that when working in business and hearing about yet another new initiative from head office, a new and exciting vision of the future, we did not always take action immediately because we knew it was likely to change, thus saving ourselves and our teams a great deal of wasted time and effort. We are sure we are not alone.

Far from being motivating and encouraging innovation, we believe that leaders who simply throw out unreasoned pictures of the future, and thus place unreasonable requirements on people, actually close things down. People working for them become more cautious in expressing the truth and too tied up in justifications for lack of progress to focus on what really matters – a successful outcome.

So, if being unreasonable is not a recipe for success, what is?

Bringing people with you

There has been much debate about whether leaders should be liked and be likeable. Traditionally it was deemed unnecessary for a leader to be liked, respected perhaps, but it was not necessary to be liked to get a high level of performance from those working for you.

More recently, research carried out by Charn McAllister, Sherry Moss, and Mark Martinko, in the US (Published in the Harvard Business Review Newsletter of October 2019) indicated that being liked is probably one of the key ingredients for being a good leader. Teams who like their leaders will be "happier at work, go above and beyond what is required of them, experience greater well-being, and perform at a higher level." Of course, there can be debate about what "being liked" actually means. The research showed that there was a correlation between liking the leader and saying they are transformational, ethical, and authentic. So, you don't have to be friends with everyone working with you but being liked does help and you most certainly have to bring people with you if you want to bring about change in your organisation and make it stick.

There is a whole section about communication and influence in Chapter 4, so we won't discuss the subject at length here, but suffice it to say, having good communication skills is a great help in the job of bringing people with you. It is not necessary to be a great orator, although it helps, but you do need to be able to listen to people, to keep your antennae out and to judge the mood before you take decisions or make any major announcements. Sometimes it is helpful to ask a few people what they think reactions will be and, by the way, the idea isn't to use those people to test out your plans like respondents in a market research survey, but genuinely to help you gauge how and when you should present your ideas.

Another major element in this mix is trust. "Trust is the new currency of our interdependent, collaborative world" according to writer, Stephen M.R. Covey (son of Stephen Covey, author of *The 7 Habits of Highly Effective People*). The days where people will just follow their leader regardless of what they, themselves, believe have largely disappeared. At a time when we want people to express their opinions and take advantage of diverse points of view, that must be a good thing, although there are exceptions to this of course, at times of emergency when speed of action is paramount. So, if you want to bring people with you, you will have to trust them, and they will have to trust you.

But how do you build trust? Jack Zenger and Joseph Folkman (2019) looked at data from the 360° assessments of 87,000 leaders and were able to identify three clusters of items that form the foundation for trust. The first was building positive relationships. This involved balancing results with concern for others, resolving conflict, and giving honest feedback. The second was good judgement and expertise. Leaders must be well-informed and knowledgeable, and use good judgement when making decisions. The third was consistency. This meant being a good role model, keeping promises and following through on commitments as well as being willing to go above and beyond what needs to be done. The researchers found that level of trust is highly correlated with how people rate a leader's overall leadership effectiveness.

Let us look at some of these attributes in more detail. We have already highlighted the idea that empathy is important (note the examples of leaders who have, to date, at least, been seen to be most effective at steering their nations through the coronavirus pandemic). Being kind and generous of spirit helps create supportive relationships that contribute to success. Tom Carter, Head Teacher of King Edward VI Grammar School in Essex told us: "Be kind to people. Be generous. You get loads back in return by being kind when you can."

Some people fear that being seen to be kind will make them appear weak, but that is not the case. Having empathy and concern for others is not about being superficially "nice." In fact, being "nice" all the time is one way of causing people to doubt you. Actions that promote trust include giving honest feedback, resolving conflict, and making tough decisions, which will sometimes be unfavourable to other people. This inevitably means that to be effective, a leader has to face up to unpleasant tasks and facts, but if people understand *why* a particular course of action is being taken, they are more likely to respect the decision and work with it. Explaining *why* something is happening rather than just explaining *what* is happening is a better recipe for success. It helps to bring people together. If everyone believes they are in the same boat (leaders and those working for them) and understands how it feels, it is easier to negotiate rough seas. There will be more sharing of information, more collaboration, and more support.

In Zenger and Folkman's research the most important factor for whether a leader was trusted was whether they built positive relationships. Having empathy is clearly an important part of that. Consistency, which you might have thought to be paramount in building trust, was important (it is hard to work with someone if you can't predict how they will behave) but not as important as building positive relationships. Perhaps it is because when you have good relationships people are prepared to forgive you if you slip from time to time.

It's interesting to note that this is not a new idea.

> "I suppose leadership at one time meant muscles; but today it means getting along with people." So said Mahatma Gandhi.

Creating energy

Energy is described as: "the strength and vitality required for sustained physical or mental activity". You may not immediately associate energy with leadership, but one thing is certain, unless an organisation has energy within it, it is unlikely to make any substantial progress. One former colleague made a habit of turning up for meetings early just so he could sit in reception and get a feel for the place he was visiting. He would look at the usual things, how well he was greeted, eavesdrop on a few conversations as people walked past, and he would also take note of energy levels, whether people were purposeful or whether they exhibited lassitude or boredom. We must be a little careful here as there are "energetic" organisations that are not at all effective, quite the opposite in fact. You probably know of organisations that employ a lot of enthusiastic people who generate a great deal of frenetic activity of the wrong type. Good leaders must have energy themselves to energise, enthuse and engage the interest of people working with them. If you think back to people you have worked with, you will probably recall how infectious their energy was. It rubs off and provides inspiration and motivation. The problem comes when you work with someone who is like Tigger – constantly bouncing about – when it can be utterly energy-sapping. To be an effective leader you need as much useful input from other people as you can get, you need them to be energetic and enthusiastic, but you also need to recognise that there are limits. No one can operate at full tilt all the time and a leader must plan to make sure that time and energy is spent on the most important activities.

In an article in Forbes, *Cultivating the Essential Ingredient in Leadership: Energy,* Brett Steenbarger (2018) quotes from a conversation he has with former US navy SEAL Lieutenant Commander Johnathan Fussell about the lessons he had learnt as a combat leader. Having worked with many elite military units Commander Fussell described having to compress the time cycle of planning, rehearsing, executing, and reviewing into a very short period. Effective leaders plan and anticipate likely scenarios, but they are ready to respond to what actually happens.

> Recognizing their limited bandwidth, leaders operating with such time constraints must actively and proactively engage team members to process the right information at the right time. Great combat leaders shape an environment that allows the team to effectively disseminate the intelligence that is needed within the available bandwidth.

So, what does "energising" actually mean? There are several elements to it. The first is generating buy in, or as much buy in as possible from the people around you. Not everyone will agree with everything but the more someone agrees with a course of action the more they will be committed to it and the more likely they are to put energy into making it work. The leader's job here is to influence, to demonstrate good reason for something to happen. Former UK Cabinet Minister, Ed Balls, was firmly of the view that to have any prospect of success you must get people to talk about any new idea or initiative, so they start to engage and feel they have ownership of it. You need to get wide involvement and you must get buy in from the very top.

Providing positive feedback plays a large part in generating energy and motivation and the importance of providing encouragement for everyone, junior and senior, cannot be over emphasised. It helps people to know they matter. Without feedback, it is like working in a dark room, not knowing whether you are on the right track, and even the most self-motivated of people will begin to flag. Feedback, of course can be negative as well as positive but even negative feedback can be motivational if it is delivered in the right way. The key is to focus on what is positive, and if something does need to change, to emphasise the new behaviour that is required rather than to stress what is wrong. The problem with many feedback sessions is that individuals on the receiving end focus on the negative aspects and forget the positives. After all, our brains are designed to detect threats, and for most people, certainly if they care about their work, being told something is wrong by your boss is a threat.

Being optimistic and upbeat yourself is indeed infectious. You may have heard about "radiators" and "drains." Radiators are people who invigorate you by their presence. They acknowledge problems but look for solutions rather than dwelling on what is wrong. Drains, as the name suggests, leave you feeling depleted. This is backed up by evidence from research conducted with 650 employees in a range of organizations which found that people who were identified as "energizers" significantly increased the morale, engagement, and job performance in those around them (Heaphy & Dutton, 2008). Remember Martin Luther King said, "I have a Dream." He didn't say, "I have a nightmare!" (used by former politician, Ed Milliband at a CBI conference).

But being optimistic raises another question – should you, as a leader protect those working for you from bad news? The answer is that you can't because you have to be honest. But how you communicate it will make a huge difference to the effect it has. You can either "rally the troops" or make them so depressed they will go away and hope the problem disappears.

Being optimistic does not mean ignoring or failing to face up to problems. About one thing you can be sure: bad news will seep out and ongoing problems, if left to fester, will drain energy. One of us remembers tolerating poor performance in a person we thought was a well-liked team member. Not wanting to cause more friction in a team that had already been through a great deal of change, we took no decisive action until matters reached the point where something had to be done. When that individual left the team and was replaced by someone else it was like a breath of fresh air. There was more energy, more commitment and motivation and one of the existing team members, far from being upset, expressed relief that someone new was in the post. Taking decisive action that you know to be right, even though it may be unpleasant at the time is the only way to prevent problems from derailing optimum performance. We sometimes underestimate how much our co-workers and employees understand about a situation and it is much better to say it as it is, to point out the reasons for an unpopular action, than it is to leave it to peoples' imaginations.

Forgetting the ego

A leader must be visible, but remember, when the sun shines too brightly you can't see anything else. It was interesting that several people we interviewed spoke about "ego-based decision making" and a culture of "self- centeredness," which a few people even felt was promulgated though the leadership programmes they had attended. Some leaders were perceived to be focussing on the achievement of short-term results and goals because that was what they needed to do to progress in their careers. One interviewee talked about needing to create "media soundbites whilst ignoring the full context." This was very demotivating, and it made that person feel undervalued and disassociated from the decision-making and from the real purpose of their job. Ego-based leadership (akin to some of the more extreme forms of charismatic leadership we described earlier) leaves little room for empathy or consideration of others but piles on pressure to achieve results and demonstrate success come what may.

It has been said that "ego is the enemy of good leadership." As individuals rise through their careers, they have more people looking up to them, more power, and more freedom to operate. More people will agree with them and there will be fewer challenges to their views and decisions. Over time, their confidence and belief in their own performance will grow. Now, there is nothing wrong with believing in your self-worth. If you are not sufficiently confident in your own abilities, you are unlikely to be able to instil confidence in others. However, when that confidence spills over into self-centredness and inability to accept challenge and listen to others, there is a serious problem. As Head Teacher, Tom Carter told us:

> Humility is important. It has to be balanced – you don't need to say you are awful at everything, but you don't need to go around seeking publicity for everything either. If you try to see yourself as you truly are, then you will be rooted in reality.

At the beginning of this chapter, we discussed how the environment in which leaders operate has changed. One of those changes is increased complexity. It is not possible for one person to know and understand everything and a skilled leader should be prepared to listen, should know where to go for advice and exercise judgement on whether to take it. The problem with self-centred leaders is that they tend to have a narrow vision because they look for evidence to back up their own beliefs rather than seeing things for what they really are. They also surround themselves with people who agree with their views or are unwilling to voice any disagreement. In doing this, they can fail to see important facts that point to alternative interpretations of what is happening. One of our interviewees, John Healey MP told us he would deliberately search out people who would be prepared both to inform and to challenge his views.

A leader must be visible and not be afraid to shine without overshadowing others, and they must also be approachable. There is a story – possibly true – that a Thai Queen and her daughter drowned when their royal boat capsized on the way to the Bang-Pa-In Royal Palace one summer. There were many witnesses to the accident who said it happened because people did not dare to touch the Queen – even to save her life – because it was a capital offence. We have both worked in organisations where the top man or woman has created a culture of invincibility. In some situations, this has had a positive effect, notably in a crisis when decisions must be made fast. But outside those rare circumstances it does mean people either won't voice their dissenting opinions because they fear the consequences, or they waste time in having to find ways to do what they feel is right anyway. Ego-based leaders can be very lonely and when things start to go wrong, they tend to have less support to fall back on as the people they surrounded themselves with fade into the background when the true picture emerges. It has been said: "If you want to go fast, go alone. If you want to go far, go together."

There are many examples of organisations that have come adrift, despite the apparent success of their leaders. A book published in 2020 "Lights Out: Pride, Delusion, and The Fall of General Electric," by Wall Street Journal reporters Thomas Gryta and Ted Mann (2020) discusses the leadership of Jeffrey Immelt, former CEO of GE. General Electric was founded way back in 1892 by Thomas Edison, amongst others, and grew to be the premier power and electric company, valued at some $600 billion at the beginning of the 21st century. However, after Mr Immelt's departure in 2017 his successors discovered things were not what they seemed. They "had found a dry well where they expected cash," according to the authors. They report that:

> The board didn't entirely understand how GE worked, and … Immelt was just fine with that….The well-compensated board members were chosen for their willingness to cheer Immelt on — and he readily ejected directors who objected to his plans.

The authors also note GE's established divisions were expected to meet earnings goals that were far removed from reality. "Under Immelt, the company believed that the will to hit a target could supersede the math."

You will remember from the description of the charismatic leader that a lack of checks and balances can be one of the pitfalls that occurs under that type of regime. It is easy to be carried away in the waves of enthusiasm and apparent success and no one wants to be seen as a spoilsport, but it is still important to carry out reality checks now and then. That applies whether you are the leader yourself, reflecting on your own performance, or someone working for the leader. It takes courage to listen to dissenting voices and admit that you are sometimes wrong. Far from regarding this as a weakness, most people will see it as a demonstration of strength and integrity.

Being the exemplar

Whether you like it or not, if you are a leader, you will be noticed, and your behaviour will be under scrutiny. Pippa was once gently rebuked by some of her team for looking annoyed at Mike who was playing with a chocolate wrapper at a formal dinner whilst listening to a boring speaker. Apparently, she had a habit of showing her annoyance (not always at Mike!) without realising it and she had no idea she was being watched. So, even in mundane situations you need to be self-aware, occasionally seek feedback from others and be prepared to listen to it when it is offered.

You and your senior colleagues will shape the culture – the "way things are done around here" – and you reflect the organisation's values, so you need to be seen to being doing the right things. You set the standards, and you must also abide by them because there cannot be one rule for leaders and another for everyone else. If there is, you are undermining what you set out to achieve. It's surprising what people notice and how even the smallest of things can have an adverse and unexpected effect. We know of one senior manager who decreed that there would be only one wastepaper bin in the open-plan office and that all the individual bins that had been in situ under desks since the office had been set up, would be removed. This was done for a good reason: to dissuade people from printing out unnecessary emails and wasting paper because they were soon thrown away. Most individuals had a little grumble but understood the reasoning and accepted the loss of their bins with equanimity. That was until they discovered the manager had kept their own bin. This caused much more dissent when they realised the manager expected them to take the few steps to the central bin but was not prepared to do it themselves. The grumbling shifted to other sources of irritation that had never been fully exposed, and what had once been an office where work proceeded smoothly and to a high level became a hotbed of discontent. The moral of this story is: be careful what you ask others to do because you must be prepared to do it yourself.

Although as a leader you are always "on show," you cannot constantly keep up the pretence of being someone you are not. It becomes stressful and tiring, others will see through you, and your actions will appear inconsistent to them. It is hard to build rapport with someone who is constantly changing, because you will always be wondering what their response will be on that particular day and whether you can fully trust them. Whilst you must be true to who you are, that doesn't mean you have carte blanche to say and do whatever you want, when you want. There has to be some filtering according to the circumstance and the audience.

In preparation for writing his book "Discover Your True North," William George (2015), Henry B. Arthur Fellow of Ethics, at Harvard Business School, conducted in depth interviews with what he calls "authentic" leaders. One of the points he notes is that these people are skilled at tailoring their style to their audiences and the imperatives of the situation. Sometimes they will need to be tough, and they will inevitably displease people, sometimes they will be inspiring, building consensus. Whatever their stance, they still manage to remain authentic. As leaders gain experience and develop greater self-awareness, they become more skilful in adapting their style, without compromising their own character.

Be aware of your impact

In the year 1170, King Henry II is reported to have said: "Will no one rid me of this turbulent priest?," the turbulent priest being Thomas Becket, Archbishop of Canterbury. Whether King Henry really intended this or not is a matter of conjecture, but his words put in train an unfortunate course of events and shortly afterwards four knights took it upon themselves to travel to Canterbury and confront and kill the hapless Thomas Becket. This led to demands for the King to be excommunicated whereas Thomas Becket was venerated which was definitely not what Henry had wanted.

When you are a leader people take what you say more seriously and, especially if you are deeply involved in your work, it is easy to forget the extent of the impact your words on other people. Added to this, whatever you say is likely to be exaggerated further down the line. You may think you are putting a small touch on the tiller, but that small touch can have a much bigger effect than intended at the other end. In most cases, your words are unlikely to cause a murder to happen, but they may not lead to the result for which you had hoped. So be careful and measured in how you express your thoughts or instructions and consider whether they are likely to bring about the result you require.

As people get to know you, they will get used to the way you behave and will be able to predict how you will respond. People say things like: "His bark is worse than his bite." That is not necessarily a bad thing because when they understand your motivations it helps to build rapport. But remember that, however friendly and amenable you are, you will always be the boss and what you do and say will make a difference to people. You will inevitably have to make unpopular decisions at some stage, and you will have to pass on difficult news, so you must try to be even handed with everyone and maintain a professional stance. Almost without noticing it, one can fall into the habit of only talking things over with one or two people who are friendly and share the same views, whilst you communicate with others only when necessary – usually when something is wrong. That will be noticed. Many of us on the receiving end have had the experience of recognising the caller and dreading the call – or even avoiding it – because we know that person only calls when there is bad news.

Supporting people and trusting them

To create the sublime music we hear when we listen to a concert, the conductor of an orchestra must bring together talented musicians who have the right instruments and lead and direct them to ensure they work in harmony. Like the conductor, leaders need employees who are qualified and skilled to do their jobs and who have the resources to do what is needed. The best results come when those people are also be interested in what they are doing. This is not only true of employees, it also applies to elected representatives. One of our interviewees told us that it is very clear when ministers are occasionally handed roles in which they have little interest. Things don't quite work as well.

It is possible to be effective for a short time when one of the ingredients is missing (people often have to work around not having sufficient resources, for example) but that effort cannot be sustained over a longer period. Fatigue and disillusionment set in and once that has happened it takes a long time to recover. Like the gardening analogy at the beginning of the chapter, if you don't provide the plants and soils with the nutrients and care they need, it will take a long time for your garden to flourish again.

In talking to people, we frequently hear hints that they feel their organisation is taking advantage of them. Take the example of managing without the right tools for the job, whether those tools are appropriate systems, expertise or having enough people to do the work. At first, everyone tries to cope because they want to do a good job and perhaps because they receive positive feedback, and this motivates them to carry on. But as time goes on, this wears thin. When they finally ask for more resources, they are met with the question: "You are managing as it is, so why do you need more?" You may recognise this stance which has echoes of Weber's traditional leader who only allocated resources when absolutely necessary.

Perhaps we are asking the wrong question here. Instead of waiting until the need for something becomes acute and people must ask for it, leaders at all levels should be proactive in observing and asking people who are doing the job what they need in order to be more effective. Always questioning people about their motivations and asking them to justify every action and every request has a ring of mistrusting about it. That is not to say that a certain level of scepticism and justification is not appropriate, particularly when resources are coming from the public purse, but if there is too much it builds bureaucracy, wastes time, and prevents people from taking action and encourages them to delay asking for something until is it too late. To quote one of the people we interviewed: "Individuals know what good feels like...we need to be given the freedom to do the right thing."

One of the most interesting examples of trusting employees comes from Brazil. The organisation concerned is a commercial company, Semco, but there are lessons that can be applied to the public sector. Ricardo Semler (2001) took over the company from his father Curt. Initially it was successful but after a while, employee relations deteriorated, Semler began to suffer from overwork and business declined. It was clear that urgent action was needed to put the company back on course. A new Head of HR joined the firm and worked with Semler to make the company a better place to work and give employees more say in how things would work. The change was to be quite dramatic. For example, employees were able to set their own working hours, thus avoiding some of the chaos of the Sao Paulo rush hour, and they were even allowed to set their own salaries, benchmarking against similar firms, and know what everyone else was earning. As you can imagine there was scepticism and there were initially some problems, but they stuck with it and it worked and the company became successful again. Trusting people to do the right thing paid off. As Semler said: "We'll send our sons anywhere in the world to die for democracy, but don't seem to apply the concept to the workplace." We tend to set up systems and processes to cope with the lowest level of trust and integrity when in fact most people are trustworthy and want to do the right thing.

An excellent example of trusting people emerged from one of our interviews, this time closer to home in National Health Service Clinical Commissioning Groups (CCGs). We spoke to Marcus Warnes, Accountable Officer for Staffordshire and Stoke-on-Trent CCG. Marcus, who firmly believes in flexible working and trusting people to do the right thing, took over his role in 2017 and was working hard to introduce his ideas into the organisation. When the coronavirus pandemic made it necessary for people to work from home, he was able to put his beliefs to the test more rapidly than he had expected. He and his team had an unspoken contract with their staff – we'll trust you and you deliver what is required but if you think you are having problems, come and talk to us. This has worked well and despite pressures of work and the turmoil caused by dealing with the pandemic, staff morale is higher than it was 12 months ago. As Marcus said: "We try to accommodate people and to trust them to work, and they are responding to the trust we put in them. Now we have a happier and more productive workforce that feels part of something bigger."

One of the many insights that came from police officers we interviewed was the high level of support they felt from their colleagues and immediate teams, perhaps the result of the danger to personal safety they sometimes faced. One Chief Super-intendent told us: "There is a real feeling of not wanting to let people down.... wanting to stand and fight together." However, some of those we interviewed were not so confident about receiving support from above if things didn't turn out well. In certain situations, such as hostage taking, decisions have to be made rapidly and they must be based on judgement as all the facts cannot be known. Sometimes the decision will be the right one. Sometimes it won't. Officers having to take these decisions need to know that they will be supported either way, providing they took the action in good faith. Knowing they are trusted and that they will be supported helps to preserve morale and enables them to take very difficult decisions on how to act. As former Chief Inspector Mark Evans told us: "The provision of a safe space to operate in allows 'hearts and minds' to flourish and in my mind has as important a role (if not more so) as well thought out processes and procedures."

Those working in the public sector are openly held to account for their actions, and rightly so, but there is still room for treating people as adults and trusting them to do the right things. For this to happen it is also necessary to manage expectations and build a culture in which stakeholders are also more trusting and tolerant of risk and uncertainty.

Avoiding silos

One question we are often asked is: "How to we break down silos?" Of course, the ideal situation is not to let them occur in the first place. Silos come about when there is a lack of communication across teams, when there is strong identification with one department or leader at the expense of the organisation as a whole and where there is competition for resources. They are most definitely the enemy of effective working because they can result in poor relationships between teams, unwillingness to cooperate and even in people withholding information for the benefit of their own "side."

Alas there are many practices and initiatives instituted by management, ostensibly in the name of achieving efficiency and effectiveness, which lead to the development of a silo mentality and performance management is one of the worst offenders. We will discuss performance management and its unintended consequences in more detail in Chapter 10 but here we'll focus on the implications for leadership.

Silos can be divided into two types – those created by structures and those created by people's behaviour. In both cases, the problem starts at the very top when leaders fail to consider the impact their policies or their behaviour will have on the way people work.

Structural silos can be seen in many large and complex organisations such as the NHS – although change is afoot. Let us take the NHS as an example because it has, traditionally, been characterised by its organisational and professional silos. Social care, for example, was in a different silo from health care. However, this is now changing with more emphasis on collaboration and integration. At Poole hospital, for example, health service and council staff work together to create packages to enable patients to be discharged from wards and free up beds for others who need them. The cross boundary working and breaking down of silos helped to halve the Trust's "delayed discharge" rate.[1]

We have already discussed the idea of the police having more impact on crime by working with other agencies to support troubled families. Working across boundaries helps. Focussing on what needs to be done, tracking back to see who needs to be involved and then working in partnership with them to do it, is far more effective than looking at the problem from the perspective of each agency. Partnership is important in this process and, oddly, the pandemic has forced partnerships to happen more quickly. As one of our interviewees from the NHS said: "The culture of competition hasn't helped. Now everyone is forced to work together as a result of Covid, it's better."

Silos can also be caused by "tribes". By this we mean groups of people, often forming within specific functions (but it can be specific teams) who are perceived as having a strong group identity. One of the problems is that "outsiders" are often reluctant to approach these people and this makes collaboration and communication difficult. In the private sector it is a well-known joke that people from finance and marketing cannot talk to each other because they see the world in a different way and they speak a different language. The same has been said of consultants in the NHS. Whether it is true or not, perception matters. If one group is seen as unapproachable there is a problem.

Silos caused by people's behaviour are equally damaging. If the Board or senior management team behave in a territorial way, that behaviour will become ingrained into the culture and it will be reflected right down the organisation. Let us take the example of competition for resources. This is not necessarily a bad thing because it should (in theory at least) encourage people to focus on what is really needed and it should discourage waste. However, whilst beating others to acquire resources may be perceived as the capability of a strong leader getting what his or her department needs, it is not particularly conducive to effective working. The competition can become an end in itself, a type of empire building with time and effort wasted on justification and bureaucracy rather than achieving the end result. It can disintegrate into a situation where everyone is fighting for their own corner rather than collaborating in the wider interests of the organisation.

It is very easy for silos to appear and they don't take too long to emerge. On speaking to people in the Civil Service, we heard several times that they felt departments and functions were too siloed. Standards and requests for information or action were pushed out according to the priorities of that department, with little reference or care about what was happening elsewhere. The priorities of other departments were ignored.

So, how do you avoid silos? We have already seen that the coronavirus crisis has forced change towards collaborative working in record time, but that change may not be sustained as the crisis recedes and normality returns.

The first step is to ensure structures and processes do not encourage silos in the first place. These include policies such as how you cascade goals and how you measure performance and reward people. If you take too simplistic an approach it will only serve to drive people to meet their targets and ignore others who trying to meet their own. You reach the situation where you have many individual streams happily flowing along but not the one large river you want. We discuss this is more detail in Chapter 10.

The second step is to keep in touch with people and find out what is really happening, rather than to make assumptions. The results of silo working are often hidden, they can be missed opportunities or little spokes being put in wheels. In themselves they are probably quite small but when you add them up, they can have a big, negative impact. That is not to say that everyone is trying to sabotage the organisation. It can just be something simple such as information being passed on late because it benefits another team and home team priorities take precedence. It's harder to discover these things formally as they are unlikely to be revealed in open meetings and sometimes people don't even mean to do them, but when you get to know people and can chat informally, they begin to emerge.

There are more formal strategies for breaking down silos and encouraging cross-team working. The first and most obvious is to keep attention on the higher-level goals and what the organisation is ultimately there to do. Remember Chief Superintendent Stamper's words to police officers: "What are you doing today to prevent crime, detect crime and keep people safe?" It is easy, especially in larger organisations, to focus on departmental goals and issues and lose sight of the overall purpose, but everyone must be aware of, and be aligned with the overall purpose of the organisation. Clearly, there are subdivisions which may have their own goals, but the overall purpose is paramount.

The second approach is to provide opportunities for people to get to know each other and for them to understand the work of their colleagues and the pressures under which they have to work. When you work in a silo, it is tempting to think you are the only group which has unreasonable demands placed upon you. We know one organisation that did this rather well. There were several regional teams, and it would have been very easy for each of these teams to exist in their own silo as the staff primarily worked from home or, in a few instances, from small offices. To avoid this happening, the organisation arranged twice yearly residential conferences which everyone had to attend. At these conferences, there were formal elements of training combined with presentations from one or two of the regional teams and from people at Head Office talking about overall goals, purpose, and strategy. Very importantly there was also plenty of opportunity for socialising. The socialising was especially effective because as well as the general gossip and chit-chat there was serious discussion of what had been said and swapping of ideas and best practice. New alliances were forged, and individuals were able to get to know their colleagues in other parts of the country and understand that they were not the only ones struggling to deal with problems. This meant they knew who to call if they needed support in tackling a particular issue. Not everyone wanted to come to these conferences because taking two days out of a busy schedule can be tough, but afterwards they nearly always thought they had benefitted from their attendance. It is hard to measure the results of that exercise and it was not inexpensive, but it certainly oiled the wheels of effective working.

One final word about silos – as a leader you must be careful that you are not unintentionally creating them yourself. There is a balance between supporting your own team, which of course you must do, and doing that to the detriment of the organisation as a whole.

Shaping the culture

The word "culture" is often used to describe the personality of an organisation, but what does that mean and what implication does it have for effectiveness in the public sector?

Culture is formed from the underlying beliefs, values and attitudes prevailing within an organisation. It takes time to develop as it comes about from the cumulative behaviour of people over time and so changing it is not a quick fix. Once it has been established the good elements must be maintained and reinforced. There is no single culture that is "correct," although there is what has been described as a "toxic culture" where the health and well-being of employees is affected. Nobody wants to work in these organisations because there is too much conflict, stress and low morale and there is usually a rapid turnover of staff which makes things worse.

The culture must suit the purpose of the organisation. To take a very simple example, you may consider that a culture which encourages high risk-taking would not be suitable for the prison service, although innovation may be helpful.

It is important to understand the prevailing culture in your organisation and to assess whether it supports its effectiveness, because a culture that may once have served it well, may now be holding it back. Let's take an example from the private sector – banking. In their earlier years banks were sited in grand buildings that reflected their stature. They exuded a sense of grandeur and security. People wanted to know that their money was safe. The bank manager was a pillar of the local community and the guardian of their money. He was often paternalistic and cautious in his decisions and he had probably enjoyed a long and successful career with the same bank. There is a wonderful description of bank employees in Charles Dickens' A Tale of Two Cities when he describes what happens to young men as they are: "Kept unseen like a cheese until they had the full Tellson's flavour and mould upon them". But the environment in which banks operated was changing. Financial markets were being deregulated and there was a need for the culture to change. Banks had to become to be less formal and more approachable and friendly, and over time, the traditional, rather cautious bank manager whom everyone knew, disappeared. The drive to improve results led to a rise in risk taking and pressure for more sales. Local branches lost much of their autonomy and banks became more impersonal and, you could argue, less in touch with their communities. Some of that change in culture was important in order to keep up with changes in society. Being more approachable meant more people could be encouraged to access the services afforded by banks and that gave those people more opportunity to put their money to better use, but some changes, such as the pressure to take ever more risks was a major factor in the 2007/2008 financial crisis.

There are several ways in which you can view culture. Professors Kim Cameron and Robert Quinn from the University of Michigan researched organisational effectiveness and success. They developed what is known as The Competing Values Framework. There are four boxes. The two on the top are Clan, where people collaborate and leaders are perceived as mentors and facilitators and Adhocracy, a creative orientation where leaders are viewed as innovators and visionaries. Both are high on flexibility and discretion with Clan having an internal focus and Adhocracy and external focus. Underneath those two boxes are Hierarchy where leaders are organisers and coordinators and it is about "control and efficiency with capable processes" and Market where leaders are drivers and it is about competing and customer focus. Both are on the stability and control axis with Hierarchy more internally focussed and Market external (Figure 2.1).

It's worth reflecting on this values framework and considering how it may apply to your organisation, or even your part of the organisation. There are elements in each of the boxes that aid effectiveness, so, although it may be appropriate that the predominating culture lies on the side of flexibility, for example, it may also be necessary to have elements of control and efficiency from the Hierarchy box.

We have already said that culture arises from the underlying beliefs of those working within the organisation. People often join an organisation because they identify with its values and purpose. Many employees in the NHS, for example, are there because they want to help and care for other people. Sarah Marsh's (2015)

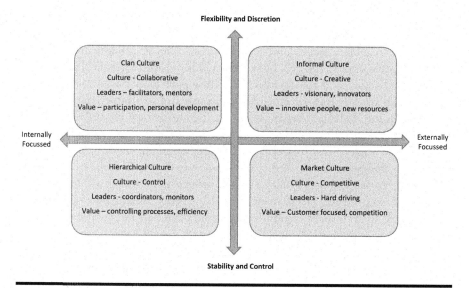

Figure 2.1 The four main culture types.

Source: Adapted from Cameron & Quinn.

survey of teachers carried out by the Association of Teachers and Lecturers Union showed that almost 75% of teachers joined because they wanted to make a difference. Some 86% enjoyed their job because they liked working with children and 76% because they liked to help their pupils enjoy learning. The NHS needs people who care for others and education needs people who want to help children. These are good things. However, it does make for a strong culture that is resistant to change. We will deal with how to effect change in more detail in Chapters 6 and 7, but it is worth noting some points about shaping the culture here.

When you reflect on the culture of your organisation, the first question to ask is why people are working there and what they care about. If you want to make changes you will need to be able to present new ideas in a way that will have resonance for them. It is a big mistake to come in and assume your changes are the right ones – people with experience of doing something are probably doing it in a certain way for a reason and you need to know what that is. On the other hand, they may be doing it in that way because "it's always been done like that" and you need to know that, too. Trying to change or shape culture is a delicate balance between retaining the traditional ethos and bringing in new ideas to make the organisation more effective.

Some time ago we interviewed Paul Woodward, who was at the time Chief Executive of the Charity Sue Ryder Care (Bourne & Bourne, 2011). Sue Ryder supports people with specialist palliative and longer-term care needs and at the time employed some 3400 staff and 10,000 volunteers with income from a variety of sources including primary care trusts, local authorities, retail, and fundraising activities. On joining, Paul realised the charity was not performing as well as it could. In fact, it was losing money and something had to change. There was a great need for the organisation to adopt a more commercial approach, but Paul knew this would be difficult to achieve given the prevailing culture. He needed to get existing staff and volunteers to understand the situation and elicit their ideas on how to approach and rectify it. To this end, he embarked on a series of two-hour interviews with key people across the charity asking them for five things they wanted to keep and three things they wanted to change. He also asked what they wanted from the Chief Executive and what advice they would give him. Interestingly, most people came up with ten things they wanted to change and three they would like to keep. Paul reported the findings of his research at a staff conference and in this way set the stage for implementing change. His strategy of involving people, taking note of what they said and keeping in constant communication paid off as staff and volunteers saw the need for change in order to preserve the organisation to which they were committed.

We must add a word of caution here and that is about checking what is really happening in the organisation as a whole. Culture is an ethos that is woven into the fabric of everyday work and it should permeate throughout. If there are pockets where something different is happening, then as a leader you need to know about it. One of the leaders we spoke to was aiming to create a "no blame" culture, encouraging flexible working where individuals were trusted to do their best. Wandering through the office at 5.30 pm on a Friday evening he saw a lone individual sitting at his desk. On asking why he was still there when everyone else had gone, he was told that his line manager was not happy with his time keeping so he had to sit at his desk. That type of presenteeism did not reflect the nature of the organisation he was trying to create, and he had to talk to the manager to explain why his actions didn't fit with the new ethos and discuss better ways of dealing with poor timekeeping. It is important to observe what is actually happening, because you must reinforce the culture you are aiming to create and applying rules in one place and not in others can lead to dissatisfaction.

Creating capacity and diversity

The effectiveness of an organisation depends to a large extent on the ability of its employees at every level, from those who set the policy to those who carry it out and those who enable it to be carried out such as support functions including finance and HR. It goes without saying, then, that part of the leader's role is to ensure the right people are recruited and retained. They must have the appropriate skills and knowledge to do the work, but they should also share the underlying values and be in tune with the overall purpose of the organisation. However, sharing underlying values does not mean recruiting people who are all in the same mould, for that is a recipe for stagnation. Much has been written about diversity and the need for those in the public sector to reflect the makeup of the nations they are serving. There is also a need to ensure there is diversity of thinking and interest to add new perspectives and insights, to avoid group think and overconfidence in one course of action.

Here is an example from the private sector that illustrates this point well. A small engineering company with a good reputation amongst its clients was involved in designing and supplying water treatment equipment for the oil industry. Nearly everyone working there was a first-class research engineer, interested in exploring new ideas and creating new solutions. The company's services were excellent, but it was not performing so well financially. When a newly appointed market analyst produced a report setting out applications for which existing work could be applied, it was met with little enthusiasm. The engineers were not interested in making tweaks or slightly re-inventing the wheel, even if this would make the company more profitable, they wanted to spend their time working on exciting new ideas.

New recruits should be a good "fit" with the organisation, but they do not need to be clones of existing successful employees. In fact, it is important they are not. Effective organisations are able to accommodate people who hold different views and have different perspectives on the world because those people bring in new insights and talent. The thread that holds them together is the sharing of the values of that organisation.

Lee Iacocca, former chair of Chrysler was once reported as saying, "I hire people brighter than me and get out of their way." Yet many leaders feel threatened by the idea of employing people who may turn out to be a challenge, preferring instead to surround themselves with those who are unlikely to voice different opinions even if they hold them. This may feel more comfortable but is unlikely to lead to successful outcomes.

We started this section by outlining the changing role of leadership. No leader of a large and complex organisation can have all the skills and experience needed to run it. Knowing where the gaps are is essential, as is ensuring there is a little sand in the oyster's shell to spark some new thinking. If you recruit bright and able people, it acts like a magnet because those recruits help to make the organisation more successful and as the saying goes: "Success breeds success." You start to create a virtuous circle where success attracts a higher calibre of potential new recruits and your organisation becomes more and more attractive to talented people.

The second part of Iacocca's statement is also pertinent; "… get out of their way." Recruiting the best people and then watching over their shoulders all the time smacks of lack of trust. Talented people need to have the freedom to act and be granted the authority that comes with their position and micromanaging is not only inefficient, but it is also not effective. In the early days you must support new recruits and ensure they know you are available to them when they need you, and from time-to-time you will need to check how they feel things are going. But, retaining talented people is just as important as recruiting them in the first place, and they are unlikely to stay if they feel they have joined an employer who will not allow them to use their skills.

There is a further reason to recruit the best people and to resist the temptation to constantly exercise your control over them, and that is for your own well-being as a leader. As you cannot do everything yourself and you cannot be everywhere at once, you must have a good team to support you. One of the senior people we interviewed spoke about the importance of creating a strong executive team and then giving them freedom to do what they felt to be right. When asked how he managed to be resilient at times of high pressure he said:

> You can switch off if you have a team you can trust. My team knows I trust them, and they trust me. We also have a proper communications process in place, so it runs itself rather than being totally dependent on one member of the team.

Note

1 https://www.ft.com/content/ee50b4bc-285b-11e8-b27e-cc62a39d57a0

References

Bourne, M. & Bourne, P. (2011) *The handbook of corporate performance management*, John Wiley & Sons, Chichester, UK.

Covey, S. (2020) *The 7 habits of highly effective people* Reissue edition (19 May 2020), Simon & Schuster, London, UK.

George, W. (2015) *Discover your true north*, Jossey-Bass, San Francisco, CA.

Goleman, D. (1996) *Emotional intelligence*, Bloomsbury Publishing, London.

Grant, K. & Williams, R. (2019) Leadership in the public sector, a renewed call to action, reflections on leadership and people practice, Series 1, No. 2, December, https://www.napier.ac.uk/~/media/worktribe/output-2376960/leadership-in-the-public-sector-a-renewed-call-to-action.pdf

Gryta, T. & Mann, T. (2020) *Lights out: pride, delusion, and the fall of general electric*, Houghton Mifflan Harcourt Publishing Company, New York.

Heaphy & Dutton (2008) as cited by "Do some people energize you while others drain you?" *Psychology Today*, https://psychologytoday.com/us/blog/your-personal-renaissaince/201811/do-some-people-energize-you-while-others-drain-you

Kennedy, J. F. (1961) "The decision to go to the moon," *NASA History Office*, https://history.nasa.gov/moondec.html

Marsh, S. (2015) "Five top reasons why people become teachers and quit," *The Guardian*, https://www.theguardian.com/teacher-network/2015/jan/27/five-top-reasons-teachers-join-and-quit

McAllister, C., Moss, S. & Martinko, M. (2019) in the US (Published in the *Harvard Business Review Newsletter* of October 2019.

Parry, Grant and Sheehan, 2019 Cited in Grant & Williams (2019) https://www.napier.ac.uk/~/media/worktribe/output-2376960/leadership-in-the-public-sector-a-renewed-call-to-action.pdf

Semler, R. (2001) Maverick!: *The success story behind the world's most unusual workplace, random house business*, London.

Steenbarger, B. (2018) "Cultivating the essential ingredient in leadership: energy," *Forbes*, https://www.forbes.com/sites/brettsteenbarger/2018/01/21/cultivating-the-essential-ingredient-in-leadership-energy/#582f3b2de1e4

Zenger, J. & Folkman, J. (2019) "The three elements of trust," *Harvard Business Review*, https://hbr.org/2019/02/the-3-elements-of-trust

Chapter 3

The skills of leadership

Doubt is uncomfortable, but certainty is absurd.

Voltaire

Dealing with uncertainty and managing risks

It is a fact. The world in which we live is an uncertain place. We can make assumptions about our lives and live with uncertainty and the risks we face – and have to do so every day. When I wake up in the mornings, I automatically assume I will make it back to bed that night, for example, but there is always the risk I may be run over by a bus when I go out. Having an appreciation of risk has served humankind well – some early humans who were careless probably ended up being eaten by hungry sabre tooth tigers. So, we must all live with uncertainty and manage the risks arising from it.

As we live our daily lives, we tend not to think too much about uncertainty. However, during periods of change or special and unusual events, we try to seek certainty and patterns where none exist. During the coronavirus pandemic there was much reporting of conflicting scientific evidence which was only to be expected. We like to think science has all the answers to our problems and that there is one answer to each problem, but we have to learn to live with the fact this isn't the case. Even when we detect a pattern, it may not be cause and effect.

People deal with uncertainty in different ways. Some feel the need to take control of everything themselves. From our own observation, we see this applies even to people who espouse the idea of delegation and who, in more certain times, allow their teams to have the freedom to operate. When the chips are down, though, they revert to the style with which they feel most comfortable and come in to take charge. They take what they believe is the tried and tested route, which means they are not open

DOI: 10.4324/9781003099895-5

to alternative approaches. Whilst strong leadership is important, storming in to take over the reins from others undermines their confidence and is a great demotivator. If you do this, you are essentially saying: "Move over. I can do this better than you. I know better." In some exceptional situations and with the right approach, taking over may be the right course of action, but in most cases, it is not helpful and it takes a long time to rebuild trust.

For other people, uncertainty makes it almost impossible for them to take a decision. They keep seeking more evidence which may not even exist. They delay action because they fear that finally taking a decision will crystallise the risk. What they forget is that not taking a decision is in itself a risk.

Over-control and under-control are both counter-productive when it comes to effectiveness and it is important to reflect on how you respond yourself and how those closest to you respond. If you are aware of what you are doing and how you are affecting those around you, you will be able to steer a steadier course.

So, how can you begin to cope with uncertainty?

In an article "Strategy Under Uncertainty," Hugh Courtney, Jane Kirkland, and S. Patrick Viguerie (2000) all from McKinsey, identify four types of uncertainty – clear future, where a single forecast will suffice, alternative futures, where there are a few discrete scenarios, ranges of future, where there may be a limited number of key variables but the actual outcome may lie anywhere within it, and true uncertainty, where it is virtually impossible to predict what will happen. The latter is quite rare, but the authors use the example of companies considering major investments in Russia in 1992 when it was not possible to predict laws and regulations relating to property rights and transactions, or the viability of supply chains and demand for previously unavailable consumer goods and services.

This model is a helpful way of taming the ambiguity. It is important to learn to live with a level of ambiguity and uncertainty but applying some form of logical analysis to it helps to prevent it from becoming overwhelming. Taking stock of what you know and don't know is a good start. Think about US Secretary of Defence, Donald Rumsfeld's famous quote:

> There are known knowns. These are things we know that we know. There are known unknowns. That is to say, there are things that we know we don't know. But there are also unknown unknowns. There are things we don't know we don't know.

We will explore that idea further in a later chapter. Examining potential risks, considering responses and actions, and assigning priorities will help you feel more in control.

Having said this, there is a balance to be struck between creating rigid processes and responses and being agile and working with rapidly changing and uncertain situations. The creation of scenarios and contingency plans forms an essential part of managing uncertainty and contributes towards achieving a successful outcome, but it is important to remember that they will not be perfect. There is only a certain extent to which you can plan and imagine "what ifs?". Too often leaders make plans and forecasts and if they don't work out consider them, and the people who have produced them, to be failures. In complex situations there are just too many variables to predict a precise outcome. If you, as a leader try to make out that a given scenario is more concrete than it really is, you are not being honest. It may provide short term relief but when things don't turn out as expected, people will become disillusioned and will lose their trust in you. In addition to this you may also cut out other better, options for action because you are set on pursuing one course.

One of the traps to be aware of at times of uncertainty is confirmation bias. That is selecting evidence and messages that confirm your own beliefs which can be a comforting practice when you are faced with situations of ambiguity. As Warren Buffet said:

"What the human being is best at doing is interpreting all new information so that their prior conclusions remain intact."

One well-known study was conducted by Stanford University (Lord, Ross & Lepper, 1979). Half the participants in the study were in favour of capital punishment and half were against. Participants were all asked to read descriptions of two fictional studies, comparisons of US States with and without the death penalty, after which they had to say whether their opinions had changed. Then they were asked to rate whether the research was well conducted and convincing. Half the participants were informed that one study supported the deterrent effect of capital punishment and the other undermined it. The conclusions were swapped for the other half. Having read detailed descriptions of the two studies almost all participants returned to their original beliefs referring to details that supported their views and disregarding those that didn't.

In a world where there is a welter of conflicting information swirling around, confirmation bias is a way in which the brain can make a mental short cut. Although it may alleviate the load on our brains and make us feel reassured about our own beliefs, it can lead us to interpret information incorrectly, blinding us to what is really there and making us cling to our own position in the light of evidence to the contrary. So, be aware of how you are processing the information you see. Make sure you read entire articles, or you may find your eyes are drawn to the sentences that reinforce what you already think. Read articles you know are going to challenge your preconceptions. And, although it seems obvious, ensure your evidence comes from a trusted and independent source, or at least one where you know what the prevailing beliefs are.

Although most of us tend to think uncertainty and risk are negative and we take steps to reduce them, it's worth remembering risk-taking has a positive side. Without taking any risks nothing would progress. We heard several times in our interviews that people working in the public sector are risk averse. They are very aware that the money they are spending is coming from the public purse. "Every penny spent on a digital solution in the NHS is a penny not spent on Grandma's hip replacement."

We also heard that people are reluctant to take risks because if it works out well there will be little praise, but if it goes wrong the penalties will be severe. There is undoubtedly a balance to be struck between tolerating risk and being ultra-cautious in trying to eliminate uncertainty and ensuring everything is right. It is, in any case practically impossible to eliminate all risk.

One of the people we spoke to in connection with projects in the NHS told us:

> There's a risk that people don't challenge themselves enough in terms of what could have been delivered ….Is that because they didn't set out with the right vision? Or is it because they trimmed the scope to something they could deliver in time and on budget? If the latter I would have had a fit because it is sort of OK, but not quite. Do we fail to be ambitious enough because we could fail to do something?

In our view, that is a very thought-provoking comment.

At times of uncertainty, we are forced to change the way we operate, we have to become more resourceful, we're often driven to share opinions and take advice from others which we wouldn't normally do. Any complacency is challenged. Change is accelerated. We are more prepared to cut though bureaucracy. So, in some ways uncertainty provides an excellent impetus for us to try out new ideas and to learn. Several of our interviewees, for example, spoke about how the uncertainty of the coronavirus pandemic had suddenly made it imperative for them to work more closely with their counterparts in other agencies, something they had been wanting to do for some time but had been unable to drive though.

What matters is how you handle uncertainty and risk. We have already said that as a leader, you must be an exemplar. People will take their cue from you and if they see you are comfortable with uncertainty and ambiguity then they will be more comfortable, too. If they see you are unwilling to tolerate any risk, they won't take risks for fear of making mistakes. That may or may not be appropriate, depending on the work you are doing. You and your senior team are the people who decide what level of risk is appropriate and you will influence the culture and the appetite for risk.

Exercising judgement

Dealing effectively with uncertainty and risk requires good judgement. There is rarely a lack of data and information on which to make decisions. On the contrary, there is often just too much to assimilate in the time available and the temptation is to wait until the next piece of evidence comes along, and then the next and the next, delaying the moment when a decision has to be made. The problem with this is that, when the crunch point comes and action must be taken, there is not enough time to plan and communicate what is required. With the growth in availability of information people expect the right decision to emerge. Sometimes it does. With reading and listening, an answer to a problem can sometimes become clearer and clearer. However, complex problems don't have simple answers and often there is no right answer, anyway. It is a matter of judgement and being able to explain why a decision has been made and persuading people to accept that judgement and work with it.

Good judgement can come with experience, but it doesn't always. If you have faced a situation before, then you should have a better idea of what you will be facing. But your experience will only be helpful if you are able to reflect and learn from what has happened in the past – good and bad. It's also true to say that relying on experience can make some people over-confident. If they assume experience in one narrow area applies to a wider field or if they fail to notice the world has moved on and circumstances have changed since their last success, then their judgement is impaired. There is no substitute for reflection and critical thinking. Leaders who are overwhelmed tend to repeat the same mistakes because they are not strong enough to acknowledge something went wrong and don't take the time to think about how it could have been done better.

People who exercise good judgement are usually acute listeners. Listening intently is hard to do as most coaches know, because as you hear the words the other person is saying, your brain is frantically working out what they mean, looking for any hidden meaning and working out what your next question or your response will be. You may even be finding it hard not to be distracted and think about what you need to buy for that night's supper. It takes a huge effort to concentrate but it is rewarding. When you listen intently, you will notice the tone of the words, the body language of the speaker and will pick up on any hesitations or omissions and you will be less likely to make the wrong assumptions about what they are going to say. In addition to this, paying full attention to someone is a courtesy which will help you build a better relationship with them. Think about your own experience. How do you feel when you are talking to someone and they constantly look away and nod at other people or glance down at their phone or watch?

Good listening should lead to good questioning. Repeating what has been said helps you to check your understanding. It is a practice well worth following because it is easy to assume you have understood something when in reality you haven't quite grasped it. We have already pointed out the importance of knowing the source of your evidence, but when someone tells you something, you need to know the point at which the facts end and their own opinions come in. Ask them. Also think about why someone is suggesting a solution. What is their angle? What do they stand to lose or gain? Don't take what you hear at face value but equally don't ask superficial questions for the sake of it or to show off your own knowledge. Listen to what is being said, take time to formulate your questions. What is it you really need to know?

Be curious about what is happening around you – if you can, go and see something for yourself rather than relying on what other people tell you. There are some things that data and information cannot supply. Some years ago, on an assignment in Kenya, Pippa met with representatives from an association for small scale farmers.

What the briefing papers and articles could not convey was the real difficulties they faced but also their palpable enthusiasm for looking at new ideas. Seeing something for yourself will give you a more rounded feel for what is happening.

If you come across something that doesn't fit, investigate it before acting. In his excellent article, "The Elements of Good Judgement" (Harvard Business Review Jan–Feb 2020), Sir Andrew Likierman cites the example of a Soviet Lieutenant Colonel, Stanislav Petrov, who in 1983 saved the world from near disaster. On being told that soviet satellites had detected a US missile attack on the Soviet Union, he decided the 100% probability reading was too high and so reported a system malfunction rather than obeying his instructions to pass the information to his superiors. It was the right call as satellites had mistaken sunlight reflected from clouds for missile engines.

There is another side to this and that is how you, as a leader, react when those reporting to you exercise their judgement or not. In a much lowlier situation than the one described above; a course organiser was preparing papers for a short course as per instructions. The instructions said: "Ensure notes for *The Effective Leader* are given to all participants." The organiser knew the course was called *The Effective Supervisor* but duly supplied the *Effective Leader* notes as instructed and was astonished to be reprimanded for following instructions. It soon became clear in that organisation that people were expected to use their initiative and exercise judgement or at least ask, rather than blindly follow the rules.

Writing about the importance of leadership, Sir Andrew Likierman in his Harvard (2020) article says:

> Those with ambition but no judgement run out of money. Those with charisma but no judgement lead their followers in the wrong direction. Those with passion but no judgement hurl themselves down the wrong paths. Those with drive but no judgement get up very early to do the wrong things. Sheer luck and factors beyond your control may determine your eventual success, but good judgement will stack the cards in your favour.

Managing relationships and handling conflict

Throughout this section, we have emphasised the importance of building good relationships. We often hear the saying: "It doesn't matter what you know, but who you know." That is right, but it isn't confined to knowing the great and the good. It's also about knowing people who know about something you don't and being able to trust them. If you know where the gaps are in your knowledge and you know people upon whom you can call when you need to fill those gaps, you will be in a much better position to create a successful outcome.

We need to describe in more detail what we mean by "relationship." When you are in a senior position there is often no shortage of people willing to help, with advice flowing in from all quarters. There are many people with whom you will have a "relationship" but what matters when it comes to effectiveness, is the quality of that relationship (and, of course, the quality of the advice). Strong relationships usually take a long time to build. Having a strong relationship with someone means you don't have to be in constant contact with that person. You can ring them up and know they won't mind, and you will know they will give you support and unbiased advice which you can trust. (Of course, it works both ways. You need to do the same for them.) The danger, as we have already said, is if you choose to build strong relationships only with people who share your own views and will take your side on every occasion. It is helpful that those working closely with you have an affinity with your underlying values and aims, but this is not the same as accepting all your views. If you have a strong relationship with someone, you can agree to disagree with them and there is no harm in being seen to "capitulate" and change your mind in the face of what they tell you.

At this stage we would like to put in a plug for coaching. A coach won't tell you what to do, at least not in the normal course of things, but they can act as an unbiased and confidential sounding board and ask incisive questions to help you see a problem from a different perspective. We had an interesting conversation from someone within the NHS who saw it as part of his role to coach promising people in his team. He told us just how much he, himself, had learnt whilst doing this. He had no real idea, for example, of the depth of problems faced by people from ethnic minorities. So, there is learning on both sides.

The people who are in your immediate circle, those who report to you and those to whom you report are clearly most important. You need to understand them, know where they are coming from and what their motivations are by talking to them and asking for their opinions and thoughts. To do this you also have to be generous in sharing some of your own feelings – a relationship is two-way after all, and they need to understand you, as well. Be careful this isn't too forced, though. We know of one organisation where an employee satisfaction survey revealed staff felt senior managers were too remote. All senior managers were urged to get out, walk around and talk to people. Alas, this didn't have quite the intended effect. Almost overnight open plan offices were regularly visited by people who had rarely been there before. On seeing senior managers looming towards their desks, some staff members took off for a coffee whilst others stopped work and sat there wondering with growing angst why the HR Director was making a bee line for them.

There are also people who flit in and out of your working life, often specialists who have a skill in a narrow area, upon whom you can call when a need arises. These are important people, and it is good to stay in touch and build a strong relationship with them, but remember what their particular skill is. They may have been very helpful in supporting you and providing advice on *a* and *b* but no matter how much you like and respect them and feel loyalty towards them, their advice and support on *x* and *y* may not be sound.

Let's move on to how to handle conflict. Unless you are surrounding yourself with clones, you are likely to have to face some conflict. We're all human, after all. Some level of challenge is healthy but too much is a waste of time and takes the focus away from getting the right things done. If you are trusted and respected then you can minimise this type of conflict, but you cannot obliterate it completely. If you think there isn't any conflict or dissent then something is wrong. Either you have only "yes-men and women" in your team or you are not in touch and are not picking up on what's going on. So, how do you deal with it? The first thing to say is obvious, you must deal with it because the longer it goes on the worse it will get. Talking to people reasonably, bringing them together in a room for discussion is the usual tactic, but sometimes, if there is major conflict you need a more formal strategy to deal with it.

Back in the 1970s, two US academics, Kenneth Thomas and Ralph Kilmann conducted research into conflict resolution and produced the *Thomas-Kilmann Conflict Mode Instrument* to help identify individuals' response to conflict situations. It is helpful in deciding how to tackle a conflict situation. Thomas and Kilmann (1994) described five approaches

Competing: this is when each side in a conflict focusses on their own needs without thinking about the other side. It can be suitable in situations where you believe you are morally or legally correct.

Avoiding: as the name suggests neither side wants confrontation, and this can be appropriate if the time is not right, and you want to postpone handling the issue.

Compromising: finding middle-ground can help you reach a win-win outcome.

Collaborating: digging into the problem more deeply can sometimes bring a solution to the surface that satisfies all parties.

Accommodating: this is where one party gives way to the other side, and it is suitable if you need to maintain relationships.

It is our firm belief that it is better to work with others – ideally to collaborate or to compromise if you can – rather than to set yourself in competition with them. This does require a level of trust, generosity, perhaps, but solutions reached in this way are likely to be more sustainable. The more you can do to smooth the way, the more effective your operations will be.

When working on a major project, Mike went out of his way to minimise possible conflicts and future squabbles with suppliers by paying trusted suppliers upfront rather than as the work was done, which was the more normal practice at the time. It did raise some eyebrows, but by doing this, suppliers were motivated to get on with value-adding work, without having to spend time filling in numerous time sheets and justifications. Everyone was focussed and motivated to achieve a successful outcome and it led to excellent working relationships.

In another example, one organisation we know of, decided to offer free office space to staff from its contractors. That may have seemed a generous offer, and no doubt may have seemed extravagant to some of the accountants, but it not only took away the problem of people having to travel to meet from various offices dotted

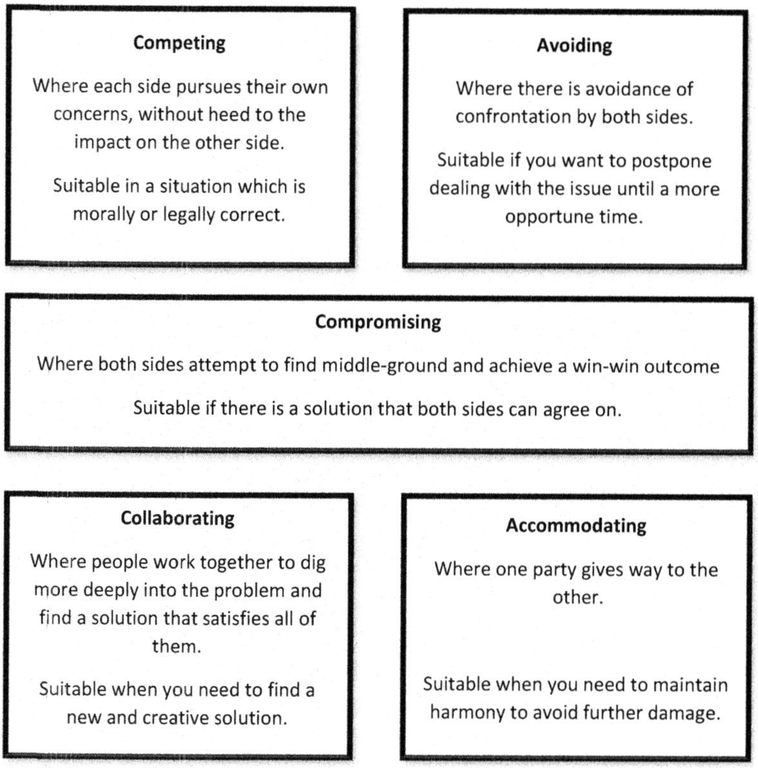

Competing	Avoiding
Where each side pursues their own concerns, without heed to the impact on the other side. Suitable in a situation which is morally or legally correct.	Where there is avoidance of confrontation by both sides. Suitable if you want to postpone dealing with the issue until a more opportune time.

Compromising

Where both sides attempt to find middle-ground and achieve a win-win outcome

Suitable if there is a solution that both sides can agree on.

Collaborating	Accommodating
Where people work together to dig more deeply into the problem and find a solution that satisfies all of them. Suitable when you need to find a new and creative solution.	Where one party gives way to the other. Suitable when you need to maintain harmony to avoid further damage.

Figure 3.1 Kilmann and Thomas' five approaches for tackling conflict.

around the place, which took up time, it also speeded up communication, reinforced relationships and meant everyone in the office was working towards the same end.

Creating resilience and managing pressure

A certain amount of pressure is helpful in providing stimulation but the notion that you must put people under pressure to get the best out of them is, in our view, outdated, mistrustful, and likely to cause more harm than good. To start with, people are all individuals. Some respond well to pressure and others don't, but, in any case, very few people are able to work productively and effectively when they are under pressure for long periods. Sooner or later, it will lead to stress and underperformance.

There is some research to back this up. Dr Hendrie Weisinger (2016), a psychologist and Dr J P Pawliw-Fry from the Kellogg School of Management studied 12,000 people who were working under pressure and found the idea that pressure made them more productive was a myth. Effectiveness is about achieving a successful outcome and that is a long-term goal. If you put people under too much pressure, they will be tempted to cut corners and forced to work to the next short-term goal. Creating a pressurised workplace will result in a fall in the level of performance over time and ultimately to higher absences and the loss of good people.

It is better to make people excited about their work, rather than put them under pressure to achieve. Ensure they know what the end goal is and why it exists. Paint a vivid picture of it. Ask them what they can offer towards achieving it. Give them responsibility, be tolerant when things go wrong and learn from mistakes. Get people to work in teams, support each other rather than compete, and make sure you celebrate their successes. In this way you will create energy rather than zapping it through unnecessary pressure and people will want to come to work rather than dreading it.

Having said this, pressure exists and particularly so in the public sector which is in the glare of the media and the public eye. Creating an environment in which pressure is maintained within healthy bounds takes a long time. As no-one works alone and what you do affects other people and their work loads, it is important for all departments to recognise that and to work together to ensure there are no time bombs of pressure ticking away in the background (see Figure 3.2). So, where do you begin?

Where does pressure come from? Often it comes from trying to achieve impossible targets, and we will deal with that in more detail in Chapter 10. Sometimes it comes from trying to work when you don't have sufficient resources. At other times, it comes about when individuals feel undervalued and believe they are not being treated fairly. Or it may be the result of miscommunication and misunderstanding, of suspicion and doubt.

Whatever the reason, managing it starts with good and open communication. By that we mean an environment where everyone feels they can express their opinion without being judged or blamed. Too often, even senior people feel unable to point out problems or express a contrary viewpoint for fear of undesirable consequences. We have already spoken about the importance of taking the time to get to know people and build good relationships because this oils the wheels of communication. If you can ring someone up, go and see them and talk openly about a problem you are much more likely to diffuse a sticky situation than you are if all you can do is email them.

The problem of hierarchies and protocols was mentioned numerous times during the course of our interviews. You do need protocols – a free for all won't work in most situations – but the problem comes when people feel so daunted by hierarchies that they can't talk to someone of higher rank because they believe their views will either be ignored or used against them. It is not only more junior people who have this problem. One of the very senior people we spoke to said:

> It's like being in the headmaster's office when you submit plans and are told to go away and come back with a better one. It's demoralising and you can end up with a plan you know you can't deliver. Thankfully, we have a different approach now and that works.

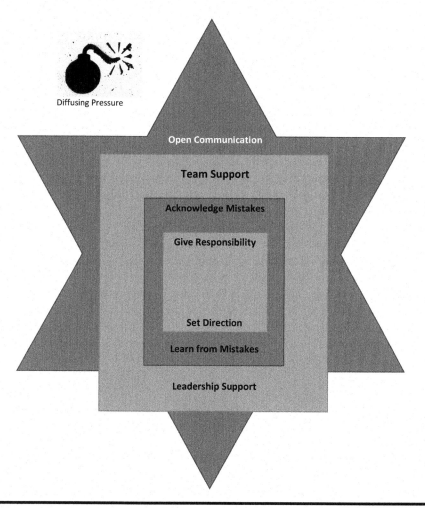

Figure 3.2 Diffusing pressure.

Fear of making mistakes often causes pressure. Of course, mistakes are not exactly desirable but they are inevitable and if, as a leader, you are not aware of any then either you are not in touch and they are being hidden from you, or everyone is playing safe and there will be no innovation, creativity, or progress.

Matthew Syed (2015), author of *Black Box Thinking*, talks about the importance of learning from mistakes and compares two fields in which mistakes can be catastrophic – the airline industry and health care. In aircraft, black boxes record voices and technical information; pilots and air crew are encouraged to report problems and every mistake is analysed to prevent it from happening again. In healthcare this has not always been the case. Some 400,000 people die each year in US hospitals from preventable error (according to the Journal of Patient Safety) and that is like two Jumbo Jets crashing every day. Perhaps it is a little unfair to compare airlines and health services because disease and injury are highly complex and there are many variables, but the point is still well made. Learning from mistakes is essential to avoid any recurrence and to learn from mistakes you need to create an environment in which that learning can take place.

Although it may seem counter-intuitive, giving people responsibility and trusting them to get on with their work is a good approach to creating an environment with the right level of pressure. As long as those people know what they must achieve and have reasonable resources with which to do it, it is far better to let them get on with it than to micromanage, as we have already seen. When people are given responsibility, they are able to develop and test out their ideas, and they have more confidence in what they are doing.

But of course, sometimes bad things happen, and this causes pressure. One of the people we spoke to talked about the importance of being a buffer rather than an amplifier. Hiding bad news is unadvisable, even if well intentioned, because it will leak out sooner or later, and people will feel either betrayed or that they are not trusted. However, amplifying bad news isn't good either because that leads to unnecessary alarm and, if it happens too often, like the story of the little boy crying wolf, no one will pay attention. There is a level at which bad news is acknowledged, accepted and everyone gets on doing their best to cope with it, knowing they have the support of their leaders and their teams.

Setting direction and standards

We are aware that some people reading this will feel the approach to leadership we are describing – trusting people, building relationships, allowing flexibility – is too soft. It goes against the grain of some organisations in the public sector. But adopting this approach still means setting direction and creating and maintaining high standards.

It goes without saying that if you want to achieve high standards, you must employ good people in the first place and then you must retain them. To do that you need robust recruitment processes, but to bring in the right candidates you also need to be an attractive employer. Human consulting firm, Mercer regularly conducts a survey into global talent trends. Their research reveals that employees in organisations that lead with empathy (care about what matters to their people) are more energised and willing to learn. They are more satisfied with their employer and are therefore less likely to leave. Research also shows that employees are looking for flexibility in work patterns (the rigid 9–5 working day is no longer desirable), they want to sense that their employer is considering their well-being and they want to feel they are working for a purpose. So, the good news is that money isn't everything. The public sector is there to provide services for the good of society and that chimes well with people who are looking for a purpose in what they do. The bad news is that some of the hierarchical and rigid cultures we have heard about in certain areas of the public sector are unlikely to be attractive, and that aversion to hierarchy and rigidity is likely to increase as time goes on and individuals become less tolerant of just being told what to do. However, it is possible to set standards and direction without imposing strict rules and processes.

Several interviewees stressed the importance of setting and communicating a precise purpose and set of priorities. One of the people we spoke to explained this very clearly:

> We struggled with clarity in the past. There were too many priorities; people didn't know what their role was. The vision came out and before you knew it, it had been reinterpreted. Now we have .... a clear strategy and set of priorities, accountable delivery and role clarity. This makes things easy for staff. It is hard to believe, but in the past one person had to go around to 20 different meetings to get a decision on one thing.

So, you set a direction and strategy and make it clear what everyone's role is in achieving it. The next job is to set priorities, goals, and milestones and this is when you also agree measurements and standards (we'll deal with this aspect in much more detail in Chapter 10). But it is not quite as simple as that. You need a clear strategy and a plan but as one interviewee put it: "You need a plan with fluidity underneath." What she meant by this was that people should know and understand the strategy and plan, but they should also understand that the environment changes, sometimes rapidly, and so, whilst the desired outcome may remain the same, the route to achieving it may change. Having a clear direction combined with understanding the need for flexibility is vital so that plans in themselves do not become too constricting as changes occur.

Military strategists are experts in the art of planning and executing effective campaigns, so it is helpful to look at what they say on the subject of setting direction and standards. Helmuth von Moltke became Chief of the Prussian General Staff in 1857. He understood that in battle campaigns the value of advanced detailed planning decreases as time passes and conflict draws near or is in progress. Commanders have to make decisions based on constantly changing situations. He promulgated the idea of "Auftragstaktik" (mission tactics) which encouraged commanders to be flexible and to react to situations as they developed.

The US Marine corps doctrine[1] expresses it well:

> We must learn to fight in an environment of uncertainty, which we can do by developing simple, flexible plans; planning for contingencies; developing standing operating procedures and fostering initiative among subordinates... success depends in large part on the ability to adapt to a constantly changing situation.

So there is a balance between ensuring there is a strategy and plan with associated priorities and also building in the understanding and the capacity to cope with changing situations.

Let's turn from setting direction to setting standards. We have already explored the idea of the leader as the exemplar. It is leaders who shape the culture and the standards they set reflect the culture and are there to uphold it. When it comes to standards people will be watching to see what the leader does, how the leader reacts. At the time of writing, Sir Keir Starmer, leader of the opposition Labour Party in the United Kingdom is faced with a tricky decision. Jeremy Corbyn, the previous party leader was suspended from the party following a report into antisemitism. Sir Keir, faced with the decision on whether to allow Mr Corbyn to return as a Labour MP (rather than an independent MP), decided not to allow him to return despite the dissent this would cause within the party. Whatever the rights or wrongs of this case, Sir Keir is sending out a message about not tolerating antisemitism.

Standards form part of the operating system of the organisation. By setting standards and applying them consistently you are showing people what you expect. By setting clear strategy and plans you are doing the same.

It is important that you enforce standards – if you don't, they won't be taken seriously. However, the way you hold people to account for meeting standards really matters. It can be constructive or destructive, and that goes for individuals being held to account by other individuals and organisations being held to account by regulators. We heard from some interviewees how inspections from regulatory bodies are dreaded, hanging over them like a black cloud and diverting their attention away from the activities they know they should be doing. Whilst they recognised regulators were important for scrutiny to ensure standards were upheld, and, as one person put it: "To keep us on our toes," they also felt regulators needed to understand better the context in which performance was being delivered. There is already a great deal of debate about this subject. If you take the regulation of schools, for example, some schools operate in far more challenging environments than others. Adverse reports can affect teacher retention and recruitment and add to those challenges. There is also the question we raised earlier of evaluating performance of activities that add most value in achieving a successful outcome, and not merely measuring success in maintaining processes or procedures which may be important and easy to measure but are not ends in themselves. Not all interviewees were critical of regulators, though. Some felt they were helpful in upholding standards and highlighting areas where improvements could be made.

There is a balance between being objective and being involved and a regulator must act with professional integrity, but it is important that the regulatory system should not take focus, resources and motivation away from achieving a successful outcome. It should be seen as being useful and supportive by those subject to it.

Note

1 Extracted from "Flexibility: An Essential Principle of War" by Thomas Eisiminger, US Army.

References

Courtney, H., Kirkland, J. & Patrick Viguerie, S. P. (2000) "Strategy under uncertainty," *McKinsey Quarterly*, June, https://www.mckinsey.com/business-functions/strategy-and-corporate-finance/our-insights/strategy-under-uncertainty#

Likierman, A. (2020) "The elements of good judgement," *Harvard Business Review*, Jan–Feb.

Lord, Ross, & Lepper, (1979) *Can rational argument actually change people's minds?*, lifehacker.com

Syed, M. (2015) *Black box thinking, the surprising truth about success*, Hodder & Stoughton, London.

Thomas, K. & Kilmann, R. (1994) *Producing useful knowledge for organizations*, Jossey Bass Business & Management Series, San Francisco, CA.

Weisinger, H. J. P. & Pawliw-Fry J. P. (2016) *How to perform under pressure: the science of doing your best when it matters most*, John Murray Learning, London.

Why pressuring your employees to perform is sure to backfire, Inc.com

Chapter 4

Changing the thinking

You've got to think about big things while you're doing small things, so that all the small things go in the right direction.

~ Alvin Toffler

Establishing the what's it for? And keeping that in mind

In the leadership section, we discussed how you can create an environment for change in the way you behave and interact with people. In this section, we will look at some of the other elements which are essential for effectiveness – influencing people to think about effectiveness, handling communication, managing change, and building effectiveness into your operations.

Most people who work – whatever the type of organisation – will tell you one of their greatest problems is having enough time. Yet organisations, or more precisely the people within them, persist in implementing initiatives and asking employees to undertake actions which drain time without adding value. And it's not just about wasting time, there are more serious consequences because focussing on one area means you focus less on another which has the potential to be more fruitful.

Once a course of action is decided upon it can be hard to stop it in its tracks if it isn't working. No one wants to lose face and, anyway, a great deal of effort and resource has probably already been put into getting it started and persuading people of the value of the new idea in order to get their buy in. New initiatives can be like snowballs rushing down a hill, speeding ahead, gathering more momentum, and more snow until they finally crash at the bottom of the hill and eventually melt without trace. They may begin slowly but as they progress, they have greater needs, attracting more staff, bigger budgets, new IT, more KPIs…… all of which are required to bolster up the original idea. That is fine as long as the original idea was well thought out – but it isn't fine if the idea was flawed and the effort and cost isn't outweighed by the benefits.

DOI: 10.4324/9781003099895-6

One of the MPs we spoke to told us about his experience of introducing a new initiative. In the end, the combination of logistical complexity and cost meant it was not worth implementing and, in any case, the original impetus for action had subsided. After three years, he pressed the stop button. He admits this happened later than it should have done, but it was hard to do because people had already put so much effort into driving it through. In addition, he had wanted to make a success of it for his own personal reputation as a Minister. Sometimes you just have to take the bold step and admit a course of action isn't working or is no longer necessary.

If you can get agreement on the answer to the question: "What's it for?" it will illuminate the strategy and the route you need to take to realise the outcome you are looking for. In fact, it has many advantages. It provides a guideline against which you can check to see if the initial idea is still relevant and it helps in communicating direction and purpose and in deciding what the measures of success should be.

Let's take a very simple example. You want to run an event to highlight findings from your research into business confidence and you have a budget of £x. If you say just that to your team organising the event, they will have some information, but not enough to secure a successful outcome. If you tell them the event is to ensure results of the research are made known more widely in the business community to enable people to understand challenges other businesses are facing and thus prepare their own operations, your team will have a better idea of what it's for. They may choose to hold the event in a less expensive venue so they can invite as many people as possible, they will invite journalists, they will embark on a social media campaign. On the other hand, if you tell them the event is to discuss implications of the findings with business people to get their feedback for the purposes of deciding on policy, they may choose to invite small groups of people who will make useful contributions and choose to use some of the budget to pay for a professional facilitator. The pictures of a successful outcome and the approaches are entirely different. Too often we tell people what we want to do without focussing them on the higher purpose.

The other pitfall is to think everyone pictures the same outcome when in reality they don't. Pippa had a meeting with the Board of a small company to discuss the implementation of a performance measurement system. At the outset she had been told the company had a very clear strategy to which everyone was committed and all they needed was a set of measures to ensure their strategy was being implemented effectively. Discussion with the Board showed that a couple of people had very different views of the actions they needed to take in order to succeed. It had been assumed that all members of the Board had the same understanding when in fact they didn't and this meant they were not working to the same goals.

Let's look at another example. What is the NHS for? After some searching, we found the following: NHS.UK – what we do. We aim to: improve health and care outcomes. Improve people's experiences of health and care services. Reduce pressure on frontline services. Make health and care services more efficient. We're focused on meeting the health and care needs of people across England…

Now, the NHS is a hugely complex organisation and obviously most people are looking at its website for a specific purpose, probably because they are not feeling well, and they need some help. However, from the description on the website, it is not immediately clear what the NHS is really there for. Is it there to protect the health and well-being of the inhabitants of the nation (which would imply research, preventative care and health advice as well as treating people who are sick and injured) or is it there to treat people and improve outcomes from that treatment?

You can also ask what education is for. Is it there to help produce good citizens, people who will contribute in some way to the society in which they live, or is it there to get pupils through examinations? If education is there to prepare "good citizens" are the current measures of success (exam attainment, for example) the right measures? Are they the only measures? Is it fair to judge the success of a university by the salaries of its alumni as has been suggested? Alumni may go on to lead highly valuable work carried out by voluntary organisations, for example, but their salaries are likely to be lower than those leaders who chose to work in the private sector.

The implication of this is that following through to the ultimate "what's it for?" means we also need to consider wider measures of success.

Concentrating too much on any individual element will take focus away from the final purpose. Let us take an operational example. If a country has purchased, say 50 m vaccines, that is good in itself, but 50 m vaccines are useless unless they are effective vaccines for the purpose and they are administered to the right people at the right time. The successful outcome only occurs when the number of people with the disease against which the vaccine protects, and the number of hospitalisations are reduced to a given level. The chain of actions necessary to achieve that result should be the major focus of attention. Each step in that chain needs to be effective (and as efficient as possible) but it must lead directly towards achieving the final outcome. If it does not, then that step should be carefully considered and if it fulfils no purpose, it should be removed from the chain.

So, the question: what's it for? applies not only to new projects and initiatives but also to small everyday decisions which can have a significant impact on success when added up. If you ask that question at every stage, it helps to cut out actions that add no value and it keeps you and your teams focussed on the outcome you want. There is an excellent tool, the success map, which helps you to clarify the steps and decisions you need to take to reach your goal. See Chapter 10 for a description of how it works. You can find out more about the value chain which helps in mapping out links in the chain that makes up a process in Chapter 8.

Another reason for asking the question "What's it for?" and for following it through to its ultimate purpose is to uncover other solutions to the problem you are trying to solve. Is the ultimate purpose to build a new road between city a and city b? No, of course it isn't, or at least it shouldn't be. Building a new road is an output. It is one possible solution to a problem, amongst many other possible solutions. The problem in city b may be that it is in economic decline and in need of regeneration, in which case there are other actions you could take. Perhaps the purpose is to bypass small villages and reduce traffic congestion, or it could be to reduce journey times, in which case you could build a high-speed railway. The further you can track down your ultimate purpose the more you are able to explore a wider range of solutions. Conversely, if you pin it down too early, you fix your output, and it may not be the most effective one for tackling the problem you want to solve.

Once you start to think about ultimate purpose rather than concentrating only on the smaller steps in the chain, it opens your mind to a wider range of possibilities. If suppliers of electricity see themselves in the business of providing heating and lighting for spaces, rather than merely as providing power to homes and businesses, it enables them to consider other ideas for products and services. A car manufacturer makes cars but ultimately enables people to travel from one place to another. They provide personal mobility. That could lead to ideas such as providing on-demand electric cars for people living in cities. Entrepreneur and engineer, Hugo Spowers, had the idea of manufacturing hydrogen cars but instead of selling them, asking people to pay a monthly fee in return for maintenance, repairs, insurance, and fuel. Thinking about ultimate purpose enables you to free your mind from the constraints of following one route to reach an outcome.

At some stage you have to place a marker in the sand and agree the outcome you want and the means of achieving it. You must reach a common understanding on the ultimate purpose, on what it will look like and what the indicators of success will be. We had some enlightening conversations when researching how public sector organisations in the United Kingdom and the United States tackled the issue of agreeing and focussing on the benefits and outcomes they wanted to see from major projects. Project leaders were concerned about making the best use of taxpayer dollars and pounds, and they regarded the identification of benefits from the outset as being of key importance. Where possible they quantified benefits and used modelling to predict possible outcomes. However, they also understood that qualitative benefits were important. Although quite a few of these were almost impossible to quantify, some people held the view that these hard-to-measure factors were the most valuable in terms of delivering successful outcomes. The difficulty was how to justify them.

Our research showed that consulting stakeholders from the very beginning was particularly important for success. Stakeholders provide different perspectives from policy makers and many of them had alternative views on the question: "What's it for?" Some of these were good ideas that had not been considered originally and of course, involving stakeholders also acts as a means of bringing them on side during the course of the project. Yet, in some cases project leaders were hesitant to involve stakeholders early on in case they delayed the start of the process. Delay is rarely a good thing, but it is better to know about potential problems and resistance from the outset rather than when the project is in full swing. Consulting a wider range of people at the beginning brings in new ideas and helps to bring potential conflicts to the surface, leading to a smoother operation and a better outcome. There is a good example of this from the banking sector. A bank was introducing a new computer system. The proposal for the new system was sent to the regulator and rejected.

It was revised and again rejected. Finally, one year into the planned three-year timescale for the project, the new system was accepted. Nevertheless, the project was completed on time. People involved with implementing the project acknowledged that the time spent in planning and replanning wasn't wasted. In fact, it enabled the implementation to be better and quicker. The challenge from the regulator had helped to refine their thinking and led to a better outcome.

There is another example from NHS Digital (Williams et al., 2019). When electronic systems for dispensing and prescribing were introduced, one might have assumed that pharmacists and patients would welcome not having to deal with pieces of paper. However, for some pharmacists, paper was helpful in allowing them to "pick" medicines as they prepared to fulfil patients' orders. Others had poor internet connections. Some patients also liked to come out of the GP's surgery armed with a paper prescription. Knowing all this in advance was helpful in encouraging people to use the new systems.

The more people you consult, the more ideas you will have, but the more conflicts you will have, too. There is a useful process, The Performance Prism, for working through stakeholders needs and wants and deciding how you can reconcile them. We cover this in more depth in Chapter 11.

From our research we know that the intention is always to align ultimate purpose and project objectives. However, these do sometimes drift apart for many reasons, from operational constraints and changes in political will to insufficient preparation. In the best processes there is periodic checking to ensure the outcomes initially envisaged are still the right ones and that the project or initiative is still on course to deliver them.

Once your project or initiative is underway, you will be building in all the measures of progress and efficiency, measuring money spent and time taken, but in doing this it is important not to lose sight of the end purpose. Efficiency is important but it is always secondary to purpose. As we said at the beginning, you can spend time and money doing the wrong things well.

Thinking about the whole

Just as it is essential to establish what the ultimate purpose of your actions is and to keep the end in mind as you progress, it is also important to see your organisation as a whole because it is more than the sum of its individual parts. Let's take short detour into the animal world to illustrate this. An individual ant is highly unlikely to survive on its own if it becomes lost because it relies on the rest of its colony for its continued existence. An ant needs warmth from the nest, partly generated by all the other ants. It relies on knowledge about the best place to forage and it finds security in numbers. When ants go foraging and discover there is no food, they leave behind a pheromone to let other ants know that area is not worth exploring. If an apple is dropped, not all ants will immediately attempt to explore and eat it. If they did and the apple happened to be poisonous, then all of them would die. Just like employees in an organisation, each ant has its allotted task within the colony. Some ants lay eggs, others find food, they build nests and defend their territory from other colonies. No-one can predict exactly what will happen in the ant colony because each ant will react to the stimuli it faces and other ants will take their cues accordingly. They adapt to what is happening around them as they go along. So, like a hospital or a school, there are many interdependent parts that function together to make the whole and to be successful they need to work well together. The individual elements must be aware of what else is happening inside the organisation and outside it and adapt to what they see.

How can this come about? In the leadership section, we discussed some of the characteristics of successful senior managers and leaders. These people focus on relationships, they look at linkages and connections and they are aware of what is happening around them. By creating a framework within which their teams are free to operate, they allow flexibility and room for people to adapt to what they see around them. You can think of it rather like filling in a form. Some forms are so prescriptive, usually with boxes to tick, that you cannot communicate what you really need. You can only tick the box that approximates to what you want. Other forms, however, give you freedom to note down what you truly need and to provide clarification for the boxes you have ticked. They may take slightly longer to process but save time in the long run because you have clarity of communication.

Communication and influence

We will change tack here to look at the importance of communicating effectively. No matter how well you define your outcomes, if you do not communicate well, you reduce your chances of success. You also reduce perceptions of your success and perceptions matter because they affect the way people respond to you as a leader. If other people do not perceive you to be competent, they are unlikely to buy into your ideas and it will be harder for you to achieve your aims. Political strategist Lee Atwater said: "Perception is reality." We do not entirely agree with this statement, because at some stage reality becomes apparent and perceptions change, but he does have a point, nevertheless. Perceptions can affect what happens in the future because they change peoples' behaviour.

We won't discuss in detail the important and intricate relationships between the government and its agencies and the various forms of media, but we have observed and talked to people about the principles of good communication which is like the oil in a machine enabling everything to run as it should.

One of the recurring themes in this book is working with stakeholders. We spoke to Elayne Grimes who had worked extensively in communication roles with police forces and she talked to us about how you need to bring people with you, and how hard that is when you have conflicting objectives. Drawing on her experience in Scotland, she explained the difference between government priorities and local needs. Local people are interested in problems that affect their daily lives, such as dog fouling and litter (usually a case for councils rather than the police) and issues such as anti-social behaviour, whereas the government's priorities tend to focus on drugs, terrorism, and organised crime. Whatever the government's priorities, local needs must also be met and in doing this you pave the way for better relationships with the police. If people trust the police, they are more likely to support them and if, for example, they see something unusual or out of the norm, they will report it. So, dealing with seemingly small local issues can actually help in preventing serious offences.

Communication should be linked to both the long-term, national goals, tackling drug crime, for example, and to the local issues that trouble people on an everyday basis. Elayne held the view that you should: "Work to national and strategic goals but operate and communicate locally to build trust."

There is a delicate balance between operating nationally and operating locally, and we will look at partnership working and the argument of whether you should centralise or decentralise later in the book, but here it is sufficient to say that employing people who understand local differences is essential for good communication. People in the Hebrides will have very different concerns from those in London.

It is also true that different groups of people have different concerns which must be addressed in order to get a message across effectively. Road deaths are horrible, and it is part of the role of the police to prevent them. Talking to young people about the number of deaths does not work because dying is not something they generally contemplate. However, they can more easily identify with the idea of being disabled. When police in one area invited a young woman, who was in a wheelchair because of a car accident to speak to young people, the audience was shocked to see how the accident had affected someone like them, and they responded to her. It was a successful tactic.

One of the former MPs we spoke to had also been a councillor. He explained the importance of looking at social media to keep in touch with local concerns. One example he gave us was the strength of feeling about shortcomings in local bus services and shelters which he uncovered when looking at Facebook. Most councillors drove to meetings and they rarely used busses, so they were totally unaware of the problem.

So, when it comes to communication, focus on the outcome you want and then work back to decide how to achieve it, bearing in mind you will probably need to use several approaches tailored to local and demographic differences.

One highly effective approach is to use the power of storytelling. We heard an excellent example of how useful this can be from someone in NHS Digital. There was some reluctance amongst GPs to use the electronic prescription functionality. A case study presented by one doctor, however, was highly persuasive. Her business partner, the other GP in the practice, had sadly died, leaving her with the whole burden of running the practice. She was distraught at losing a valued friend and overwhelmed by the amount of work she had. She examined everything she might be able to do to reduce the workload and decided to try out electronic prescribing with as many patients as she could. It transformed her practice, allowing her to cope until she found another partner. GPs around the country would be able to identify with that situation making it far more effective than simply saying: "Using this system will save you *x* amount of time."

Most communication has an element of influencing in it. If you are giving an instruction, you are persuading someone to do something. If you are providing information, you want them to use it, when necessary. If someone trusts you, they may just do as you want, but in most communication and certainly in mass communication, you will need to use the basic marketing tactic of stressing the benefit, as in the case of the doctor. This doesn't always happen.

We were doing some work in the Middle East, talking to government officials about measuring and managing performance. One of their aims was to inform the population about how money was being spent and what the government was doing for them. Many of the communications were somewhat dry with factual information about infrastructure projects, for example, or improvements in processes. It was only when we asked participants to "take off their official hats" and think about sitting at home, that their perspective changed. We asked them what the drive to speed up processes would mean for their own families. Then they began to think about benefits to individuals, such as being able to get a passport in a few days rather than a few months and they realised how they could capture peoples' attention.

This applies to the United Kingdom, too. We had some interesting discussions with people working in NHS Digital about communication. Clearly, finance is very important. Health care is hugely expensive. But, as a couple of people in the study commented, the man or woman in the street would be more interested in being able to get an appointment sooner with their GP than in knowing £10m had been saved. That is not to say £10m is not important, but for the purposes of effective communication, if you want to get a message across you have to find the benefit for the individual.

Choice of words is another important consideration. Words are very powerful. We heard about one organisation where clients were routinely called "punters" by staff. When new management took over, they found it hard to improve customer service because staff had little regard for customers. They couldn't identify with their needs and their problems. They were just seen as purchasers of goods and services. So, words not only affect the culture of the organisation and behaviour of people within it, but your choice of words can also impact on how people receive your message.

Communications must be crafted with care and attention to detail because even a small, unintentional miscommunication can do a great deal of damage. Whilst the composer of a message may read it in one way, the reader may perceive it in another. One Head Teacher we spoke to talked about how he felt it necessary to draft many versions of communications to parents and pupils, before deciding on the final text, because he was aware of the impact his words could have. He did this despite having a very heavy workload because he knew how important it was.

We've talked about the words you use and how you tailor your message to your audience. How you deliver your message is also important. Javed Khan, former Chief Executive of Barnado's, had to work and communicate with many different groups of people including a large body of volunteers, who are at the heart of the charity's work. He had no direct authority over volunteers as they can choose to leave whenever they wish, so he had to use powers of persuasion, particularly when he was trying to introduce new ideas or change. In his view you must have clarity of purpose at the outset. People need to believe what you are saying, not just understand it. Complex messages must be made simple, you must repeat those messages and make them highly visible.

We should be clear about one point here: we are not advocating avoiding the truth in communications or manipulating the facts. Just as reality eventually emerges from the many perceptions people have of what is happening, so the truth will come out. One of the main tenets of effectiveness is building trust. If you mislead people, they will not trust you and you will not easily regain that trust. Delivering a diluted message is also a good way to lose public confidence, because people will wonder what is missing and will create their own theories. We have all probably become too focussed on wanting certainty where none exists. Sometimes it is better to say, "I don't know" and to explain what is happening to put right that lack of knowledge. Direct communication from the person who knows the facts as they stand is the best solution.

Managing change

> There is nothing more difficult to plan, more doubtful of success, nor more dangerous to manage than the creation of a new system. The initiator has the enmity of all who would profit from the reservation of the old institutions and merely lukewarm defenders in those who should gain by the new ones.
>
> Niccolo Machiavelli

If you introduce a new IT system into your organisation it is very visible. Most people will understand why it is there even if they don't like it and think it is an imposition. They can see it, they can be trained in its use, and, over time, you hope they will see the benefits from using it. On the other hand, building effectiveness into the culture involves change which is intangible. It involves influencing people to alter their expectations (not to constantly look for short term results, for example) and to change the way they think. It means changing habits that have been built up over a lifetime of work. It will probably mean encouraging people to take more risks as layers of bureaucratic safety blankets are removed. Some of those people involved in the change will be employees over whom you have direct control, but some will be elected representatives and members of the public who can only be subject to influence.

Creating a change in culture will not happen overnight. It takes a long time to achieve but it can be done. Think about attitude to alcohol and particularly to driving. It seems alcohol formed an important part of peoples' lives even in Neolithic times, about 6,000 years ago. There is evidence from Neolithic sites that inhabitants in Britain knew how to make malt and ale from grain, but whether they drove while under the influence of alcohol is a matter for debate as the wheel was probably invented many years later. Leap forward to the mid-20th century. There was an expression "One for the Road," meaning have one last drink before you drive onwards. Nowadays it is hard to believe that was a common expression. More than 50 years of UK governments' road safety campaigns have managed to change attitudes dramatically. In a survey conducted a few years ago, 91% agreed drink driving was unacceptable and 92% of people said they would feel ashamed if they were caught drinking and driving. Over 88% of people say that they would think badly of someone who drinks and drives. This compares to over half of male drivers and nearly two thirds of young male drivers who admitted drink driving on a weekly basis in 1979 (Government Press Release, 2014). This fundamental change in attitude was achieved through a combination of hard-hitting advertisements and campaigning and legislation with strict enforcement of the rules.

We asked our interviewees how they tackled change. Sometimes, but very rarely, it is a case of saying: "Now we are going to do this." More often than not it is a question of recognising that embarking on a programme of change is a major undertaking and asking why you want to do it and whether you are doing it for the right reasons. If the answers are satisfactory then begins the job of talking to people to get them on board and ensuring the right resources are in place. Sharon Taylor, Leader of Stevenage Borough Council emphasised the importance of building a good relationship with officers so you can have an open discussion about how something can be done and whether it is feasible, the sort of relationship where they feel able to politely tell you "if you have a bee in your bonnet." John Healey MP told us how important it was to get the attention of people who can make things happen, to ensure you have the authority and the reporting lines you need to get the job done. At ministerial level you need the backing of the Prime Minister and possibly the Chancellor. In all cases people told us successful change was only achieved with careful planning combined with knowing very clearly what you want to achieve, getting people on side and finding champions who would be positive and enthusiastic in their support.

Change is always a step into the unknown. It can be seen as a threat. If there is too much change (and from our interviews we know this is often seen as a problem when a new minister comes in or government policy changes) then you can be forgiven for taking the attitude, "Here we go again." People who have been with the organisation for a long time have seen so many changes they become cynical and sometimes they don't really expect to alter what they do. They just circumvent any change. So, there is a balance between bringing in new ideas and ensuring there is continuity. On the one hand we hear about reluctance to consider new ideas – one former MP told us of his experience of going into a room with a good idea and being demotivated when he met with 10 civil servants telling him why it wouldn't work. Another told us about the importance of smashing the "reflective layer" between groups of people to enable constructive dialogue. On the other hand we have heard about sectors such as education where there is perceived to have been far too much "chopping and changing." There is a balance to be struck between sticking to what is working and exploring new ideas.

It is worth looking at some of the academic literature and research. David Gleicher, a consultant at Arthur D Little (Cited in Bourne & Bourne, 2015) way back in the 1960s proposed the argument that organisational change will only happen when dissatisfaction with the current situation, the desirability of the future goal and the knowledge of the first step to get there will combine to outweigh the costs involved. He expressed this idea in a formula: $K \times D \times V > C$

Where:

K represents knowledge of the first practical steps.
D represents **D**issatisfaction with the status quo.
V represents the vision of the future and its desirability.
C represents the cost, both material and psychological of doing something.

The multiplication signs are included to show how the factors combine and it also means that if any factor is missing then the value reaches zero and change will not happen.

As this book is all about working with the end in mind, we would add to this another element: **O** which represents having a clear and shared picture of what the outcome will look like. Without that it is hard to assess and communicate the desirability of the vision of the future.

Working through each of the factors and building them into your plan for change is a good start. How can you establish the level of dissatisfaction with the status quo? How can you encourage people to see new possibilities? How can you promote the desirability of the vision of the future?

You can be sure that there will be some resistance to any proposed changes. One of the most widely used approaches to change was developed by psychologist, Kurt Lewin (1947) who explained that change is a transition, a journey from one state to another. He is perhaps best known for his "Force Field Analysis," which proposes mapping out the forces which will drive people towards or away from a desired state. Positive forces may include, for example, rewards and incentives, regulation, public opinion, attractiveness of new ideas. Restraining forces may include threat to personal position, comfort with the status quo, unsupportive structures. This is an easy-to-use tool which can be used to identify where resistance will lie and how positive forces may be strengthened (see chapter 7 for more information).

Change within the public sector is not only a matter of influencing employees, but also a matter of influencing members of the public and stakeholders such as the media. Much of what we said in the leadership chapter applies here. If people trust you and believe you are capable and think you are working in their interests, then they are more likely to accept change. If you have taken time to build relationships with key people, including journalists, they may support you rather than constantly challenging.

Often, resistance to change comes because an idea has become firmly lodged and keeps being repeated without evidence or scrutiny. For example, one interviewee told us there had been a view in central government that the quality of local leadership was not sufficient to allow them to devolve certain activities. On thinking about this he realised that whilst some local leaders were less capable than others, there were many who were very capable, and that development of local capability was actually being hampered by not allowing more local responsibility. A completely different example of adherence to routines comes from the private sector and this shows just how ideas, actions and processes can carry on for years without being challenged. A chemical company was measuring the toxicity of the local canal. Apparently, they had a Portacabin with a tiny laboratory for this purpose. When the new plant general manager asked what it was for, no one knew. Further investigations revealed that a barge full of chemicals had been sunk during the Second World War, toxicity was being measured and this activity was still continuing, to little purpose, 40 years later. Here is another rather amusing example. A company had a form with a column headed NAT on it. On asking what it meant, a young graduate was told: "Don't worry about that. You just put zero in that column." When he persisted with his question as to why it was there, he found someone who remembered it stood for "number of air raids today." It takes a long time to break habits and established protocols and changing attitudes and beliefs is even harder.

It is worth checking the extent to which the mountain of resistance you face has some evidence underpinning it or is, in fact, the result of out-of-date information and ill-informed opinion. Your course of action will depend on the answer to that question. The process of getting people to look at and accept evidence is not straight forward. Using evidence such as graphs and numbers, for example, may contribute towards a change in attitude and opinion for part of your audience, but those methods are unlikely to work for everyone. Some people will not understand them, and others will be cynical. People often take the attitude: "statistics can be used to show whatever you want them to show." They have a point.

Earlier on, we cited the example of a young doctor, struggling to cope following the death of her partner, sharing her experience of using a new digital application which helped sway other GPs to try a new system. Storytelling is not new. Aristotle considered it at length and included in his deliberations the importance of "Pathos," the speaker's ability to evoke emotions in the audience. Images are also far more important now in the kit bag of tools of persuasion. Just think how most people exchange photos and videos on a daily basis. Pictures of the suffering of patients and doctors in intensive care wards shook viewers into the realisation that the Covid-19 pandemic was serious and they must obey lockdown rules.

In his book, *Nervous States,* William Davies, a political economist at Goldsmiths, University of London, discusses the drift away from the supremacy of facts and reason which have dominated Western societies since the Enlightenment to the acknowledgement of feelings. He talks about facts produced by experts and technocrats not capturing lived reality for many people and he argues that we have moved from a "verbal public sphere to an image-based sphere." Communication and persuasion are important elements in the process of implementing change. If you are to manage change successfully it is essential that you understand your audience and how you can combine the various channels and approaches to reaching them. This is true whether you are embarking on a major campaign, such as drinking and driving we discussed earlier, or contemplating the overhaul of your performance measurement system.

So far, we have discussed the importance of assessing whether the change is being done for the right reasons, getting key people on side, securing resources, and reporting lines and formulating a communications plan. One of the most difficult elements is how you deal with people who are disruptive to proposed changes.

Professor Paul Strebel from The International Institute for Management Development (IMD) suggests categorising people into four types according to how they respond to the change.

- ■ Change Agents: respond actively and see it as an opportunity
- ■ Resistors: respond actively and see it as a threat
- ■ Bystanders: respond passively and see it as an opportunity
- ■ Traditionalists: respond passively and see it as a threat

Knowing your people and how they are likely to respond helps in planning how to tackle resistance and win people over. However, you cannot persuade everyone. The key is to put effort into getting as many people as possible to engage with the change and not to focus too much time on the few people who won't. Of course, you need to know why they are resisting (they may have valid reasons) and try to support them, but after a certain point affording them the light of attention is more likely to make them dig in further. Sometimes you just have to let people go.

Here is an example from the education sector. A training centre within a university was originally set up primarily as a means of building relationships with the financial services sector. A significant number of those working in it were there because they enjoyed the public relations aspect of the role and there was no particular commercial pressure laid upon them, although it was desirable to cover costs. However, in the search for additional sources of income, the university decided the centre needed to become more commercial and brought in new leadership to strengthen commercial aspects. The first six months were tough. Several highly regarded employees decided to leave. When the new General Manager reported on progress to the Dean, she expressed her dismay and concern at the loss of these people. In responding, the Dean asked her to consider why those people joined in the first place and whether they were truly suited to the change in their role. Buoyed by his confidence she went on to recruit people who were more commercially focussed, and the centre began to flourish in meeting its new objectives.

When change is underway, bring in symbols showing something is different. One of our interviewees was involved in the establishment of a new agency. Following consultations with staff they introduced smart, well cut, high-quality uniforms which made employees look and feel more professional, and this was one of the symbols of change. Remove symbols of the past, old protocols, legacies of previous systems. This may seem superficial but linking changes in the way things are done with visual cues people see every day reinforces the idea that change is happening.

It is important to ensure everything is aligned with the changes you want to make. This includes not only the visual cues but also reward systems and management and measurement of performance. It is easy to overlook the fact you are asking people to do one thing and continuing to reward them for doing something else. So, analyse any symbols, systems, processes, and behaviours that are likely to be associated with old ways and consider how they can be changed to match what is required now.

There is one final point to make here. In the leadership chapter, we talked about "being the exemplar." This is critical when it comes to change. If senior managers appear to doubt the change will be successful and if their behaviour and actions are not consistent with new requirements, then there is little hope of success.

You can read more about the detailed process in handling change in Chapters 6–9.

What is effective thinking?

This section has been about changing the way people think, whether that is to encourage them to think longer term or to accept change, so it is worth spending just a little time exploring thinking itself. What makes some people more effective than others? A fair amount of research has been conducted on this subject and we will draw on some of it in this summary.

Daniel Isenberg (1984), Professor of Entrepreneurship at Columbia University, studied thought processes of senior managers and found some interesting results. One surprising finding is that most effective senior managers do not follow the expected model of rational sequential thinking. That is clarifying goals, assessing the situation, formulating options, estimating likelihoods of success, taking a decision, and then acting on it. This is particularly true when they face complex problems. They use intuition justified by data and logic. Bear in mind that intuition is not the exact opposite of logic and sometimes intuition comes from sensing a problem. We spoke to former crime commissioner, Nick Alston, who related the story of a local police inspector who told him something strange was going on and they needed to get on top of it. He could sense something was different. His intuition turned out to be right – it was the beginning of county lines operations in that area. So, in this form intuition is about sensing when there is likely to be a problem. Intuition facilitates the bringing together of individual pieces of data, information, and experience into a whole. As Isenberg describes it: "an aha" experience.

In most complex situations you do not have all the facts and you probably cannot wait until you have them because a decision must be made. We are not making the case here for acting on gut instinct alone. Clearly evidence and data are important, not least to avoid falling into the trap of taking action on the basis of incorrect assumptions. Sometimes, however, you have to make a judgement call and you will have to trust your instinct.

Far from being unreliable, there is evidence to back up the idea that you should trust your gut instinct, especially if you take a little time to consider where it may have come from. Researchers in Pennsylvania studied students tackling multiple-choice questions in a test, looking at how confident they were in their first instinctive answers and whether they went back to revise them. They found most students were good at assessing their uncertainty about an answer and when they went back to revise their answers, it was the correct decision. First instincts were not always right but *instincts in the confidence* for that answer tended to be correct. Without us realising it, our brains are always comparing what is happening now with what has happened in the past, so intuition may indeed be based on experience.

William Davies (2018) discusses in his book "Nervous States" the idea that The Enlightenment has "run aground" and sets out the struggles between reason and feelings. He observes that European countries founded an intellectual architecture, Royal Societies, Universities and so on, that codifies knowledge and focuses on reasoning. However, we have now become more attuned to real-time events and media and this leads us to place more attention on feelings and emotion than evidence and facts. "Knowledge becomes more valued for its speed and impact than for its cold objectivity, and emotive falsehood often travels faster than fact." As Davies points out, telling people they are safe is no use if people do not *feel* safe. If they don't *feel* safe then they will take matters into their own hands. This comes back to our point about trust and integrity. If people trust you, then they are more likely to do as requested, as well as feeling able to contribute their ideas and efforts to achieving common aims. That trust will be eroded, however, if they discover you have not acted with integrity.

So, evidence and rational thinking are important, but only up to a point. They go hand in hand with paying attention to your own "gut instinct" and understanding the importance of how you and other people *feel*.

The proverb "practice makes perfect" or variants of it, exists in many languages. The idea is quite simple, the more you do something the better you are at doing it. But there is an extra dimension which should be added and that is learning and reflecting on your performance. If I practise playing the piano without learning from my mistakes, I will just become more fluent at playing a piece of music with mistakes in it.

You may be familiar with the four competence levels which people go through when learning a new skill:

Unconscious incompetence – you are not aware you lack the competence to do something; to move to the next stage you will need to recognise that fact and have the desire to gain the competence you require.

Conscious incompetence – you are aware you lack the competence and set about finding ways of gaining it. You will make mistakes and should be learning from them.

Conscious competence – you know you have the competence but have to think about what you are doing.

Unconscious competence – where skills have become habits which you carry out without too much thought. Take the example of driving. After several years of driving, you automatically know what to do when you see a pedestrian crossing or see a car slow down in front of you. Most people can happily talk to passengers or listen to the radio without it affecting their driving skills.

People who operate effectively reach the stage of unconscious competence and they do this by gaining as much experience as they can, by reflecting on what they are doing and by learning from their mistakes. They are also aware of the stages of competence of those who work for them. They know when individuals and teams need extra training and knowledge, they also know which individuals and teams are best suited to fulfil a given task. This is why scenario planning and practice is so important. If you think about the army, soldiers spend a considerable amount of time training for combat. They are presented with scenarios that reflect the types of situations they are likely to face, so when they become involved in an actual event, they know what to do and can spend more time on higher level thinking rather than thinking about the basic actions.

The other characteristic of people who operate effectively is that they think about organisational and interpersonal processes. This was identified by Isenberg in his research into how senior managers think. They consider questions such as: "Who the key players are, and how I can get their support? Whom should I talk to first?" In essence, they think about ways of bringing the right people together to create the most effective outcome.

Ron Carucci (2016) conducted a ten-year longitudinal study designed to isolate skills of top performing executives and he revealed similar findings. Exceptional executives know the whole business and "have deep knowledge of how the pieces of the organisation fit together to create value and deliver results." They "focus on strengthening the organisation's seams to minimise poor coordination and fragmentation…." Interestingly, Carucci also highlights the finding that these high performing executives make decisions based on a balance between instinct and analytics. They use experience and emotion and they also use data and analysis.

Most areas of the public sector are highly complex. Even if a department is handling what may appear to be a simple process, it is likely to be made more complicated by the number of stakeholders involved or changes in emphasis on a fairly regular basis in line with new policy. In his research, Carucci found that effective executives were able to prioritise what was important, to understand what the trade-offs were and choose among them. This is important because, as we shall see later when we discuss key performance indicators, creating a whole raft of goals can obscure rather than enlighten the essence of what is needed to achieve a successful outcome. That is not to say that effective people work with tunnel vision, focussing exclusively on the problem in hand, rather that they know where the priorities are and keep alert for what is happening on the periphery.

Another tool for effective thinking is "problem framing," in other words how you describe a problem in order to come up with a solution to it. How you frame a problem makes a significant difference to the way you tackle it. It is sometimes useful to do it with other people, each of whom is likely to have a different perspective on the matter, and to see if you can agree on what the core issue is, and what the approaches to solving it might be. Doing it as a group helps ensure you haven't overlooked any important aspect but when you are thinking on your own, try to be objective, to be dispassionate and separate yourself from the problem before looking for solutions. There are various techniques for doing this. One we like, introduced to us by Margaret Adey, a wonderful coach in Cambridge who helped Pippa negotiate her way through a tricky time at work, is to take a bird's eye view. This involves sitting back and taking time to imagine yourself as a bird, a seagull perhaps, looking down on what is happening below. It may sound strange, but it works for many people because rather than looking at a problem and feeling you are entangled in it, you are able to separate yourself and see it from a higher-level viewpoint. The further up you go the more you should be able to see the problem in its entirety.

So far, we have talked about rationality and intuition, about feeling, learning, and problem-framing. We have discussed how effective people work on understanding how the whole organisation works and knowing the strengths of individuals within it. We have discussed the role practice plays in creating habits and freeing up space to think about other things and how effective people prioritise whilst keeping the larger picture in view. That is quite a lot to do, so the question is how do you do it without becoming overwrought. One approach to remaining calm and in control is mindfulness, which is taught on Cranfield's courses, including to senior government officials as part of the Project Leadership Programme. Some people are still sceptical about this approach but there is scientific evidence to support its benefits (Halliwell, 2010). In people who regularly practise it, mindfulness has been associated with differences in the areas of the brain associated with decision-making, attention, and awareness.

Creating the space to think and not immediately moving to act is one of the characteristics of successful people. It may be an inbuilt survival instinct to react immediately in response to an unpleasant stimulus, but unless, of course, you are in the way of a lorry which is careering out of control, it is usually better to pause, to take a breath and consider what the best course of action should be. Things are not always what they seem at first glance. If an employee comes to see you, angry and upset at the treatment they have received from a co-worker, the temptation is to feel angry on their behalf. But of course, you need to hear the other side and you need to hear the other person's recollection of events without being partial. The key is to be mindful, to notice how each person is behaving and reacting. You should listen carefully to what they are saying, the tone of their voice, the words they choose and watch their body language. By behaving in this way you are more likely to establish the truth about the situation and be able to gauge the severity of it and find a more appropriate solution than if you had taken immediate action.

A former colleague at Cranfield (now at City University), Psychologist, Dr Jutta Tobias Mortlock (2017) set out a clear description of how she uses mindfulness in a Huff Post Blog:

> I often explain mindfulness as a practice that "creates space" – mental space for myself, to help me make sure that I use the (often small mental) pause wisely between what the world brings to me and how I will respond.

References

Bourne, M. & Bourne, P. (2015) *Successful change management in a week*, Hodder Education, London.

Carucci, R. (2016) "A 10-year study reveals what great executives know and do," *Harvard Business Review*, January.

Davies, W. (2018) *Nervous states: how feeling took over the world*, Vintage, London.

Government Press Release (2014) "92% of people feel ashamed to drink and drive as 50th anniversary THINK! Campaign is launched - GOV.UK," www.gov.uk

Halliwell, E. (2010) *Mindfulness 2010 report*, Mental Health Foundation, Mindfulness_report_2010.pdf (mentalhealth.org.uk).

Isenberg, Daniel (1984) "How senior managers think," *Harvard Business Review*, November.

Lewin, K. (1947) "Frontiers in group dynamics," *Human Relations*, Vol. 1, No. 1, 5–47.

Tobias Mortlock, J. (2017) "What is organisational mindfulness and how can we develop a mindful culture at work?" *Huffpost*, October.

Williams, T., Vo, H., Bourne, M., Bourne, P., Cooke-Davies, T., Kirkham, R., Masterton, G., Quattrone, P., & Valette, J. (2019) "A cross-national comparison of public project benefits management practices – the effectiveness of benefits management frameworks in application," *Production Planning and Control*, Vol. 31, No. 8, 644–659.

Part 2

Approaches for making it happen

In Part 1, we looked at why effectiveness is important and how it differs from efficiency. We examined some of the challenges that arise when striving for effectiveness including pressures to set and attain short-term goals at the expense of focussing on longer-term outcomes. We discussed ways in which you can create an environment that is conducive to effectiveness, concentrating on leadership, influencing the way people think and looking at issues such as communication, managing change, and developing effective operations. In Part 2 we will get down to the nitty gritty of how you make it happen, with particular focus on structure, planning and executing change and measuring performance.

DOI: 10.4324/9781003099895-7

Chapter 5

Creating supportive structures

Make everything as simple as possible, but not simpler.

~Albert Einstein

Simplicity and complexity

One of the themes emerging from the discussions we had with people in the public sector was how they struggled to work their way through complex, bureaucratic structures, whether that was trying to get committees from six different parts of a service to agree on a course of action or trying to read pages and pages of information to pick just the right words necessary for a funding application to have chance of success. When it came to the latter, several people told us you needed to "understand the rules of the game" and fit what you required into those rules rather than describe the true need. As one, perhaps cynical, person told us: "…you have to translate daft ideas into something useful."

The problem with simplicity is that it is not easy to achieve, especially when a situation is already complex. It is much easier to start with a simple solution and try to ensure it remains simple than it is to de-complicate something when people are already used to working in a certain way.

Of course, running government and working in the public sector is not the same as running a factory and a production line. The use of public funds means higher levels of transparency and lower tolerance of risk and that, in turn, means more scrutiny and checking. However, there is a balance. As one person put it: "When we do something there is an army of people following up and checking. Everyone is scared and looking over their shoulder." Several people told us about instances where

DOI: 10.4324/9781003099895-8

committees were focussing on checking how very small amounts of money had been spent from very large budgets, whilst missing the point that a successful outcome had been achieved. This was highly demotivating for people concerned and led to a culture of watching the pennies rather than concentrating on whether those pennies were being spent effectively.

To put this simply there are two issues here: creating the simplest and most direct structure possible to create a successful outcome and ensuring processes, including those concerned with scrutiny and checking are adding value. We have described in previous chapters how processes become bound into everyday work without being questioned. Efficiency comes into this, too. Can data collected on one form, for example, be used to move the process on, and also be used for the purposes of scrutiny? Sometimes it helps to be ruthless and ask people why a process exists and what would happen if it were to be abolished. That is hard to do because there will nearly always be a group of people who like doing that process or who put greater weight in its purpose than it deserves. The same is true of simplifying structures. One person told us: "There are some 300 councils and really there should be about 120 to create the optimum size." Clearly, not everyone will agree with this, but each council has a different way of working (sometimes owing to important local differences, of course) so some simplification in provision of basic services such as refuse collection would appear to help create more efficient and effective outcomes. But, as we said before, once complex structures have been created, it is hard to simplify them.

There is another dimension to this, and that is tolerance of risk. Cutting back on layers of scrutiny inevitably means accepting a higher level of risk. In situations of emergency, you have to take risks. Evacuating people from a burning hospital ward involves risk, but a calculated risk that is lower than leaving people in situ to suffer from smoke inhalation or worse. After the event there will probably be an investigation which will check whether procedures were followed correctly and probably also whether those procedures were appropriate or whether anything could be learned. In such a situation you can never have procedures and processes to cater for every eventuality so you must rely on effective leadership, judgement, and decision-making. Whilst it is essential to examine processes and procedures and to adapt and change them when necessary, adding ever more complex ones is likely to be less effective than ensuring you have the right people in the right place and that they are free to exercise good judgement. The problem is that stakeholders may expect to see additional processes as proof that lessons have been learnt which results in knee jerk reactions, adding complexity rather than building capacity to better manage situations in the future.

One of the potential failings of auditors is to check process but not the competence of the people running the process. Therefore, you can be over- reliant on the process because you don't have competent people. The more competent the people, the fewer processes you need. The less competent the people, the more processes you need.

Simplicity (as far as is possible), common sense and capability of individuals should all be in place.

Centralising or not

Centralising v decentralising is a much-discussed topic in both the public and the private sector and it was raised by several people we interviewed. It applies to almost everything from buying travel tickets (the centre can get cheaper tickets by bulk buying, but people can purchase them cheaper locally and use off peak services, you know the arguments....) to running a health service. The same principles hold true for central/decentral organisational structure and central/decentral leadership and decision-making. In fact, the two are closely interlinked. You cannot have an effective decentralised structure if you don't also decentralise the leadership, decision making and the authority.

To a certain extent it goes in waves. Activities are centralised and then there is a push to decentralise them as the diktats from the centre become too onerous or unacceptable at a local level. Once decentralised, activities gradually become centralised again, as the centre begins to feel the need to tighten up and exercise more control and the whole cycle repeats.

There is no simple answer to this – and the extent to which activities in the public sector are centralised or not depends on Political perspective – but there are some principles which are worth exploring.

If an activity is fully decentralised, you allow the freedom to be creative and innovative. Reflecting on her teaching career, one of our friends told us how in the past she would construct lessons for her primary school children, based on what was most likely to engage them and make learning fun. That may be looking at the snow outside and learning the science of snowflakes, making drawings, and reading poems about them. Or it might be learning about ancient Egypt, drawing to scale pictures of the pyramids and imagining what it would be like to live in those times. Having worked in different schools and with children from different backgrounds she understood each child had different needs. She followed a teaching plan but had the freedom to deliver the learning as she saw fit. With the advent of testing and a more centralised approach, however, she felt constrained in doing this and felt her lessons were less effective for it.

However, another teacher, Graeme Hawkins-Dady, told us about a school he first worked in – pre national curriculum. "There was a lack of structure and no common purpose," he said. "It was up to each teacher what was taught and there was no guidance from the centre, which made it difficult for both the pupils and the teachers." So, decentralisation allows creativity and some tailoring to individual circumstances, but in the absence of an overarching framework it becomes hard to assess standards and realise expectations. There is a balance to be struck.

There is no doubt that sometimes you need understanding of the local area to offer effective services. One interviewee told us about the government's well-meaning attempt to centralise provision of food to vulnerable people during the coronavirus pandemic. "93-year-old-Mrs Smith in the High Street received chickpeas, which she had never eaten before, and an enormous bag of pasta which was too big for her."

Later on, in the course of the pandemic, food was delivered based on knowledge of the local area and what people who lived there were most likely to need.

Centralised structures and approaches can work against achieving successful outcomes. We heard about one example where young offenders were "sentenced" to apprenticeships. None of those young people re-offended, which would probably not have been the case had they been sent to an institution. However, the scheme relied on involvement from probation officers who were funded and managed centrally rather than locally, and it was not possible to increase their number. As a result, the scheme could not continue.

When local people are tasked with creating a successful outcome for their own communities, they are often well motivated. As one of our interviewees put it: "Devolution gets rids of artificial splits and makes people work together for the benefit of the local area."

So, decentralising has a host of benefits. Rob Whiteman, Chief Executive of CIPFA who was previously Chief Executive of the UK Border Agency, said: "Don't review what should be devolved. Review what should be reserved." What he meant was, don't start by looking at activities that could be devolved, start by looking at the activities which you should retain centrally. Clearly, an activity like defence should be centralised, but is it sensible to have a centralised approach to provision of local services?

As we have seen from the examples above, decentralising can encourage really good outcomes but it can also result in bad outcomes and so it must be combined with public accountability. That is part of the dilemma. As Rob Whiteman pointed out, there is always a tension between good organisational leadership and governance, and a concentration on good outcomes. How do you monitor and hold a local organisation accountable without stifling creativity and innovation and limiting their ability to act in the local interest? We will discuss that later, but first, let us look at some of the principles.

The book, Mission Command, edited by Donald Vandergriff et al. (2019) is an anthology of essays offering perspectives on the concept of mission command, which is, according to Army Doctrine Publication 6-0: Mission Command, US Army, "the exercise of authority and direction by the commander using mission orders to enable disciplined initiative within the commander's intent to empower agile and adaptive leaders in the conduct of unified land operations." Although these essays concentrate mainly on military issues, they offer useful insights into the debate about centralising v decentralising. In the introduction, Stephen Webber explains how the book came about – professionals from military, public service and law enforcement backgrounds in the United States, Norway, and the United Kingdom drew on their experience to call for an evolution of leadership culture, "emphasizing decentralized execution enabled by mutual trust and shared understanding across an organization." The essays discuss how culture must evolve to allow this to happen and also the role of training and organisation. The underlying concept, however, is the creation of an environment with a culture of trust and open communication in which individuals are carefully selected for their attributes and trained to enable leaders to have sufficient confidence to delegate responsibility.

We have already discussed in the leadership section, the importance of trusting people, with the example of the company, Semco, in Brazil (Semler, 2001). It is clear from many of our interviews that people believe processes and regulatory regimes are designed to cater for the lowest levels of performance. In his essay, Peter Vanjel expresses it well: "Rather than accepting risk in trusting the judgement of junior leaders…, we have inserted a written caveat with which to constrain these leaders or hold them accountable if things do not occur as intended."

We have had many comments on the lack of trust the centre (usually the government, in this case) has in local and decentralised organisations and how this is sometimes reflected in the operations of certain regulatory bodies. Here are a few of them.

"We suffer from fear of risk. Everything is very controlled."

"My job's on the line if I get this wrong. The system builds in inertia. The less you do, the less you risk."

On talking about the regulator, one of our interviewees said: "It hangs over our heads like a black cloud. It takes attention from what we should really be doing, and it has a damaging impact as everyone is worried about it. The stakes are ridiculously high." There's another dilemma. If you don't give people the opportunity to develop and expand that capability, then you cannot expect it to improve.

This brings us back to the theme of trusting people and cooperating to focus on achieving a successful outcome, rather than creating competition and distance. Nevertheless, you do need accountability and some form of direction to avoid complete chaos. So how can that be achieved?

The first step is to ensure there is a clear framework of desired outcomes and standards that is understood from both the centre and the devolved area. There must also be an understanding of the ways in which performance against those outcomes and standards will be measured and what resources will be required to be able to meet them. (We will delve into measurement in much more detail in Chapter 10.) In setting standards and performance measures, the centre must be prepared to tolerate differences in the way the outcome is achieved, and the devolved area must be prepared to justify why major differences have occurred or are necessary. For all this to happen you need dialogue and understanding and a certain tolerance of risk.

Let us take a simplified and hypothetical example about housing. The Government has stated the outcome of its policy is that everyone in the country has access to adequate housing – with clarification on what "adequate" means. This gives regions freedom to be creative in how to achieve this outcome. Some may decide to build council homes, others affordable homes for people to buy. Some may decide to embark on the conversion of existing buildings and others may decide on new schemes such as providing grants and loans for individuals to renovate derelict buildings. All these schemes should result in achieving the desired outcome of ensuring everyone has access to adequate housing, but the outputs will be different. In fact, the outputs are likely to be very different from those which would have been achieved had the government stated that they wanted "*x number of new houses to be built in the country.*" Setting out the broader requirement of ensuring adequate housing for everyone allows more innovation and tailoring to suit regional differences, it gives more autonomy and is more likely to engender commitment to achieving the aim. However, it also makes it more difficult to measure (it is easy to measure the number of new houses built), some schemes may fail, the way some areas approach the problem may not fit entirely with the political ethos of the centre and, it has to be accepted that providing homes in a multiplicity of ways does not make for a snappy headline in the media.

The example above relates to government policy being executed in the regions, but the same is true of devolving power to act within a single organisation. Helmut von Moltke, a Prussian Field Marshall known for his modern method of directing armies, pointed to the need for agility and speed of action which can be achieved when "people on the ground" are empowered to use their initiative. When speaking of subordinate commanders he said they must "…judge the situation for themselves and must know how to act independently in consonance with the general intention… the advantage of the situation will never be fully realised if the commanders wait for orders."

Now we come to the nub of the problem – how do you "keep a hand on the tiller," hold people accountable for their performance whilst still allowing them the freedom to act in the local interest? (Figure 5.1)

We don't want to repeat what we said in the leadership chapter but the first requirement for successfully decentralising activities is to create a climate of trust and confidence and to build channels of communication. That may sound obvious but from our discussions we understand senior people often don't feel able to pick up the phone and talk freely to other people because it is not what is expected of them. Likewise, people working locally don't want to talk to others heading the

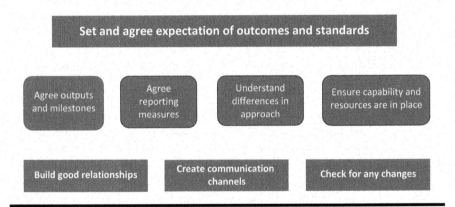

Figure 5.1 Managing accountability and freedom.

central team. Direct communication is essential because if you speak through a third person your message is always open to interpretation. It seems layers of bureaucracy and protocol stand in the way of communicating directly and building relationships. Although it takes time, meeting people, listening, and talking to them, genuinely trying to see issues through their eyes is an investment. It is time well spent.

Agreeing outcomes is about creating a shared picture of what success will ultimately look like. It means setting out a framework, an outline which is filled in by the people who are actually going to do the work. It takes time to negotiate and to ensure everyone has the same picture in their minds and to agree what the signals of that success will be. You will have a head start if you already have a good relationship with those people.

Outcomes by their nature happen in the longer term so you will need to measure outputs to check progress is being made. What those outputs are, and how to measure them is best decided by those responsible for producing them. This allows freedom to operate and also engenders commitment to achieving goals. It is at this stage that you must resist the temptation to propose or stipulate in detail *how* something is to be done. You will need to understand *why* a course of action is being proposed and ask searching questions to check motivations, but unless there is good reason to seriously doubt the approach, you should set direction and expectations and allow those doing the work to get on with it.

It is important to have an open discussion about capability and resources because it is harder for both sides and damaging to a relationship when one party either removes resources or has to ask for more. Sometimes this will happen owing to unforeseen circumstances, but it is better to be honest at the start about the reality of what is needed.

Whether you are decentralising a function, a project or a whole service, change will occur over time, so it is important to keep track of how things are going things are ask what is different. This not only helps you to keep in touch and feel more reassured about what is happening, but it also demonstrates your interest. If you have built good relationships and constructed robust channels of communications, then issues will be picked up as they occur and before they become too much of a problem.

Building partnerships

> Coming together is a beginning; keeping together is progress; working together is success.
>
> – Henry Ford

Earlier on we talked about the problem of working in silos, where each department or team beavers away oblivious to the wider implications of its work, or to the gains that could be made by collaborating with others. Whereas breaking down silos is about the *way* of working, partnership is a more formal structure set up to gain the benefits of working with other organisations. Working in a partnership that functions well is often a good way of achieving successful outcomes as you are assembling people with complementary fields of expertise who bring in new ideas and perspectives. There are, of course, different models of partnerships (public-private partnerships or joint ventures, to name just a couple) each with their own advantages and disadvantages. In this section we are going to look at the principles in relation to adding value and effectiveness, so our definition of partnership is quite simple: organisations working together to achieve a joint aim.

In their paper, Partnership Continuum (UIDP, 2012), Wayne Johnson and colleagues described the ways in which organisations interact from having a loose arrangement to becoming strategic partners. (Based in the United States, they were looking at academic, industry and government collaborations.) They set out three levels of arrangement, starting with transactional in which one party has something of value to another and is willing to provide it in return for something else. The second stage is where greater collaboration exists, sharing of ideas for mutual benefit, and the third stage is where both sides have shared goals and aspirations that they are unlikely to achieve alone. These alliances are usually long term and require substantial commitment.

Strong alliances add significant value because people in both organisations (or it can be more than two) have strong commitment to achieving successful outcomes. There is an element of emotional buy-in to success that is absent when the relationship is merely transactional and each organisation wants the best for itself – the highest amount of money for providing a service, for example, whereas the other party wants to pay the lowest possible amount. However, as Javed Khan, former CEO of Barnardo's told us: "Working with partners is both exciting and very difficult. Rather than just partnership you must have an interdependent existence. Lock arms, stand together and feel how each other's shoes pinch."

So, what are the requirements for good partnership working and forming of strong alliances? Having clear roles and responsibilities is an obvious first start. Perhaps less obvious is checking that values align. People can have the same long-term objective but because their values differ, they take different approaches to achieving it. To have a strong alliance, you must (metaphorically) speak the same language – the same words can mean something different to other people.

Alliances are not always composed of organisations of equal size, but that should not be a problem with the right approach. The key is to understand where each other's strengths are and play to those strengths. The charity Barnardo's is the largest children's charity in the United Kingdom and they offer an excellent case study of how this worked in practice with their "See, Hear, Respond" programme. During the Covid pandemic it became clear that there were many hidden victims who needed support. In response to a tender from the Department of Education, rather than doing everything on their own, they decided to build a coalition of 10–15 initial partners. Within a short time, they had over 80 partners, large and small, national, and local, and they were able to reach over 100,000 children, young people, and families in need, through this collaboration – more than the organisations would have been able to, if they were working individually. Working locally has meant they were able to identify more children who were hidden from more centralised initiatives. The added benefit is that they were also able to build capacity in smaller charities to enable them to support their communities into the future. Javed Khan stressed the importance of being humble and generous on your partnership journey and in that way, there can be learning on both sides.

Processes that work against effectiveness

Creating an effective organisation involves ensuring all constituent elements are conducive to achieving the optimum result, whether that is facilitating partnership working, providing long term funding to allow continuity, or rewarding the right behaviour. We'll talk in more detail about rewarding behaviour Chapter 13, but here we want to discuss the impact of processes on achieving effectiveness.

For the most part, people want to do a good job. They want the satisfaction of knowing they have achieved something, and they are prepared to wade through a certain amount of bureaucracy, even bend the rules up to a point. However, there is a limit. If the system is too prohibitive, actions which might have been done are left untouched because it takes too long to do them. Here is an example. One of the organisations we know believed in rewarding and recognising individuals when they had put special effort into achieving something. The reward was relatively small – usually a retail voucher. However, the process for recommending staff for this award was far more onerous than was warranted, meaning few managers actually used it, preferring to do something themselves, which took less time. Individuals received their reward and recognition within their own teams but not wider recognition within the organisation, which was a pity.

We know that in many cases collaborative working results in a more success-ful outcome. In their report "Partnerships for Better Public Services" (DoE, 2018) Saimah Heron and colleagues point to the challenge in promoting collaboration in an inherently competitive market. On one hand there is a push for partnerships, on the other "procurement processes and short timeframes to bid for the contracts are designed to encourage competition and innovation in the market and often consti-tute a systemic barrier to collaboration." Robust procurement processes are import-ant to ensure value for money, security of supply, and standing of supplier. They exist to minimise risk. But "value for money," for example, is open to interpretation and value for money in the short term may not be good value in the long term. What we are advocating here is a closer analysis of the consequences of such processes and whether they really support successful outcomes.

Another process which was raised several times in our interviews was that of bidding for funding. There were complaints that the process itself was akin to a game where you had to understand the rules and use the right words, rather than focus on real need. Another common complaint was that funding streams were frequently too short. As one person told us: "You cannot put a sticking plaster on deep seated problems. It can take ten years or more to support problem families." So having a funding stream for a short-term initiative is unlikely to be effective.

Productivity is often in the news and it can be viewed from different perspectives and measured in different ways. One way of looking at it is technical productivity, that is managerial efficiency, how efficiently something is produced. Allocative productivity, on the other hand relates to spending money in the right places and on the right combinations of services or products to achieve the best outcome for society. Both matter, but it is important to ensure the easier-to-measure technical efficiency does not obscure the longer-term allocative measures.

Finally, there is the issue of continuity of structure and process. Whilst innovation and new ideas are essential for progress, too many changes detract significantly from both efficiency and effectiveness. We heard time and again from interviewees that new ministers came in with new ideas, wanting to make their mark (even within the same government) and this resulted in everyone having to rethink their plans, only to discover that person was moving on before too long, leaving behind "zombie initiatives." The same has been said of permanent staff who move roles frequently both internally and externally, taking with them their experience of operating in that role and their understanding of what has happened in the past. There is a balance between stagnation and a system that is so fluid that nothing takes root.

So, processes matter. You can see from the examples above that that they can either facilitate effectiveness or undermine it and you will need to balance the strictures of the process with the latitude and professionalism of the people using them. If you have a simple uncomplicated process you don't need to allow much latitude in decision-making. If you have more complex issues to be resolved you need to allow people freedom to exercise judgement and act but ensure they are trained and have the expertise to do so.

References

DoE (2018) Department for Education, PARTNERSHIPS (publishing.service.gov.uk)

Semler, R. (2001) "Maverick!: The success story behind the world's most unusual workplace," *Random House Business*, London.

UIDP, University-Industry Demonstration Partnership (2012) *Understanding & developing the pathways for beneficial university-industry engagement*, Partnership-Continuum1.pdf (uidp.org).

Vandergriff, D., Webber, S., Peter Vangjel, P., Brender, L., Luccio, D., Roberts T., Wilson, D., Fox, T., Long G., & Labarbera J. (2019) Mission command II, the who, what, where, when and why: an anthology, Amazon Fulfilment, Wrocław, Poland.

Chapter 6

Effectiveness and planning for change

A plan never survives the first encounter with the enemy
(adapted from Helmuth von Moltke)

So why do we plan? Our answer may also take a lead from President Eisenhower's words: "Plans are useless, but planning is useful." Let us have a closer look at this.

There is a (possibly apocryphal) story about the corps of Austrian cavalry who became lost in a blizzard in the Alps. They had reached the stage where they were totally dispirited and ready to give up, when one of their number found he was carrying a map. So, they all gathered around the map and made a plan as to where they needed to go. The result was that they found their way back to their barracks and all lives were saved. It was only some time later that someone had a closer look at the map and found that it wasn't a map of the Alps, it was a map of the Pyrenees.

Back in the mid-2000s, Mike ran an executive MSc at Cranfield in Managing Organisational Performance. Participants came from as far afield as South Africa and New Zealand in addition to participants from the United Kingdom. At that time, there was concern over the possible impact of a flu pandemic and the Centre for Business Performance did some detailed contingency planning for that event, especially around the issue of potential disruption to international travel. The flu pandemic did not happen, but a couple of years later the Icelandic Volcano, Eyjafjallajokull, erupted causing widespread disruption to air travel in the Northern Hemisphere. Interestingly, it turned out that the plans for the flu epidemic were very useful for dealing with the problem created by the volcano. So planning was useful on this occasion.

DOI: 10.4324/9781003099895-9

At the beginning of 2020 in the early stages of what later became the Covid 19 pandemic, Mike remembered the contingency planning that had been done over a decade earlier. Staff working on the Cranfield Project Leadership programme couldn't work from home on personal laptops for security reasons, as the client was the UK government and data security was paramount. Looking ahead and based on what had been foreseen in earlier planning for a different event, Mike approved a set of laptops, enabling staff to work from home in a secure manner. Had these not arrived, the programme administration couldn't have continued when the University campus was closed during the first lockdown. The earlier planning had sensitised Mike and the team to possible problems and so they were able to take early action.

One of the reasons for planning is to think through what might happen and what to do about it if it does. Working with a team means people will have some common experience to fall back on when the unexpected happens. Scenario planning was used widely in Shell back in the 1970s and 1980s to help managers think about alternative ways of dealing with future shocks to the system. The idea wasn't to create a solution, because the source of the future shock couldn't be anticipated, but it was to prepare people so they could respond more quickly when the need arose in the future.

What do we mean by planning?

When you talk about planning, what are you thinking about? Are you thinking about your ultimate goal and how you are going to achieve this in broad terms, or are you thinking about all the detailed activity, work breakdown structures, Gannt charts and critical path analyses required to work out exactly what is required to deliver the project?

More often than not, you think about the latter, but we will argue here that detailed planning without an overall understanding of the purpose and outcomes of what you are trying to achieve is dangerous. The danger is that the ultimate goal gets lost in the detailed planning, which can develop a life of its own. We will also argue that high level plans without a more detailed understanding of what is required for actual delivery is also dangerous. In this situation, leaders can believe that the plan is totally deliverable within the timescales set and budget provided, when in fact, it is not.

What is the purpose of planning? There are many reasons for planning, including to understand:

■ How something is going to be delivered.
■ How long it will take to be delivered.
■ How much it will cost to deliver the plan.
■ Whether it is feasible to deliver the outcomes.
■ Whether the outcomes are worth the time and effort needed.

Items in the list above are all good reasons for planning, but planning isn't as simple as this when it comes to implementing policy effectively. Most public sector change is complex, often emergent and frequently influenced by politics. So, in this chapter we will start by asking the question: "What kind of change are you planning?" We will then continue the theme by looking at different scenarios.

What kind of change are you planning?

Before you do anything else, you should answer this question because it will determine how you plan. Start with understanding what you know and what you don't know.

US Secretary of Defense, Donald Rumsfeld gave a wonderful speech in which he talked about the "known knowns," the "known unknowns," and the "unknown unknowns." He was accused of being overly complicated, but these are questions you really need to understand at the planning phase of a change. The diagram below captures the four quadrants you need to consider (Figure 6.1).

The known knowns are the things you are sure of, often things that have been done before or for technical reasons are very predictable. For example, if you have built a bridge before, you will understand the civil engineering of bridge building. The "known unknowns" are the things you know you don't know. In the bridge building example, the civil engineering may be well understood, but there may be aspects about the ground on which the bridge is to be built which needs further investigation. So, from a planning perspective this is a risk, and you need to decide at which stage the ground needs to be surveyed so you reduce the risk.

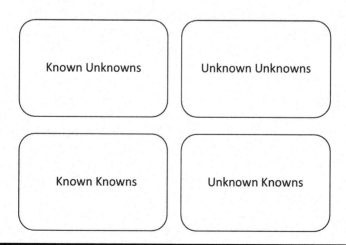

Figure 6.1 The four quadrants to consider in planning.

As you move across the figure to the right-hand side you move into new territory and the bridge building example becomes less appropriate. There are things that you do, in fact know, but you don't realise it. These "unknown knowns" are also referred to as tacit knowledge. It often comes about when you do something so frequently that is becomes almost automatic. But it also happens in teams. There may be a member of your team who knows things that others don't. It is important to bring this knowledge to the surface so that it can be shared and used when needed. "Unknown knowns" don't normally trip you up in delivering a project but finding out what they are can save you a considerable amount of time and effort.

"Unknown unknowns" are by their very nature very difficult to manage, simply because you don't know what you don't know. These are usually sensed by experienced individuals who have an uneasiness about something but can't quite put their finger on it. The more difficult and complex the change, the more likely these problems are to occur. There are two ways of dealing with this issue. You can simply proceed with the change knowing that, at some stage something will emerge, and you will have to deal with it and work through it when it happens. Or you can experiment or conduct a pilot so that you discover the problems before you embark on a full rollout. Shell have a mantra that they never embark on a full-scale project without proving the technology or approach at a smaller scale first. In this way they limit all the inherent risks and costs involved.

So what does that mean for planning? Firstly, everyone should be made aware of the type of change you are embarking on and the state of your knowledge. This is really a discussion about the risks associated with undertaking the project. Frequently it isn't a very "mature" conversation. Those sponsoring the project don't want to be distracted by what they see as *detail*, and those planning the project may hide some of the risks in order to get the business case *over the line* and the project approved.

Secondly, there are implications for the plan itself. Differences in the state of knowledge lead to differences in the predictability of the planning process and in the way situations should be handled. If you are dealing with:

- **Known knowns** – then planning is linear and straight forward. Estimates of time and cost should be relatively certain and there should be high levels of confidence in delivery. Limited contingency is required.
- **Known unknowns** – when planning you need to allow time and resource to identify and bottom out the unknowns. Estimates of time and cost will be dependent on conducting further research into what you need to find out. Once this has been undertaken and fully assessed you should have a reasonable level of certainty and high levels of confidence in delivery. In this situation, the initial plan needs to contain significant contingency which can then be reduced once the information is available.
- **Unknown unknowns** – planning under these circumstances is more problematic. During the planning phase you can identify many of the issues you

are going to face, but although there may be detailed and comprehensive plans no savvy sponsor or project director will believe it. So now you need to think about three things:

■ The relative levels of contingency required,
■ The point at which the costs outweigh the benefits, and
■ Whether the project should be broken down into manageable pieces with stage reviews and points at which the decision to discontinue or reset the change are made.

Delivery and outcomes

In the section above, we talked about what you know and don't know about a change initiative. In this section, we want to present a similar framework developed by Eddie Obeng which is often used in the project community. Obeng's framework focuses on the degree to which the required outcome can be specified and the degree to which the process of *getting to* the outcome can be specified (see Figure 6.2).

It is important to realise that there are occasions when no-one fully understands what the solution or outcome should be. This has a significant impact on the way you need to think about a change and how you plan its implementation. So, moving through the framework, quadrant by quadrant, let us illustrate some of these differences.

The bottom left quadrant is sometimes called, painting by numbers. If a change lies in this quadrant, you will know exactly what is to be achieved and how you will go about it. Activities in this quadrant may be well repeated straightforward projects

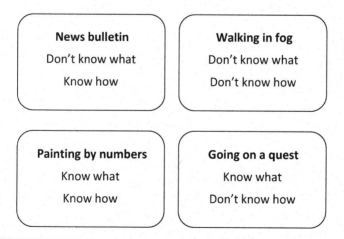

Figure 6.2 What type of project is it? The four quadrants to consider.

Source: Adapted from Eddie Obeng 1995.

where the team knows exactly what they are going to do and what they are going to deliver. In reality, there are very few public sector projects that fit into this category.

The top left quadrant is sometimes called News Bulletin because the process of gathering content and collating it into a news programme is well understood. It is done every day and has become a routine. However, the content of the news changes, so whilst people planning the activity know the process inside out, they can never be absolutely sure of what the content will be. In the public sector a simple example could be preparing a Minister's answers to parliamentary questions.

The bottom right quadrant describes many change initiatives in the public sector. People are clear on what is to be achieved but the path to delivering the outcome is not known. This is sometimes described as going on a quest, because you have to find your way through to the final destination. It could be argued that the idea behind the UK government's universal credit policy fell into this category. Bringing benefits together into one system was the goal, but achieving this integration given the extremely complicated landscape of UK benefits was far from straightforward.

Finally, the top right quadrant captures the situation of trying to make a change when, not only is the outcome unclear, but so is the process of getting there. For obvious reasons this is sometimes called, Walking in Fog!

What does this mean for planning? As we said before, it is extremely important to recognise the type of change you are embarking upon. Change where the process of delivery is known (the left-hand column) is often called technical change. There is a set of approaches that you apply and more often than not they work to deliver what you are trying to achieve. Change that falls into the right-hand column is called adaptive change because you will have to feel for the path to achieve your aim and be flexible and adapt according to what turns up on the journey.

Standard project planning tools and techniques work well for technical change because the process is known. Planning for technical change requires skill and experience but it is linear. Activities can be specified and sequenced and resources can be estimated with the result that accurate plans and budgets can be produced.

However, planning becomes more problematic if you only know what you are trying to achieve, and the path is unknown. There is no certainty. There will be previous projects of a similar nature that can be used as a basis for planning but that could well be the extent of your knowledge. Under these circumstances you should present timescales and resources as a range not as a fixed budget or delivery date. Presenting information as a range may unsettle many change sponsors because they like to see certainty, but building unrealistic expectations is a problem and, in the end, can lead to loss of trust. By using ranges, you are signalling to everyone that there is no certainty.

Evolution of change

We have been talking as if change is fixed at inception because we have simplified it to explain the planning process more clearly. The reality is that change evolves over time and this evolution is driven by the underlying type of change and complexity of delivery (see Figure 6.3). We will discuss these three types of change next.

The first type of change involves structural complexity. Many larger change initiatives have structural complexity at their core. They have a significant team and resource base that must be directed and coordinated towards delivering outcomes. If you are leading and managing these types of change you must plan effectively at a detailed level to ensure everything fits together and is sequenced to best effect. This is often a staff activity because it needs specialist skills and experienced staff who have worked on this type of project before so they can bring their experience to bear. Examples of such a change could be the building of the A14 road expansion, which became a technical project once the highly political phase of arguing about the course of the final route was completed.

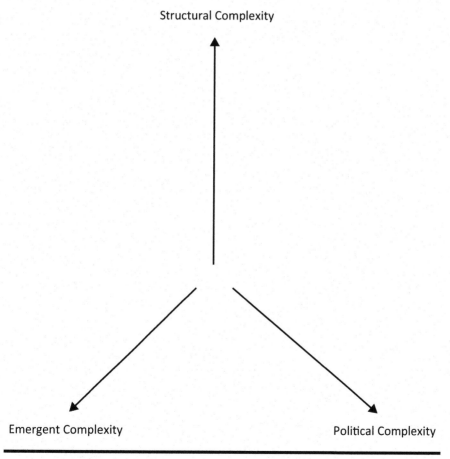

Figure 6.3 Three dimensions of complexity to be considered in change projects.

The second type of change is emergent. In this situation, you need to work your way through the complexities of the change because it isn't possible to know all the issues and problems from the outset. You have to cope with the unknown and your plan must reflect the reality of what is evolving on the ground in real time. Here, your earlier planning will be useful, but good leadership comes to the fore. Line managers need to be sensitive to emerging issues and having noticed what is happening they must realign the planning and delivery activity.

An example of this emergent type of change would be during the planning stage of the Covid vaccine programme. The effectiveness and approval date of each vaccine was uncertain as was the ideal period between shots. Decisions had to be made despite these uncertainties.

The third complexity is political complexity as changes are often subject to political interference. Political interference can make planning very difficult as there may be changes in expectations, resourcing, scope and even support. This requires intense communication and engagement between leaders and stakeholders, so that the team implementing the change can stay abreast of developments and can create solutions in line with developing political needs. An example of such a change may be the building of a new runway at Heathrow Airport, where the project from its outset has been embroiled in arguments about capacity, the best place to locate this capacity and local resistance versus national need.

In the public sector, many projects have elements of all three types of complexity. Often these different complexities come to the fore at different stages, so a project may well begin life as a political issue, but once the politics have been settled, the project starts but faces emergent complexities. As the project progresses, these complexities are resolved, and the focus moves to structural complexity and getting the change delivered. In the latter stages, the project may evolve again as the delivery moves into implementation and the project is handed from the project team to those who will operate the new way of working.

On the Project Leadership Programme at Cranfield, we emphasise the need to understand the type of change you are facing. If you treat an emergent or politically complex change as a structurally complex project it will lead to disaster. The former two require greater leadership involvement with a need to reflect and respond, whist structural complexity requires greater management focus on the coordination and detail. The leadership skills you need for political complexity are different from the leadership skills you need in order to deal with emerging complexity. In the first instance the focus is on political engagement and dialogue, whilst in the second, emergent situation, you will require a more entrepreneurial approach. Aligning leadership and management capability with the complexity of your project phases is important.

To conclude, can we suggest you consider the following issues:

■ Some planning is a staff activity, and some planning is a line management activity – the type of complexity you are facing will dictate the balance.

- Line managers are responsible for delivering the outcomes so they should own the higher levels of the plan in order that they understand how it is going to be delivered.
- We will argue that high level planning is best done as a group exercise because it engages the senior team in developing the plan, draws a wide range of expertise into the development of the plan, builds understanding between members of the team and creates commitment. We suggest using success mapping and theory of change for this process and you will find these topics later in the book.
- Detailed planning can be a staff activity, but it should be undertaken by suitably experienced staff with the appropriate expertise. Leaders must work with these staff to guide them, especially under situations of political or emergent complexity.
- Effective and regular communication between those involved in high level planning and those involved in detailed planning is absolutely essential. If that communication breaks down or is compromised for any reason, then the delivery of the plan will be put in jeopardy.
- There must also be effective communication between those involved in the detailed planning and what is being delivered on the ground. The feedback from people who can see what is actually happening is invaluable in updating and validating the original plan. Think about the type of complexity you are facing and how that can be best managed.
- The emphasis will be different depending on the complexity you face, but there should be regular reviews at the high level of the plan to ensure that the
  - ☐ Plan and intended outcomes are still necessary,
  - ☐ Stakeholders views are known and reflected in the plan,
  - ☐ Unknowns and uncertainties in the plan are understood,
  - ☐ The work planned is still expected to deliver the outcomes and benefits expected at the outset.

Reference

Obeng, E. (1995) *All change; the project leaders secret handbook*, FT Prentice Hall, London.

Chapter 7

Stakeholders and change

Stakeholder analysis

A stakeholder is anyone with an interest in what you are doing. That interest may be supportive and useful to you, it may just be a passing interest, or it may even be hostile. Hostility sometimes stems from the stakeholder's lack of knowledge about what you are doing which leads them to worry about whether it may have an adverse effect on them. Sometimes they are hostile because they believe very strongly that what you are doing is wrong.

So, it is important to understand who your stakeholders are if you are trying to change something. You need to understand where they sit in relationship to what you are trying to implement and whether they may try to prevent you from delivering your goals. From our experience, despite the widespread understanding of stakeholders in the public sector, too many projects either fail to deliver benefits or are hampered for three main reasons:

■ Stakeholder analysis was not carried out at all,
■ Insufficient time and effort were put into serious stakeholder analysis (paying lip service to the process), and
■ Analysis was carried out but abandoned and not used or repeated as the project progressed.

In this section we will present a number of tools to help you analyse your stakeholders. The tools are simple, deliberately so. Ideally, they should be used and shared by your team so there is a widespread input into the stakeholder analysis and a common understanding of where stakeholders sit and why and how you plan to engage them.

In the next three sections, we will describe force-field analysis before moving onto discuss a couple of change matrices. This is followed by sections on why stakeholders

DOI: 10.4324/9781003099895-10

resist change and the typical stakeholder experience, or change journey, over the life of a change project. In the last section we will summarise how you might plan to use these tools together to help you understand the change you are embarking on.

Force field analysis

Force field analysis is a simple approach to looking at stakeholders. It starts with asking the question: who is in favour of the change you are trying to implement and who is against it? Once you have established this you can draw a diagram such as the one below (Figure 7.1) so you can visualise the direction and strength of the push for change or resistance to it. The conversation you have with your colleagues whilst drawing this diagram is of particular importance. Do they have a common view of stakeholders? Are there any stakeholders who have been forgotten or ignored? Do colleagues agree on the relative strengths of opposition or support for change?

Once the diagram is completed, the conversation should move on to how likely it is the change will succeed given the environment in which you are operating and to how you can improve the odds of success by reducing forces against the change and increasing forces supporting it.

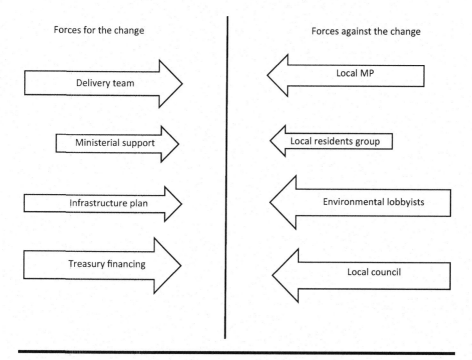

Figure 7.1 An example of a force field analysis.

Stakeholder matrix analysis

Lewin's (1947) Force Field analysis framework described above goes right back to the 1940s, but it has stood the test of time. More recently, writers on change have created slightly more sophisticated tools to help people with their stakeholder analysis.

The change response framework is one of these. This is a simple two by two matrix that looks at the perceived impact of the change on the people or groups concerned on one axis and the expected energy of response on the other axis. The version portrayed in Figure 7.2 is based on Strebel (whom we mentioned in the chapter on leadership) who grouped people into four categories. High energy people adversely affected by the change are *resistors*, whereas those adversely affected who are not expected to expend high levels of energy in their response are called *traditionalists*. People who are not adversely affected by the change and are not likely to be vocal in their response are *bystanders* and those who are likely to be active in their response but not adversely affected are called *change agents*.

Others have a slightly different version of the stakeholder matrix (see Figure 7.3). This approach looks at the attitude to the change (for and against) on one axis and level of influence on the other. Again, this is a simple technique to allow you and your team to visualise those affected by the change and how they are positioned with regard to it.

Piercy then goes on to discuss how you treat individuals and groups in each of the four quadrants. Those with influence who support the change need to be engaged. Don't take this group for granted, they need to be fully engaged throughout the change process to ensure their support is constant and their influence is there when you need it. This box tends to contain the senior sponsors or initiators of the

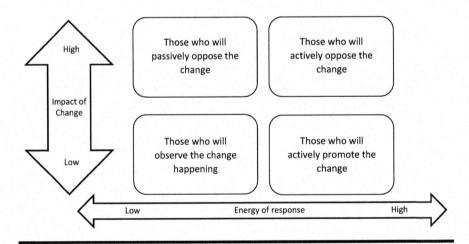

Figure 7.2 Positioning stakeholders and their possible change response.

Source: Adapted from Strebel (1994).

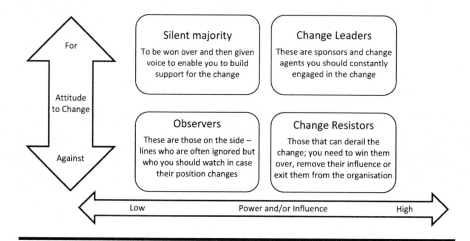

Figure 7.3 Engaging tactics for stakeholder groups.

change you are endeavouring to implement, so be aware of who they are and make sure you know of any other priorities they have that may distract them.

Those who support the change but don't have the same level of influence need to be treated differently. As you will need as much support as you can garner, ask yourself how you can increase the influence of this group. How can you make their voices heard so that they can positively influence your change roll out?

Piercy suggests that those against the change and with low levels of influence should be ignored. We don't entirely agree with this, because you may have underestimated their influence, or, indeed, their influence may change over time. Here are two examples that illustrates this point.

We often think of influence as being based on position. In the military, the higher the rank, the more influence the person has. But is this really true or does it also depend on the informal networks? If you want to change a policy, do you approach a junior minister, or do you have a conversation with the Special Adviser who advises the cabinet minister directly responsible? So, when you think about influence you need to look at the whole landscape not just formal hierarchies and relationships.

Levels of influence can change over time. One clear example of this was a recent railway project in the United Kingdom where an opposition group made up of local people were, at the outset, considered to be unimportant as their level of influence was low. However, over time the group became more active, attracted media attention, signed up local residents, started to petition local MPs and in a matter of just a few months they managed to get to a position where they had a significant influence on aspects of the project. Engaging this group at the beginning, instead of ignoring them, could have saved those running the project considerable time and effort.

Those with high influence who oppose your project present a problem. In some circumstances it is possible just to push through the change you want despite opposition, but it is far more beneficial if you can engage and work with this group of high influencers. Persuading people that a change is a good thing and winning them over is one tactic that you should consider, but of course, not everyone can be won over. For those who can't be won over, ask yourself whether it is possible to distract them or remove them from the ambit of the change. During a balanced scorecard implementation, Mike was working with a senior team through a series of workshops to help them design their performance measures. The workshops were designed to engage the whole team and to win their support but, from the start, it was apparent that two individuals were opposed to the process. It was not possible to persuade them to support the initiative as their views were so entrenched and it was likely that they would make it difficult to implement any new ideas. At the closing dinner, the Managing Director stood up and thanked everyone for their efforts and then went on to announce that the two dissenting individuals had new jobs starting the following week. The result was electric, the MD had removed his two "trouble-makers" by moving them sideways but had also signalled to everyone else the conse-quences of not being behind this project.

Our third and final matrix is one that we have developed from our discussions and interviews with politicians and civil servants in the process of writing this book. This matrix, shown in Figure 7.4 is designed to look at the proposed change from the perspective of the initiator as a key stakeholder. The degree of political ideology/expediency is shown on the vertical axis and spread of agreement on the horizontal axis.

The difficulty with most change is that it takes time and the more fundamental the change, the greater the time required. But politicians tend to move on from their posts quite quickly, so a project may only have reached the starting gate by the time the person responsible is moved to their next departmental appointment. One of our interviewees, concerned about the rapid turnover of ministers with whom he had been dealing, told us he had asked (perhaps half seriously?) at the first meeting with the new minister whether they would still be in post for the second meeting.

When we put the issue of rapid turnover of people to our interviewees, they recognised the dilemma. If you are passionate about ensuring a change takes root and bears fruit you must seek wide recognition and support for it from a range of different stakeholders, and particularly those with influence. You need to "get your ducks in a row," gathering support from a variety of quarters, ensuring resource and funding are in place before you have a chance of success. If you can do that then the initiative should survive a change of minister and possibly even a change in government.

We are suggesting that projects based on political ideology or political expedi-ency are at risk because a change in government may well reverse the change. We are also suggesting that change projects with widespread support will survive longer than change projects with narrow support.

We have named the four quadrants (i) Ministerial Whim, (ii) Ministerial Insight, (iii) Political Will, and (iv) Consensus. The labelling implies this can only be used

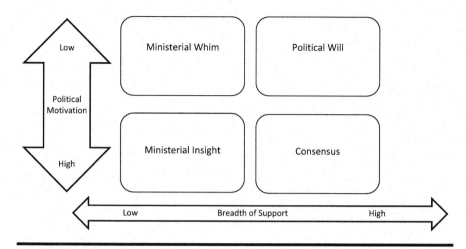

Figure 7.4 A framework for reviewing stakeholder support and political will.

as a means of assessing likelihood of long-term success for central government initiatives. However, you can relabel each of the boxes to suit your own circumstances. Even in commercial organisations, there are initiatives that are the brainchildren of the MD that are politically motivated (with a small "p") and those which have wide support, and there are initiatives started by forward-thinking people with real insight where there is as yet, little support because most people have not yet fully understood what it is all about.

In the next couple of sections, we want to look at the quadrants from two perspectives, that of the politician and that of the civil servant required to implement the change.

Starting from the perspective of the politician, creating a policy or change initiative that is politically motivated and doesn't have wide support could be seen as chasing a whim. There are a few politicians who are in post long enough to see these changes through, but the reality is that if there isn't wide support, then the change may not survive the next reshuffle. Similarly, if a minister does have an insight that doesn't garner wider support, even if it isn't politically controversial, the change is not likely to survive. *Ministerial Insights* need wider support. The quadrant we have described as *Political Will*, may well contain ideas and promises made in the party manifesto. These often are politically motivated and have wider support from across the party in power so will often survive a ministerial reshuffle. The question is whether or not they will survive a change in government.

What we are proposing here is purely pragmatic. If a change is to be initiated, developed, implemented and is to survive, there must be widespread support and, ideally low political controversy. A politician who is interested in creating real and effective change in how government or the wider public sector works (rather than just a headline) needs to try to position their policy or change in the bottom right-hand box. The change may not start there, but by building consensus and reducing the politics of the change, this repositioning can be achieved.

Now let us take a look at this from the point of view of the Civil Servant (or permanent official). Does it help to understand that a project is a *Ministerial Whim*? If it is a whim, it creates a dilemma as the Civil Service is there to implement the policies of ministers. However, if you, as a Civil Servant, recognise the project has little chance of success and you are able to advise against its implementation, it will mean that public money will not be wasted on something that will never be finished or deliver any future benefits. We are now reaching the position whereby the implementor of the change sees a different outcome from the initiator of the change, something we discuss in the next section.

Let us suggest some options that the Civil Servant or official can take. Simply rejecting or stalling the change will cause frustration, so probably isn't the best option. Having a one-one dialogue with the politician about what the change is intended to deliver may bring clarity of intent and that may in turn allow the discussion to move towards considering alternative ways of delivering change. Exploring these options could well transform the initiative from that of a whim, to something that is actually beneficial and, as a consequence, the initiative will gain wider support. Creating the clarity of intent will move the initiative from the *ministerial whim* quadrant, to the *ministerial insight* quadrant. Exploring the implementation and benefit options will then move the initiative into the consensus quadrant. In that way, it may be possible to turn a whim into a lasting and beneficial change.

In reality, there are situations where this is really hard to manage, the conversation doesn't happen, or the politician isn't prepared to engage. Under these circumstances we would suggest that the implementation is broken down into short deliverable sprints. Each sprint should have a beginning and an end. It should have a finite set of resources and time for delivery and specific measurable output and, ideally, measurable outcomes and benefits. The outcomes and benefits may not be realisable in these short sprints, but they need to be kept in mind. The idea behind taking this approach is to deliver the change in chunks, but at the end of each chunk, there is the opportunity to stop and reflect on what has been achieved and on what the next step should be. For those familiar with project management terminology, what we are describing is the agile approach where there are several discrete phases and lessons can be learnt after each phase and adjustments made accordingly for the next. As change progresses a picture begins to emerge, and it is important to take the opportunity to pause and take stock. If it becomes clear that expected benefits are not being realised, then you may decide to go no further with that initiative, but you can bank the benefits you have managed to accrue and avoid wasting effort in the future on something that is not likely to succeed.

One of the speakers on the Project Leadership Programme at Cranfield University, Katie Davis, tells the story of the project to introduce a national identity card on which she was the Director of Strategy, at the time of a Labour government. She was acutely aware that if the Conservatives gained power, the initiative would be stopped.

With this in mind, she did two things. Firstly, she used the project to improve processes in the issuing of new passports, as there was overlap and efficiencies could be realised in both processes. This meant improvements created by her project survived beyond the life of the identity card scheme. Secondly, she planned the project so it could be quickly closed down with as little adverse impact as possible. Understanding the stakeholders and wider political context can be used to think through your approach to achieve the best possible outcomes despite the vagaries of politics.

Resistance to change

In the previous section, we discussed how to categorise various stakeholder groups according to their response to change. It is also important to ask yourself why they are resisting change. There are four main reasons why people resist change:

1. Apprehension or fear
2. Self-interest
3. They see the change differently
4. Principle

Each of these groups of people sees change from a different perspective and so you need to handle them in different ways.

Apprehension or fear

Change is always disconcerting, so it is understandable that people will be apprehensive when they first hear what is being proposed. If the change is significant, apprehension can tip over into fear but you can overcome this through careful, planned communication. If people understand why change is being introduced and the impact it will have on their work and lives, it is often possible to put their minds at rest. The more change you do and the better you become at implementing change, the easier it is. But it is also possible to create a culture that is resistant to change when you try to do too much and nothing ever gets completed.

Communication isn't simply a one-way process with those initiating the change broadcasting to everyone else what it is and how it will happen. If change is to be successful, those affected by it must not only hear the message but understand what it means for them. This in turn may raise further questions as people mull it over in their minds. You need to have an open channel of communication so you can have a dialogue about what is happening as it happens and what it means for individuals. In this way, you can temper the rumour-mill which often portrays intentions as more damaging to the individual than they actually are.

Most changes require the involvement and support of a wider group who will have to go through the change and then be responsible for delivering and adapting to the new way of working in the future until it becomes "business as usual." Talking to people as the change unfurls, engaging them and getting their ideas is a good way of allowing them to shape change in their own place of work. If they have some say in how things happen, it will not only overcome anxiety, but should also bring to light any detailed issues that the initiating team had not considered.

When planning communication, you can use Gleicher's change formula discussed in Chapter 4 and build on dissatisfaction with the status-quo, create a vivid picture of the future and set out the first practical steps towards implementing the change you want to see. Providing those first practical steps and getting people involved in how those steps are implemented will greatly enhance the chances of a successful outcome.

In all communication, trust is important. Do you trust the person giving you the message? If the message is seen as being patronising or deceitful, this will be problematic as your culture of acceptance of change will rapidly deteriorate into a culture of resistance. So, choose your words carefully and consider whether there is any way they can be misinterpreted. As we all know, when you speak you may think you are imparting one message but the person hearing your words may understand something quite different.

Self interest

In any change, there are usually winners and losers. Individuals may perceive that the change is not in their best interest, and sometimes this is just a perception rather than reality, and you can overcome their concerns by talking to them. Sometimes, however, the impact is real. People can lose their jobs, their position, or their status, and you have to recognise and deal with this. How you treat people in these situations is important for two reasons. Firstly, it will reflect on the organisation. If you handle the situation badly, it may make it extremely hard to recruit in the future. Social media means bad news travels fast. Secondly, it will have an impact on those who remain, who will see the organisation either as one that treats people fairly or one that doesn't.

During the course of a career, many people will experience redundancy at some stage. It can be a very wounding experience, or it can be one in which individuals, although not happy to lose their jobs, accept what is happening and still have respect for the organisation for which they worked. Pippa experienced redundancy on one occasion along with several other colleagues and remembers the open communication, the willingness of the HR department to respond quickly to queries and the support package available to her following her departure. On the other hand, we know of an organisation that embarked upon a redundancy programme following restructuring and, despite severance terms being more generous than those offered by similar organisations, discovered the number of people who left the following year of their own volition exceeded the number of people made redundant in the first place. To make matters worse, some of those people were hard to replace.

So, if people are resisting because of self-interest, try to see the situation from their perspective. Negotiate with them. If they are concerned that a sideways move prompted by restructuring will affect their status, perhaps you can adjust their job title. There may be other actions you can take, like offering training or a future path for development. In some cases, you will have to make individuals redundant, and it goes without saying that you should be as kind and generous as the situation allows. But think also about those who remain in the organisation. How are they going to react? How can you be assured of their support in the future?

Perception of change

In creating a vision for the future, the initiator of the change will have their own personal vision of what the new world will look like. They will communicate that widely and encourage others to see the change in that way.

However, those initiating the change aren't the only ones who have an opinion on the future. The initiators aren't infallible; they could easily be wrong. If you identify the people who are resisting because they don't believe the change is being implemented in the right way or they don't believe it will deliver the outcomes you, as the initiator, expect to realise, talk to them, and ask why. If they are the people "at the coal face," they may know something you have missed. It is easy to assume people are resisting change and being awkward for the sake of it, but they may actually have a point and you should listen.

Describing the vision, the time in the future when the change has happened is the easier part. Knowing *how* to deliver that future state and actually delivering it is the harder part. Having the support of a diverse team of people who have intimate knowledge of the problems and of how things work in practice will help you create a pathway towards your final goal.

We interviewed elected representatives and permanent staff and asked them about change. It may come as no surprise to you that some elected representatives told us that permanent staff are good at telling them why something cannot be done (computer says "no," as one person told us). On the other side of the picture, some officials have told us politicians will go ahead with what they want to do, regardless of what they say.

We believe this is a common example of different perceptions of change. To move forward both sides need to understand the other person's position and for that you must have dialogue and a situation where people feel able to express their views.

Principle

So how do you deal with someone who is resisting change on principle? You should, of course, talk to them and find out what the problem is, but they are unlikely to be open to communication or persuasion. If that is the case, there are only two possible courses of action, put up with their continuing resistance, or remove them so they can no longer interfere or influence what is going on. In the public sector, the latter is often difficult, but there are costs of not removing them in terms of time and effort and indeed of general morale as these people will have an influence on how others feel.

Stakeholder journeys

Social psychologist Kurt Lewin identified three phases of change, unfreezing, moving, and refreezing. The first phase focuses on preparing the organisation for change, the second phase on making the change happen, and the final phase on embedding it so that it takes root and doesn't unravel once those managing it have left. This is a useful framework from an organisational perspective.

Individuals subject to change react in different ways at each phase. Writers in this field talk about the "change roller coaster." This can be viewed as how either performance or self-esteem changes over time whilst change is taking place (Carnall, 2007; Coyle & Page, 2006). The initial reaction is to deny that any change is needed or that it is even going to happen. As the change process persists, the mood changes and people start to blame others, then blame themselves which can lead to very low morale. But if change is going to be successful, new ways of working will emerge and, as people get used to the new environment and new ways of working, confidence will grow and so will performance until finally the other side of the change is reached and benefits will begin to be seen. In Figure 7.5, we have inserted our own thoughts and reactions to the change roller coaster, but it is useful at the planning stage to think what these reactions might be for each of your main stakeholder groups. Some will be scared, some will be angry and some will be subversive. Having a picture in advance and observing reactions will help you understand the point you have reached in your change journey.

Many writers have written about the stages people who are affected by change will most likely go through, as illustrated by Figure 7.5. The change initiator's journey is obviously important too, but this has received far less attention. In Figure 7.6, we have developed on Conner's (1992) view of the initiator's response to change by adding the phases of the change to Conner's picture of optimism and pessimism on the vertical axis and time along the horizontal axis. Conner argues that over a change life cycle the initiator starts off by being optimistic, but this optimism comes from partial ignorance. As the change progresses, the initiator learns progressively more about the nature and challenges of the change they are trying to implement, which leads to a more pessimistic view of the likelihood of success. At its deepest moment, the change can fail as the initiator "opts out" or abandons the project. This is sometimes done publicly, when the initiator declares openly that the change has been abandoned. Sometimes it is done privately, when the initiator stops pursuing the project but doesn't formally tell anyone. This can lead to a very difficult situation as

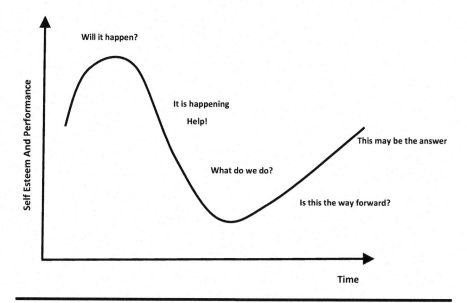

Figure 7.5 Participants' change journeys.

Source: Adapted from Carnall (2007) and Coyle and Page (2006).

people still could be working on the change which in reality is now no longer going to happen.

If the initiator reaches the stage of fully understanding the real costs and consequences of the change but remains committed, then over time this new knowledge leads to a more optimistic view and ideally to the successful implementation of the change.

Stakeholder engagement as a process

As we said at the beginning of this chapter, change often fails because initiators have paid insufficient attention to stakeholders and we cannot overestimate how important this step is. You cannot assume you know what all your stakeholders' responses will be without talking to them and continuing to talk to them. Find out why they are resisting change. Can you do something about it?

In planning change, we discussed the different journeys that individuals and initiators take. You can use these frameworks to think through the overarching plan of who you will engage when and how that engagement will happen. It is important to keep stakeholders firmly in your sights throughout the change process, to watch what is happening and how they are reacting. But it is also important to keep in touch with them once the change has been implemented to check whether your plans have been implemented and are working and delivering benefits as they should.

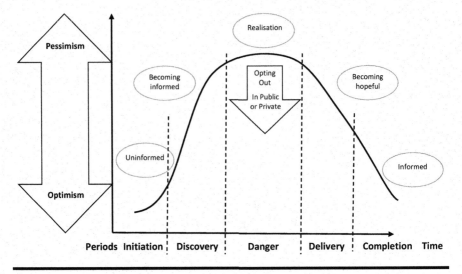

Figure 7.6 Sponsors' change journeys.

Source: Adapted from Conner (1992).

References

Carnall, C. (2007) *Managing change in organisations,* Fifth Edition, Prentice Hall, London.

Conner, D. R. (1992) *Managing at the speed of change: how resilient managers succeed and prosper where others fail,* John Wiley & Sons, Chichester.

Coyle, M. & Page, C. (2006) *Manging change,* Kogan Page, London.

Lewin, K. (1947) *Field theory in social science,* Harper, New York, NY.

Percy, A. (2010) *Art of change management,* Embassy Books Mumbai, India.

Strebel, P. (1994) "Choosing the right change paths," *California Management Review,* January.

Chapter 8

Capacity and capability for change

Creating capacity

If you want to create change in your organisation – any type of change that will result in improvements in the future, from restructuring to the implementation of a new IT system or changing the process for doing something – you will need to ensure you have the capacity and the capability not only for carrying out the change itself, but also for ensuring activities run smoothly under the new system when your change has been completed.

Capacity can be defined as the availability of the components that enable an organisation to achieve its purpose. You can achieve results in the short term by exceeding your capacity, but that simply isn't sustainable, as we explained in the leadership section. Resources such as people, finances and equipment just become exhausted and wear out when they are over-used. This is obvious, yet there is always a push for doing more with less.

Capability is the ability to do something. You may have the capacity, for example the right number of people, but if those people don't have the capability, then there is a problem.

There are several ways of remedying capacity problems. The obvious way is simply to add more resource. Let's take the example of busy retail store. If queues are too long at the pay desk, you can add more tills and recruit more people, so queue lengths are reduced. Another way is to look at changing the process. In the retail example, you may decide to add some self-service tills for people who just have a few items to buy, thus reducing pressure at the pay desks. You could change the barcode system to avoid operators having to enter lengthy numbers that are hard to read into

DOI: 10.4324/9781003099895-11

their tills. A third way is to improve capability. You can train till operators to work more quickly perhaps, or upgrade tills so they work faster and have fewer breakdowns. You can also train staff so they are multi-skilled and can work effectively in a number of departments and in a number of roles, providing flexibility in your resources as these people can work where there is most need.

We spoke to Graham Farrant, Chief Executive of the newly created unitary authority of Bournemouth, Christchurch and Poole and he gave us a good example of this. Relatively new in his role, he emphasised the use of digital technology to reduce the demands on staff, whose talents and capability could then be released for use in another area where they would add more value.

In the following sections, we will look in more detail at building capacity and capability and give you some ideas for how to analyse what you are likely to need.

Knowing what you need

One common mistake when considering capacity requirements is to look at the present and to assume the future will be an extension of the present. This is something we commonly do when we are asked to produce a budget or a forecast. Occasionally, an action will have been taken because a crisis has occurred. People or resources have reached breaking point, and something has to be done quickly so extra resources are brought in without any real planning. Looking back and using that as your base-point for future planning without fully understanding the circumstances would present an inaccurate picture.

When planning resource requirements, you need to look at the present, the future and also scan the horizon for possible events that may change the direction of travel. In his book "Only the Paranoid Survive," Andy Grove, founder of Intel, coined the phrase "Strategic Inflection Point." In mathematics, the inflection point is the point at which the curve changes in response to an event, in an organisation it is the point at which something happens to make change inevitable or essential. In the case of Intel (founded in 1968 and produced memory chips for computers), the inflection point arrived when Japanese companies came to dominate the market. Intel had to do something different and so began to produce microprocessors instead.

Good leaders are not complacent and do not assume what happens now will continue into the future. They look at potential threats, opportunities, and changes and plan for how they will respond. This planning includes examining capacity and capability to deal with the changed situation.

It is important to build some fat into the system. That is not to say that you should not aim to create a *lean* organisation, though. A lean organisation is one in which everyone focusses on customer needs and all processes are aligned towards that goal, minimising waste. Lean organisations tend to have fewer hierarchies. When we talk about building fat into the system, we mean ensuring you have enough resources, whatever those might be, to achieve the outcomes you want. An airport finance director once commented that they planned capacity based around the tenth busiest day in the year. The theory was that above that level the system would be under strain, but it could survive for a short time. If you overload the system for too long you will find rather than being efficient you will waste time and resources. You cannot build infinite capacity, but you do need some resilience.

One question you should think about is how process driven or judgement driven your organisation is. A process driven organisation will tend to be more efficient as each individual part of the process is optimised and this works well in a steady state environment. However, if you are dealing with changing environments or complex situations then you will need more professionals who exercise judgement. If they are empowered to exercise that judgement, then the organisation can build resilience as individuals have the capability to adapt. It is a case of knowing what type of environment predominates. Putting too many professionals in a steady-state environment is not ideal because their ability to make judgements is unlikely to be fully utilised.

So, you must understand from multiple perspectives what you need in order to achieve the outcomes you want now and be flexible enough to cope with change in the future.

Identifying opportunities to create capacity

Henry Ford is reported to have said: "If it doesn't add value it's waste." Cutting out activities that don't add value is an excellent way of releasing resources to use in a more productive area and thus increasing capacity. You may have come across the "value chain" conceived by American academic, Michael Porter. The value chain is a way of breaking down operations into individual elements and showing how all the activities in an organisation are linked with inputs, transformation processes and outputs.

Activities are divided into two types: primary activities, such as logistics and operations and support activities such as human resources and procurement that enable the primary activities to happen. These activities are shown in the form of a chain from input to output. Whilst the value chain is most commonly used in commercial manufacturing and service companies, there is no reason why it cannot be adapted for use in the public sector, where there are inputs and processes that turn those inputs into benefits for the public, and support services that run alongside them. The difference in the public sector (other than the obvious lack of profit motive) is the multiplicity of stakeholders, so we have adapted Porter's original model slightly to include them (Figure 8.1).

You can adapt this model to suit your own situation, whether that is creating and implementing policy or running a school or hospital. The basic idea is the same: each link in that chain must be strong and each link must add value. Let us take a very simplified example of a school. The inputs could be the teachers and the pupils, the operations would be the teaching, the outputs would be pupils with qualifications

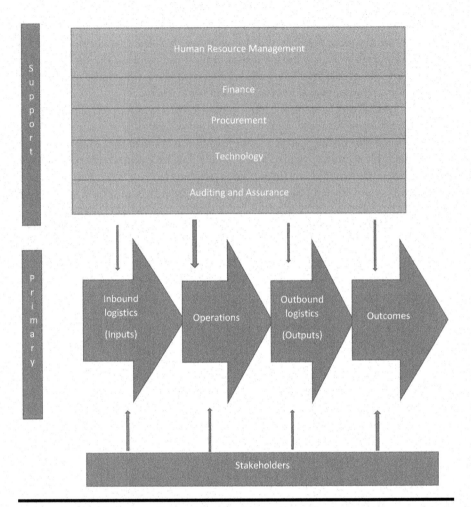

Figure 8.1 A public-sector value chain.

and the outcomes would be people adding value in society. (We realise, of course, that in practice running a school is far more complex than that.) The stakeholders would include the relevant government departments, local authorities, parents, governors, and future employers. You can look at each link in the chain and ask whether it adds value and how can it be changed to add more value. Incidentally, you can also test how resilient that link would be, should a problem occur. If teachers were unavailable as a result of a flu pandemic, for example, how could you operate that part of the process?

The process of identifying each of these stages is in itself useful because it enables you to see a whole picture whilst also seeing how each element is linked. It helps you understand what needs to be strengthened and where the existing strengths are.

It also helps you to identify where you can cut something out to allow greater capacity in another more productive area. When an organisation has been well established, there are often activities that have become ingrained because they were necessary at the beginning but, in fact, deliver very little, if any additional benefit. They exist because that is the way things have always been done and no one has questioned their value.

When evaluating the value of individual elements make sure you keep the end in mind. Streamlining the process is important for efficiency and for releasing scarce resources but if, by doing this you undermine the outcome, it is counterproductive. The picture of the chain should keep your focus on what you are ultimately trying to deliver.

The problem with support functions is that sometimes they develop a life of their own. They are only there to provide the support needed for the value chain to work and, where necessary, to ensure the organisation complies with relevant regulations and legislation. Let's take an example of how this happens. A brand team exists to project a common image of an organisation and it is quite logical to have a central team to do this. They need to provide guidelines for users of the brand, they need to have some type of policing role to ensure guidelines are adhered to. However, many people will recognise from their own organisations the term "Brand Police" where ever more rules are added, ever more people are added to police those rules and the whole system becomes sclerotic with people unable to progress with their projects because they are waiting for clearance.

How do you know when support functions are achieving dominance at the expense of the primary activities of the organisation? There are several tell-tale signs. The first, as we have described in the example above, is when you see people trying to find their way around the rules. The second is when the numbers in the support functions expand more rapidly than the rest of the organisation, in which case you need to examine if there is a special cause for this and you should challenge whether that cause is valid. The other sign is how the head of the function talks about their role. Are they truly focussed on the part their function plays in supporting the delivery of the outcomes or are they talking about internal practices and procedures and politics. The support function teams should see operational teams as their customers. They then need to align their processes, so they deliver what their customer needs.

Having said this, support functions are essential as you bring together a group of people with the expertise to deliver the services required. They should be the custodians of specialist knowledge and expertise which the organisation needs. It is also unproductive to cut out too many support staff. One example that sticks in the mind is a Cranfield Round table event where a group of senior people came together to discuss the important topic of strategy implementation. At the start, we had a very high-level conversation about the competitive landscape. However, after everyone had settled in and the conversation moved to why strategy fails, people began talking about lack of time and resources and how their organisations had reduced the number of support staff to the extent senior people had to waste time negotiating the central room booking system to find somewhere to hold their meetings. It was clear from the discussion that this was a bone of contention for quite a few people in the room.

When operational people are spending too much time on what we would call "infrastructure" activities, you know the balance is wrong. It has gone too far the other way. Another sign of an unbalanced organisation is when operational activities are being delayed. This can be either because there are not enough support staff or support functions have become too dominant.

There is a normal ebb and flow. At one time, the support roles will be too dominant, at another they will be too subordinate. The key in all of this is to keep your eyes focused on the end goal and create a balance between operations and support.

The other stream in the value chain pictured above represents stakeholders. Just as there must be a balance between support and operational teams, stakeholder involvement must be proportionate. If stakeholders are somehow hampering operations, then there is a problem. If your stakeholders are risk averse for example, you may find operational leaders in the organisation are unable or unwilling to try out any new ideas. Stakeholders have a place in adding value to the organisation's activities, but they are not the operational leaders. One clear example of this is in the charities sector where individual donors are all asking for their own performance metrics. Donors naturally want to see their donations are being put to good use, but multiple performance measurement systems confuse staff and take too much time away from operational activities.

Some stakeholders in the public sector are regulators who have varying roles. From our interviews, we know that some are viewed by operational leaders as adding value whereas others are seen as a drain, where operations must be adapted unnecessarily to meet the regulator's requirements. In these cases, capacity is taken up in ensuring the regulator's needs will be met. Regulators exist partly to uphold standards and of course, standards are essential. In addition to looking at whether standards are being met it would also be useful to evaluate the extent to which an organisation is adding value to the inputs (similar to the value chain). In a school for example, if the input of pupils comes from a deprived area and the end result is an above average number of university entrants then you may conclude that this school is doing very well, whereas another in a more affluent area with the same level of university entrants is not adding as much value. The measure of value added does happen, but in our view, this needs greater emphasis.

The general public is nearly always an important stakeholder. This is challenging because, whilst some members of the public will be highly knowledgeable, others will have little knowledge of a particular area. Most people will still have an opinion though. Public perception of value is important because citizens are ultimately paying through taxation for services and will be less willing to do so if they do not see a return. Public opinion, though, is often diverse and not always right because individuals do not have all the evidence at their disposal. This is not disassociated from the topics of capacity and capability because the aim is to identify how stakeholders can add value to a process that is designed to improve outcomes and minimise the strain or brake, they put upon it as this affects capacity. The question of the extent to which public opinion should influence decisions is beyond the remit of this book but undertaking programmes to inform and influence public perceptions is an important step in smoothing progress and gaining public support.

There is a good example of this in "The Public Value Framework," a report which discusses the use of the framework for maximising the value delivered from funding (HM Treasury, 2019). The example is of a local authority which has evidence that its policy is improving literacy in the local area and wants to devote more budget and resource to that policy. Engagement with local citizens, however, shows that they would like more budget devoted to filling potholes instead. Clearly, the authority cannot ignore potholes, but they also need to point out the long-term benefits of improving literacy. If they can persuade local people of the importance of policies to improve literacy, it will allow them greater latitude to pursue policies that will improve longer term outcomes.

Creating capability

We have spent some time concentrating on capacity, creating the time and space to do things. Now we will turn to capability. Capability is comprised of several elements. If we look at capability in relation to an individual, what makes someone capable? In some circumstances, it will be their expertise. In others, it will be their leadership abilities or talents such as skills of persuasion or communication. Or perhaps, it is their experience of what has happened in the past, of what has worked and what hasn't. We have already said that good leaders know their people. They understand their skills, their strengths, and weaknesses, and they work around them. What we haven't yet covered is the importance of developing people. Training and development is a prerequisite for creating an effective organisation. It improves performance, creates resilience by developing skills and knowledge, and it motivates. It should also be instrumental in promoting a culture of learning.

How can you expect people to know what to do if they have no training or, in some cases, little induction into their jobs? Barbara Follet told us how difficult it was for her when she first joined Parliament as an inexperienced MP with little or no training for the job. She found herself surrounded by a plethora of information and had to create a strategy for dealing with it. One of her strategies for knowing where to start was to ask herself the question: what problem am I facing here? Sir Bernard Jenkin MP also spoke about the importance of training and professional development for MPs. Whatever your position, you need training and you need to know how things work. He told us: "As an MP you cannot just pull levers and expect things to happen."

Despite this, people often feel they have no time for training or regard it as an add-on to be done when the time is right, which it rarely is.

The lead must come from the top. Senior people are responsible for creating a culture where learning is valued, where people are encouraged to ask questions, to challenge and innovate. Whilst it is easy to say, it is difficult to do in a culture where individuals are afraid to make mistakes and take risks. So, building capability is in fact an element of overall culture change. It requires a majority of people to understand that a change is needed and to share a picture of what the new culture will be. Over time culture change will happen.

The capability to deliver results depends on the prevailing culture and also the calibre of people you have within your organisation. In reality, the two overlap, culture strongly influences how people behave. It is also true that organisations that are seen to have a positive culture will attract good people. Few people want to work for an organisation that has a reputation for treating people badly.

The MOA (Motivation, Opportunity, and Ability) framework is widely described in HR literature as a framework for thinking about the delivery of good performance. From our experience of management and the research done at Cranfield (Bourne et al., 2007) around the implementation of IIP (Investors in People), we have extended each of the three elements to create a slightly more focused and practical framework (Figure 8.2).

Motivation is always an important factor in delivering performance. It comprises two elements. The first concerns engaging with people, making them feel genuinely valued and involved in achieving the goals of the organisation. This comes partly from the organisation's systems and HR policies which set the tone. It also comes from the relationship between managers and those who work for them. Let us face it, an organisation is made up of relationships and interactions between people. The second element is about the clarity of purpose of goals. People may be highly motivated, but they need to be motivated to do the right things.

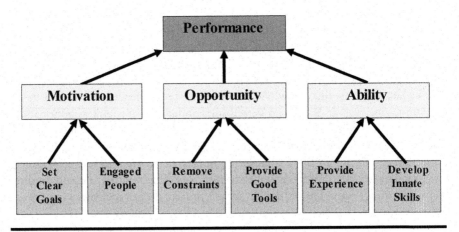

Figure 8.2 Drivers of performance.

Opportunity is about the having the possibility to do a good job. People need the right tools to do their job, if they are to perform effectively and it is the responsibility of the organisation to ensure they have them. Opportunity is also governed by whether or not people are allowed to make decisions and take actions. Obviously, employees can't have unfettered authority, there must be a framework in which they operate, but if there are inappropriate constraints, not only will activities be delayed but people will also feel disillusioned. This is a continuing theme as you will probably have gathered by now.

Ability comes from two factors. Firstly, people have innate skills which are important, but these skills need to be developed and we will describe some approaches later on. Secondly, experience plays a very big role in building ability. Having encountered a situation before means the individual is better prepared to deal with something similar the next time. So, providing individuals with wider experience is highly productive. This is why secondments, even short ones, can be effective in increasing capability.

Learning and development is not all about training courses, although they do play their part. It is also about building mechanisms for sharing knowledge. It is about learning from mistakes and looking at what happens outside the organisation and taking lessons from that. Learning comes from being given responsibility and one of the problems in working in an environment that does not tolerate risk is that managers are unwilling to delegate to less experienced people because of the inherent risk.

Coaching and mentoring is a good way of helping people to become more self-reliant and to develop their capability and confidence to take calculated risks. Sabine Losch et al. (2016) and colleagues from the University of Salzburg conducted empirical research into coaching, which demonstrated its effectiveness in developing skills and changing behaviour. The research showed it was particularly helpful in reducing procrastination and in enabling people to attain their goals. From our own experience, we see how helpful coaching is at helping people to develop insights into how they behave and the impact they have on others. As individuals, we sometimes have an inaccurate picture of how we come across because we see the world from our own perspective and based on our own experience and this affects the way other people respond. Someone we know well, who is a kind and helpful person in reality, was regarded by some members of her team who didn't know her well, as being distant and unapproachable. That meant they were reluctant to come and talk to her when they felt something wasn't right. It was only through coaching she realised this was the case. A good coach can help their coachees to understand how other people can perceive the same situation in a different way. All this helps in creating constructive relationships and avoiding unnecessary conflict and all the time and energy that absorbs.

Having discussed the capability of individuals let us turn now to examine capability at the organisational level. High-performing organisations tend to share certain characteristics. These are accountability, positive management style, action orientation, and good communication networks.

Accountability stems from people taking ownership of their work and recognising their own contribution to the organisation's success, and ownership develops from a feeling of belonging to the organisation and having a commitment to its goals. As with motivation, relationships are highly important. Accountability is strongly influenced by culture and is created over a period of time and alas, it can be ground down if the culture changes. When senior managers and colleagues are seen to be interested in performance, it becomes infectious, and individuals start to realise they must be accountable for what they do. Accountability also comes from having a sense of control and involvement in what you are doing and being recognised for your achievements. There are two important points to note here. The first is that recognition must be genuine. The second is that expectations must be reasonable. If people are constantly set tasks that are unobtainable then they begin to feel exploited.

Positive management style encourages accountability, enables action orientation, and supports effective communication. Positive management style comes from having leaders and managers who are both task-focussed and people focussed. Task focus is important for communicating direction and stimulating necessary actions. People focus is important to ensure engagement, to foster commitment and build those all-important relationships.

Organisations have a greater or lesser propensity to act on the information they have. This is partly owing to the complexity of the situations they deal with. The more complex the situation, the more difficult it is to know what should be done. The best situation is where information is gathered, analysed, and interpreted and decisions are made quickly and result in appropriate action being taken. For this to happen, it requires people to have the necessary information at the right time and have the skills and judgement to know what is important and what to do with it. People also need the authority to act. In straightforward situations, this should happen automatically. In more complex situations where the cause-and-effect relationships are not so transparent, greater deliberation, and consultation is required. When consultation and deliberation does not happen decisions and actions are delayed. A classic case is where there are too many hierarchies of management and senior managers are constantly reviewing junior managers' decisions and where junior staff are always having to ask for permission before they can take action.

In thinking about sharing learning and information, you must also reflect on channels and flows of communication to enable this to happen. There are three types of communication flow in most organisations. Top-down communication is important, so people understand direction and what is to be achieved. Bottom-up communication is equally important as senior managers need feedback on what is happening and whether it is working. The third flow of communication is horizontal and this is extremely important for coordination between different departments working together to deliver a product or service to a customer. This third type of communication is often overlooked. If horizontal communication works well and appropriate authority to act is given, then considerable time and effort can be saved by not having to pass decisions up and down the management hierarchy.

So, when thinking about capacity and capability the first thought that comes to mind is probably the calibre of people and availability of resources within the organisation. In this chapter, we have emphasised how the processes and the culture also matter. They can either clog up the works or facilitate capable people working together to achieve a common goal.

References

Bourne, M. Franco-Santos, M., Pavlov, A., & Lucianetti, l. (2007) The Impact of the Investors in People Standard on people management practices and firm performance, Cranfield School of Management Report, Cranfield.

HM Treasury (2019) *The Public Value Framework with supplementary guidance*, March, Crown Copyright, London, ISBN 978-1-912809-47-9.

Losch, S., Traut-Mattausch, E., Mühlberger, MD., and Jonas, E. (2016) Comparing the effectiveness of individual coaching, self-coaching, and group training: How Leadership Makes the Difference. *Frontiers in Psychology*, Vol. 7: 629. doi: 10.3389/fpsyg.2016.00629.

Chapter 9

Theory of Change tools

Theory of Change (ToC) is a specific approach used primarily in the third sector and the public sector, where change is complex and has outcomes for society. It can be used to guide the planning, implementation and evaluation of projects, policies, major events, or any change initiatives. The premise is that all attempts to make changes should start with a theory, comprising your assumptions of what is needed to improve a situation. Let us take the example of planning and implementing a new policy. Theory of Change takes you from creating an understanding of what is wrong (what has prompted you to believe a change is needed), through thinking about what is required to put it right, to consideration of who you will need to influence, and finally to envisaging outcomes and the intended new state. It is known as a "theory" because it is the plan, and you cannot tell in advance that it will work in the way you expect. So, you plan, you start to implement, and you track, learn, and adjust as you go along.

We are going to focus on the use of ToC in change initiatives, but the process is the same whether you are using it for projects or any other intervention. Nothing is certain about change and rather depressingly there is a whole set of literature on why it fails. There is another set of literature prescribing how you should implement change, but of course every situation is different and there is no one right way of doing it and no recipe for success. In this section, we want to focus on Theory of Change because it will provide you with a framework for thinking through *what you* want to deliver and *how* you should deliver it.

Before we describe the framework, we will discuss the process and in our view the process is more important than any tools or frameworks you use. The process is the mechanism by which you plan and review the change you are trying to implement, and it is particularly important because you can involve people in understanding and planning change. This inclusive approach is designed to capture multiple

DOI: 10.4324/9781003099895-12

118

perspectives. It helps in creating a wider understanding of what is to be achieved, why it is needed and how it will be done. Just as importantly, it should also help create commitment to implementation.

A process approach

How should you implement change? Many change initiatives go wrong in the early stages or get bogged down during implementation, so it is important to spend time planning well in advance to give the best possible chance of success. Think of the planning and management of change as a process with five key elements, based on Platts (1994).

■ Point of entry
■ Participation
■ Project management
■ Procedure
■ Purpose

Let us consider each of these in turn.

Point of entry is all to do with understanding the commitment of the team or organisation to delivering the change and the clear definition of expectations of what is to be achieved.

Participation refers to the selection of individuals who are to be involved in the process. This may be a core group, but you may also need sub-groups who will be involved in defining specific aspects, undertaking certain fact-finding studies, or taking selected elements forward. Having a clear understanding of the roles of these groups is important. As the process adopts a workshop approach and is therefore collaborative, you can build consensus and a coalition to do something which is beyond the scope of any one individual. When selecting who is within these groups you will have to consider the consequences of your decision about who is included and who is left out. Some people will be perceived as being against the change and therefore considered disruptive. But it is better to encounter any disruption during the workshops rather than dealing with it after decisions have been made. As we have said in an earlier chapter, resistance to change isn't always for the wrong reasons, so it can be useful to include some dissenters to add an element of challenge. If they have useful ideas to contribute you can take them on board in crafting the way forward. At the very least you will be presented with a different perspective and you are less likely to fall into the trap of group-think.

Project management in this case refers to the project management of the process itself, not the wider project management of the intervention or change. There are two distinct elements to this. Firstly, if a workshop approach is being used (and we strongly advise it should be) then a competent and impartial facilitator is extremely helpful. This will allow attendees to focus their attention on what is to be done. The facilitator can ensure that if any difficult or potentially controversial issues are raised, they are not simply brushed under the carpet. A skilled facilitator will also challenge assumptions when necessary. The facilitator should be the custodian of the process, keeping the team focused, ensuring everyone knows where they are in the process and what the next steps are. It is essential that workshops are adequately resourced to ensure administrative actions are completed, leaving executives free to focus on important decisions. Having someone to take minutes of meetings, make the meeting arrangements and coordinate diaries and also to follow up on actions makes a huge difference to the smooth running of the process.

Procedure refers to the format of the workshops themselves and involves leading the team through a series of discussions and debates that guide information gathering and processing and decision-making. Structure is very important here as it is easy to be side-lined by distractions, to have wide-ranging discussions that achieve very little. Each member of the team must be able to see the steps in the journey they are on and know where they are on that journey. This means that they can focus on the information and the decision in front of them rather than leaping ahead to think about issues that will be discussed later. This helps to build understanding and consensus over time. If people know their particular concern is going to be addressed later, they can suspend judgement on that aspect until that point is reached.

Purpose is the reason why the intervention or change is needed. In the public sector, it is common for different parties to have different purposes behind the change. The Treasury, for example, may have a great interest in longer-term cost reductions and efficiency gains that a change will create. However, other stakeholders may not be so interested in this aspect. If you are digitising prescriptions, patients are much more interested in convenience, doctors in the time they save and pharmacists in how it will help or hinder their dispensing and stock control. You need to analyse what the potential benefits will be for key stakeholders. If these disparate purposes can be channelled into meaningful outcomes, then implementing the change will become much easier.

So, the ideal process will have support from key stakeholders and a clear direction of travel. You will decide who to involve so you have a diversity of perspectives in the workshops and in wider conversation, and, ideally, engage the main decision makers. You will need to lay out the structure of the process like a road map, so all concerned can see the whole process and the decision points along the way. You then need to find a good facilitator who will be impartial and will keep the process on track whilst ensuring full participation. Finally, if you can create a common purpose either at the outset or through the emerging discussion this will be a benefit in the subsequent roll out of the change.

Here is one final note of caution on the process. Don't expect it to be a smooth ride. The best change initiatives frequently have very difficult process phases, partly because this is where the arguments *should* happen. The more thorny issues, entrenched positions and niggly difficulties unearthed during the process, the better. There should be lively and challenging debate, but this must happen at the right time and in the right environment. Arguments and challenges usually result in consensus and commitment to the proposed implementation because people can see why decisions have been taken even if they don't agree with them. The last thing you want is hostile disagreement just as the project starts to be rolled out.

Uses of Theory of Change

Theory of Change can be used in three distinct ways, as a

- Planning tool
- Management tool
- Evaluation tool

We know from repeated widespread application of the Theory of Change concept to public sector change projects that the structure really matters. There are different versions of Theory of Change in the literature. The planning ToC structure we describe here is slightly more complicated than other approaches, but it does create better insights.

Planning

There are two possible starting points for using a Theory of Change approach. The first is the problem to be solved and the second is the conceptualisation of the future state you hope to create. We suggest you start with the end in mind, but the two need to be reconciled so you should check the problem aligns with your vision of the future state. It is important to develop as clear a picture of the future state as you can, and to ensure there is a comprehensive understanding of the current problem. This will pave the way for a more successful implementation of the process and for achieving the outcomes you are looking for. To help the debate and possible future reviews of your Theory of Change, ensure you capture the main assumptions you are making. Remember, this is only a theory at the planning stage, so you are making assumptions and you need to remember what these are because you may need to come back at a later date and reassess on what basis you made your decisions. Figure 9.1 captures an outline of the framework we are using.

Having established the two ends of your Theory of Change, the next step is to work from left to right, populating the framework.

Who are the people you need to influence? In any change, there will be groups of both internal and external stakeholders, individuals, organisations, and even society at large. In the last chapter, we presented a series of tools to help you think about stakeholders. You can use these to inform the discussion about how these people will

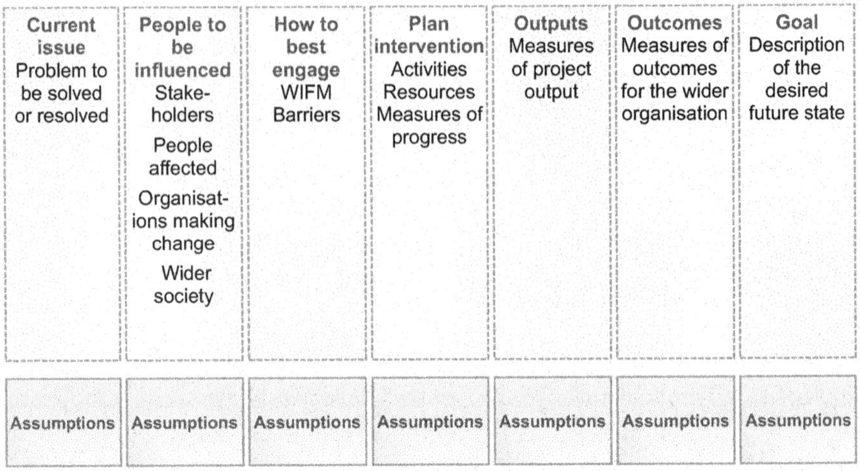

Current issue Problem to be solved or resolved	People to be influenced Stake-holders People affected Organisat-ions making change Wider society	How to best engage WIFM Barriers	Plan intervention Activities Resources Measures of progress	Outputs Measures of project output	Outcomes Measures of outcomes for the wider organisation	Goal Description of the desired future state
Assumptions	Assumptions	Assumptions	Assumptions	Assumptions	Assumptions	Assumptions

Figure 9.1 A framework for creating your theory of change.

be affected by the actions you are planning and what their reactions are likely to be. You should note down in your assumptions how you view these different groups and why.

We suggest you include all the stakeholders in this discussion even if they appear not to be influential, bearing in mind what happened in our earlier example of the railway protesters. Another pitfall is to assume you have all the expertise. A group protesting against a quarry raised funds to engage a civil engineer and as a result successfully argued to the planning committee that stringent safeguards should be in place before work could commence. These requirements were onerous and a better solution could have been reached if there had been better engagement.

Having identified stakeholder groups, you then need to think how to best engage with them. Start by envisaging the project from their point of view. Some will not understand the project and its aims, and you will need to inform and educate them whilst others will need convincing that the change is good for them (or at least won't greatly inconvenience them). Some will not like the change simply because it is change and others will resist as a matter of principle or because it is in their best interest for the change not to happen. At the planning stage, it is important to identify how you intend to engage with stakeholders but keep an open mind as you progress through your project. By the end of this discussion, you should have a broad understanding of who the important stakeholders are. You should know where they stand, the barriers to be overcome and how to engage those who support the change and manage those who don't. As you go along you need to check your assumptions are still correct, and also check that the position and reaction of your stakeholders has not changed.

The next stage is to plan the intervention. This requires significant planning time in a large complex project. Focus this part of the process on three topics:

- Activities to be undertaken, what these are and who will deliver them;
- The resources required, this may be money, but it will also be people, senior people's time and support, and probably actions required from other functions and departments; and
- Milestones and measures of progress; these should tell you how the change is progressing, but remember these are only indicators of progress.

Capturing this information at the top level is important because if any of these elements are missing then the change you are planning is in trouble before it starts. Resourcing is critical here and should include contingency. Under-resourcing the project is a major problem and if it looks as if this is likely to be the case then you should question whether there is enough will and support to take the project forward.

Outputs are the direct results of the project delivering the change. They are tangible, such as a new prison, a new software system, or a new piece of legislation. These are the things that are most under your control and often clearly defined at the start of the change. However, remember that outputs are not what the project is ultimately designed to produce; those are the outcomes.

Outcomes are the benefits resulting from outputs. So, a new prison may house more prisoners but the outcomes you probably hope to deliver may include better mental health and educational attainment amongst prisoners to prevent likelihood of reoffending, lower turnover of prison staff as a result of better working conditions, and fewer violent protests and attacks as living conditions are improved. A new software system may enable patients to reorder their prescriptions online but the outcome you are looking for is widespread use by doctors, pharmacists, and patients combined with lower processing costs and better stock control. The new piece of legislation may appear on the statute but ultimately the legislation needs to stand up to challenge in the courts and to change behaviour in the way you intend.

The final test in the process is that the outcomes you have defined should effectively represent the future state that you envisaged at the outset. This last step is critical as otherwise your team will be working to deliver something other than that which was originally required.

From a process perspective Theory of Change breaks down the design of a change into a series of manageable steps. It focuses on key aspects and has a logic that should support decision making. Having worked through the Theory of Change, it should be reviewed as a whole. Does this still make sense and does the logic hold? We would also suggest that although this planning is very useful at the outset of a project, it needs to be reviewed as the project progresses. Things will change so having a process for going back and reviewing the plan and assumptions is extremely important.

Management

In the section above, we described how Theory of Change should be used at the beginning of the process to plan the intervention. During the change journey, the team will spend a lot of time looking at progress, the amount of money spent, and adherence to schedule. This is a necessary step in keeping the project under control. However, if the team focusses solely on these project management tools, there is a danger that they will lose focus on the outcomes. We suggest that from time to time, whilst the project is being delivered that the team go back to their Theory of Change and work through what it says and check its validity. In particular, the team should look at the assumptions they made in the initial model because those assumptions are most likely to be impacted as they learn more.

Evaluation

One of the prerequisites for effectiveness is learning from what has happened. The evaluation stage of the Theory of Change approach provides a structured way for looking at outcomes and learning from them. You should be learning as you progress through the implementation stage and adapting as you go along, but it is usually not until the end of an initiative that the full implications of your actions begin to become known. This is also a stage that is sometimes completed in a more superficial way than is desirable. In research carried out into major public sector projects, we talked to people in several countries and found there was less evaluation into outcomes at the end of those projects than might have been expected (Williams et al., 2019). This was the case for several reasons. Firstly, because projects are often very long term, it was felt less could be learnt from a thorough evaluation because the environment in which they were first envisaged had changed substantially. Secondly, there was the question of where you put your measuring stick. Benefits from a major project may continue to be realised for decades. When do you stop measuring? And there were many other reasons such as changes in administration and so on. Of course, there is a point at which the resources needed to evaluate outcomes outweigh the benefits gained from learning, but it is important to make that a conscious decision, to state your reasons for not carrying out a thorough evaluation.

Returning to the evaluation element of ToC, you should, if you can, bring together the group of people involved with planning and implementation, those who know the intervention inside out. You will look in a structured way at questions such as: was the original idea correct? Did the change deliver as expected? Was the plan implemented as originally envisaged? What factors intervened to affect implementation/outcomes? Let us look at this through a series of pictures, each of which shows a stage in the structure of the evaluation.

First and second steps

In most complex interventions, there will be unintended outcomes, some will be beneficial for some stakeholders and some not (see Figure 9.2). For example, the building of a new railway will reduce congestion and enable people to get to work faster but is also likely to result in an increase in house prices in the area close to the new stations which will be good for some people but not for others.

It is important to remember that not all outcomes become apparent in the short term. If the State provides training for someone then they are more likely to get a job and in the short term that will lead to lower social support costs. In the medium term that individual is more likely to progress in their career and pay more tax as their salary increases. In the longer-term parents in employment are more likely to be able to afford a better lifestyle for their children and consequently enable them to have better life chances (see Figure 9.3).

Third step

In this stage you are comparing the intended intervention with what actually happened. So, for example, if you have a social support programme which is extended you should be able to see an improvement on your original expectations (see Figure 9.4)

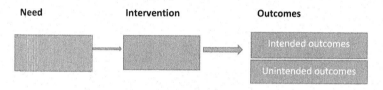

Figure 9.2 First step in your Theory of Change evaluation.

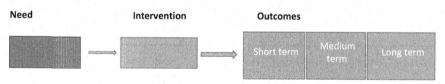

Figure 9.3 Second step in your Theory of Change evaluation.

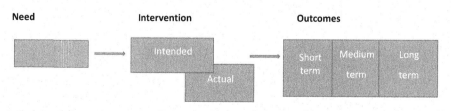

Figure 9.4 Third step in your Theory of Change evaluation.

Fourth step

Here you are looking at whether there were any special factors affecting the outcome or the intervention itself (see Figure 9.5). These are factors you had not anticipated at the outset or, perhaps, factors which played a stronger role than you had anticipated. An example of this would be a back to work programme that benefitted from an unexpected upturn in economic activity. On the other hand, it could be something like a community policing programme that is adversely affect by a local council deciding to save costs and turning street lights off at a certain time in the evening.

Fifth step

In this stage you are examining whether the process itself worked and also whether you created the outcomes and impacts you were looking for (see Figure 9.6). It can be difficult to attribute cause and effect, to say how much of the benefit that has occurred is the result of your intervention. Nevertheless, it still worth doing because it will give you a better understanding of how this type of change works in practice and that should help the planning of initiatives in the future.

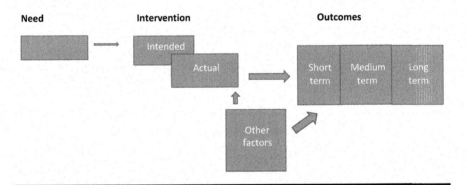

Figure 9.5 Fourth step in your Theory of Change evaluation.

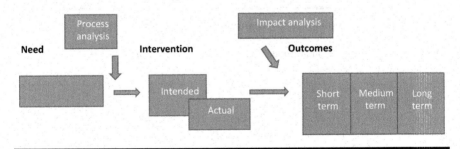

Figure 9.6 Fifth step in your Theory of Change evaluation.

Theory of Change case study

We have described Theory of Change, what it will do for you and the various stages you will need to take to follow the process. Here is a case study to show you how it works in practice. City & Guilds will be familiar to many people as an awarding body, offering accredited qualifications. Set up some 140 years ago to protect and promote the standard of technical education, City & Guilds works with partners to provide a range of products and services to help people achieve their potential through work-based learning.

City & Guilds worked with Charlotte Turner and David Grayson of Cranfield University to understand, measure, and report on the societal impact of their activities. They conducted research on the impact of skills development on the lives of beneficiaries and the wider community, interviewing a broad range of internal and external stakeholders. Their idea was to use the Theory of Change approach to develop a societal impact framework, essentially setting out the outcomes they wanted to measure, the impact they wanted to see and providing a means of assessing progress along the journey. The framework would be embedded in all areas of the organisation so they could report social metrics alongside financial information. It helped shaped their focus as well as helping in sharing the baseline evidence of their impact.

The initiative began with examining where the organisation had made a difference, identifying what success looked like and how success could be demonstrated. They then turned to how that success could be measured and how that would affect investments. Three potential impact areas were identified (Figure 9.7).

The core purpose of City & Guilds is "Helping people, organisations and economies develop their skills for growth." With this in mind they envisaged the outcomes they wanted to measure and the impact they wanted to see in each of these impact areas (Figure 9.8).

These indicators provided a focus for activities against which results could be measured. Looking at a recent report (City & Guilds, 2020), the organisation was able to show that, for example, by achieving a City & Guilds qualification in

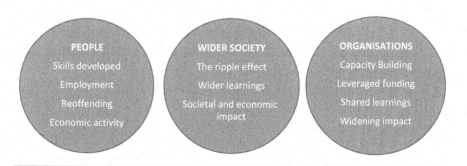

Figure 9.7 City & Guilds' stakeholder impact.

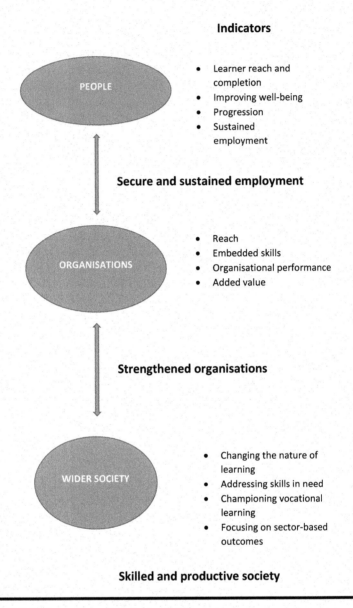

Indicators

PEOPLE

- Learner reach and completion
- Improving well-being
- Progression
- Sustained employment

Secure and sustained employment

ORGANISATIONS

- Reach
- Embedded skills
- Organisational performance
- Added value

Strengthened organisations

WIDER SOCIETY

- Changing the nature of learning
- Addressing skills in need
- Championing vocational learning
- Focusing on sector-based outcomes

Skilled and productive society

Figure 9.8 Bringing our social change to life.

Source: Adapted from City & Guilds social impact report (2020).

prison the number of proven re-offences during a one-year period decreases by up to 22 offences per 100 participants. (Figures from Ministry of Justice Data Lab.) In another example, they were able to show the ripple effect of providing grants for developing peer advisors which led to people gaining qualifications, increasing their likelihood of being employed with financial benefits for society.

Using a formal approach like Theory of Change helps in visualising and communicating an effective outcome.

References

City & Guilds (2020) *Baseline social impact report*, City & Guilds Group, London.
Platts, K. W. (1994) "Characteristics of methodologies for manufacturing strategy formulation," *Computer Integrated Manufacturing Systems*, Vol. 7, No. 2, 93–99.
Williams, T., Vo, H., Bourne, M., Bourne, P., Cooke-Davies, T., Kirkham, R., Masterton, G., Quattrone, P., & Valette, J. (2019) "A cross-national comparison of public project benefits management practices – the effectiveness of benefits management frameworks in application," *Production Planning and Control*, Vol. 31, No. 8, 644–659.

Chapter 10

Measuring performance

The performance framework

Definitions

People often use the same terms to mean different things, so before we continue, we will define key terms in the way we mean them in this book.

Objectives are descriptions of what has to be achieved in order to fulfil the ultimate goal, the strategy, and purpose of your organisation and they are cascaded down from top levels through to individuals at every level.

Choosing the right objectives to cascade is perhaps the most important activity in designing your measurement system and one that we believe leaders give insufficient attention to. There is a temptation to add too many objectives but that is a big mistake because it is not possible to prioritise everything. In an earlier chapter, we posed the question: what's it for? Apply this to your thinking about objectives. Is there a clear and direct link between the objective and the strategy and purpose? If not, use Occam's Razor, keep it simple and cut away the possibility of people embarking on unnecessary courses of action in the future.

Outcomes are benefits that arise as a result of action. They are the direct and indirect consequences of **outputs**. Let us take an example. In a prison you may have an education programme to enable prisoners to undertake degree courses. The *output* would be individuals with qualifications, but the *outcome* (you intend) would be for individuals not to re-offend, but for them to contribute to society as they take up useful jobs on their return to normal life. One very common mistake in measurement systems is to judge performance by measuring outputs (often easier to measure and shorter term) and ignoring outcomes. As one of our interviewees, Andy Reed, said "Measuring outcomes seems tediously slow in a world of instant gratification." It's a long journey.

DOI: 10.4324/9781003099895-13

Resources are the people, equipment and the systems that allow a process to function. Without an appropriate level of resources, you will be unable to achieve sustained performance. If you do not have access to the resources, you need then you have to manage expectations about the level of expected outcome. Naturally, it is possible to manage without sufficient resources in the short term – hospitals managed to do this during the Covid pandemic – but it is not possible to keep up that level of performance over the longer term.

A **process** is the set of steps that turns inputs into outputs and outcomes (see Figure 10.1)

Performance Measures quantify levels of performance and enable you to assess your progress towards achieving an objective. It is important that measures can be calculated accurately and consistently and that they measure what you want them to measure. **Key Performance Indicators** are the most important indicators.

Targets are levels of performance required to achieve objectives and also to make measures tangible to everyone. Without targets it's a bit like working in the dark.

A milestone is a recognisable point in the delivery of a change or project. Milestones are defined so you can track and communicate progress at a key stage in delivering a change or the project.

Efficiency is how well you are delivering your outputs and is often stated as outputs divided by inputs.

Effectiveness is how well you are delivering your outcomes and can be stated as outcomes divided by inputs.

Improvement initiatives are changes made to the organisation's operations to improve performance. Improvements don't come directly from measurement, although measurement focusses attention on what is important and provides feedback on progress and trends. Sustainable improvement comes from making changes to resources and processes.

The performance framework

The performance framework provides a structured means of thinking about the complex process of agreeing levels of performance required to achieve effective outcomes and setting goals and measuring them in the context of your organisation.

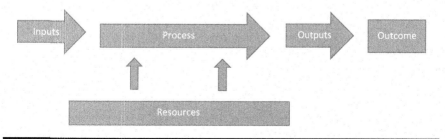

Figure 10.1 The input, process, output, outcome model.

We will begin by asking why people measure the performance of their organisations. The obvious answer is to make improvements, although in reality we have seen that performance measurement systems are used for other hidden purposes such as creating good headlines and being seen to be doing a good job. This aside, well-designed performance measurement processes applied in the right environment can help you to steer your organisation in the right direction and deliver the outcomes you want.

Some time ago, we identified five good reasons for measuring performance. We continually test these with executives across both the public and private sectors to check whether they are sufficiently comprehensive and whether they remain valid, which they do. These reasons are to:

- Establish position
- Communicate direction
- Influence behaviour
- Stimulate action
- Facilitate learning

What do they mean in practice?

Establish position

It is easy to understand what establishing position means. Before you do anything, you need to know where you are. In the private sector you might ask yourself: is my business solvent? Are my customers satisfied? In the public sector, you may ask questions such as: "How much of the budget have we spent? What are our waiting times? The answers will enable you to know what resources you still have available, to make comparisons with previous periods, between units in your own organisation and externally and to establish the gap between what you are trying to achieve and where you are currently.

When establishing your position, it is important not to use anecdotal evidence. You need reliable data collected over a period of time. Before you can understand this month's performance you need to know the previous month's. Before you compare different sections of your organisation you need a basis for making those comparisons. It is essential to measure accurately and consistently from a solid baseline. The same holds if you wish to do any meaningful benchmarking.

Establishing position forms the basis of measurement that everything else builds from.

Communicate direction

If you measure an activity, you are sending out a message that says loudly and clearly: "This activity is important." In drawing attention to a set of activities you are, in effect, communicating the direction of the organisation. This is one reason why it is especially important to measure only what matters, otherwise it becomes unclear as to where the priorities lie. If you measure the wrong activities, then the organisation will begin to veer off course. When you produce a set of measures or a "scorecard," you are drawing employees' attention to the most important goals and how progress towards achieving those goals will be measured. If they change, you need to change the measures too. In that way you communicate a change in direction to the rest of the organisation.

There is an important point to make here. People often forget that measures (or perhaps we should call them indicators, with the most important being key performance indicators, KPIs) aren't real. They often become commandments set in stone, but indicators can only be proxies for the goals you are trying to achieve. They are signals of how well or how badly the organisation is doing in terms of meeting those goals and they are only ever signals and nothing more.

Influence behaviour

Do not underestimate the influence that is exerted when you measure something. If you introduce a new set of indicators, you will capture peoples' attention and they will work towards achieving the new set of goals. That is why it is important to ensure you are influencing people to behave and work in a positive way. For example, if your measures focus on purely financial targets then you may find customer service or quality declines while people attempt to carry out their work at the lowest possible cost.

If you do not set and manage the measures appropriately you can encourage some people to "game" the measures. That is, improve the indicator without improving the underlying performance. From our experience, too many managers think that introducing a new indicator will drive people to deliver higher levels of performance when in reality this approach is more often than not counterproductive.

Stimulate action

The point of measuring performance is to collect information and use it to inform decision-making and to take action when necessary. Action means changing something. So, for example, it could be training people, redesigning a process, or buying a new computer system. Until action is taken, nothing really changes, so stimulating the right action at the right time is extremely important.

There are different types of actions. Measurement often prompts the need to take corrective action. If a process is not delivering the required output, you make changes to bring things back into line. This is often called feedback control. Let's take an example. The thermostat on a radiator is feedback control. As the temperature rises, it will trip the thermostat and turn the radiator off. As the temperature falls, it will trip the thermostat again and the heater comes back on. In that way, a reasonably constant level of heat is provided. Something similar happens with cruise control on a car to maintain constant speed on a motorway.

Action can be feedforward too. Feedforward means taking action that takes you somewhere. For example, you may be aware that a current process is not capable of delivering the improved levels of service you need, so the action could involve redesigning that process, automating parts of the process, and retraining the staff in a completely new way of working. Taking an everyday example, when driving your car, feedforward control is when you apply the brakes to come to a smooth halt at a set of traffic lights. Here is a work example of someone running a job centre. Feedback control is about looking at how processes are working currently and making adjustments to maintain a level of performance. However, a new business park has been developed nearby and several large employers are moving into the area. Feedforward control in this context will be about looking at what needs to be changed in order to accommodate a huge increase in demand for services.

The reason for differentiating between feedback and feedforward is to ensure you look at both types of action. Adjusting for the current state but allowing time to anticipate what is on the horizon and consider actions that will be required as a result.

Facilitate learning

You may think you understand how your organisation works, but is this really true? Do you have the evidence that things really work in that way? From our experience and research, we know that most people often have a partial view at best. Work goes on in the background of which leaders and managers are unaware. For example, one group of employees may have a much better way of doing something that circumvents the prescribed method, but they have never shared that knowledge. Providing the opportunity to talk about performance could well bring that knowledge to light.

When you are reviewing performance there always two fundamental questions to ask: "Are we doing things right?" and even more importantly "Are we doing the right things?"

"Are we doing things right?" refers to looking at existing practices and ensuring that they are working and delivering as expected. You may also look at existing practices from the perspective of whether they could be done better so they deliver more consistently, more quickly or in a more cost-effective manner.

"Are we doing the right things?" is a fundamental question. Here you should be asking whether or not the actions you are taking will deliver the intended outcome, and you should always be asking whether those are still the right outcomes.

Perspectives in the performance framework

The Performance Framework contains three perspectives: Measurement, which sets out essential requirements of the system; Management and Leadership, which sets out key actions managers and leaders need to take to make the system work and, finally, Pitfalls, problems that often occur. If you know what to look for, you can spot undesirable behaviours or characteristics and nip them in the bud. Each of these perspectives is seen in the context of one of the five roles of performance measurement. Figure 10.2 summarises the framework in a single picture.

We will now look at the various boxes on the framework in more detail. At the end of each description, we have set out some questions to ask in order to check that you are on track.

Measurement perspective

Establish position

It is important to know what the current level of your organisation's performance is, and ideally how it compares with others in a similar position. This "health check"

	Establish Position	Communicate Direction	Influence Behaviour	Stimulate Action	Facilitate Learning
Measurement: requirements of the system	Accuracy of measures; Making the right comparisons	Objectives aligned to strategy; Measures are good indicators of performance	Linkage between results of measures and recognition; Linkage between results of measures and reward	Timely relevant data; Presentation of data in a form that demonstrates relevance	Collect the right data to answer the right questions; Present data in a digestible form that prompts questions
Management and leadership: actions needed to ensure the system works	Manage the performance review process to ensure realistic evaluation of current performance; Create an environment for honest debate about bad news	Manage the performance review process to ensure measures communicate direction; Ensure objectives measures and targets are up to date; Set boundaries on what will and will not be done.	Manage the performance review process to encourage the right combination of cooperation and competition; Support and live the values; Being explicit about what is acceptable and unacceptable behaviour and how under-performance will be handled.	Manage the performance review process to make timely decisions based on data; Maintain a culture of using information to inform decision-making; Establish appropriate levels of authority and referral in decision-making.	Manage the performance review process to encourage the opportunity to challenge and learn; Communicate guidance on risk appetite; Create a culture of learning and challenge
Pitfalls to be avoided	Silo mentality; Covering up under-performance	Too few or too many measures	High blame culture; Reward systems that short-circuit learning	Tampering; Brushing issues under the carpet	All learning and no real change as a result; No-one taking responsibility

Figure 10.2 The performance framework.

provides information on which to make decisions about the future. Think about what you want to know, why you want to know it and what information you will need to collect. There are two big mistakes that are often made here: wasting time by collecting information just for the sake of it and only using information that is currently available. If you do the latter your information could well be irrelevant or misleading.

Ask yourself:

■ What measures do we need in order to provide data to establish our position?
■ Can we rely on the accuracy of the measures we have?
■ Do measures allow us to make the right comparisons?

Communicate direction

When you use measures to communicate what you want to achieve, you need to be extremely careful to define your goals and your choice of measures correctly.

Ask yourself:

■ Do your goals describe the outcomes you want to achieve?
■ Do your intermediate goals reflect the strategy you are pursuing to deliver your outcomes?
■ Are your measures good indicators of your goals and do they enable you to track progress?

Influence behaviour

We talked earlier about the fact that measures influence behaviour and stressed that how you use these measures is really important. Individuals and teams can usually be trusted to look at their own measures of success and take appropriate action when things are not going as expected. However, managers often see their role as having to intervene to make that happen. Their intervention can be supportive, but that is not always the case and when it isn't, it can lead to inappropriate responses.

Organisations typically use two main systems to influence people: reward systems and recognition systems. Traditionally, rewards are seen as direct monetary incentives for delivering performance, although such approaches are rarely used in the public sector. But rewards are wider than that. They are likely to operate in terms of the resources you have at your disposal. For example, if you meet your maximum four-hour waiting time, we will reward you with extra resource and if you don't, we will take resource away from you. Recognition is equally important. Being seen to be doing a good job matters, being singled out as being an exemplar may in time lead to promotion.

Ask yourself:

■ Does the way you use measures to reward people (in the widest sense) influence the types of behaviour you want to encourage?

- Does the way you use measures in your recognition process influence the types of behaviour you want to encourage?

Here is an example. We know of one organisation in which individuals were rewarded for going out and meeting people, for collecting and passing on information that was of use to their *own* department. The result of this was that when they were meeting people, they rarely took the opportunity to enquire about anything that would have been of use elsewhere in the organisation and if they did find something out, they rarely passed it on because that took time away from the work they were being measured on.

Stimulate action

We talked about taking action as a result of measures. Of course, you do not always need to act, especially if the activity you are measuring is running well and delivering what you need. But there are times when the measures signal that something has changed and you need to make corrections, or perhaps the goal has changed so you need to realign your efforts and activities. To do this you need relevant information in a timely manner so that decisions and action can be taken.

Ask yourself:

- Do the measures give you timely and relevant information to inform your decision making?
- Do they provide any insight into how you could improve even further?

Facilitate learning

Measuring performance enables you to learn. Measurement will tell you whether or not you are achieving the goals you have set and if you are meeting your goals, that's fine. If you are not, it prompts you to ask how you can close the gap. In that situation, your measurement system should also give you greater information and pointers to what the problem is.

Ask yourself:

- Are you reflecting on what the measures are telling you and learning from that information?

Management and leadership perspective

At the measurement perspective, we focused on the collection of data; is it the right data? Is it accurate? Is it collected in a timely fashion? The management and leadership perspective focuses on what managers and leaders need to do to make the system work.

Establish position

In most organisations, results of measures are considered at performance review meetings, where teams get together to review results of their own performance measures combined with other available information. The effectiveness of these review meetings is critical for managing performance, so it is important they are done well.

The management of the review meeting must enable a realistic assessment of the health of the organisation. To do this, attendees need access to the right data and have time to review it. They must have the opportunity to ask questions and to drill down to the causes of any trends that are emerging. They need to be able to understand the data in context, so they can interpret it and use it to judge what is happening to the organisation's performance.

It is important that information is widely available and shared amongst those who are able to act on it, but, alas, people are often reluctant to share bad news. The longer it takes for the managers and leaders to realise that performance is slipping, or, at least, not where it should be, the less time there is to respond.

Ask yourself:

■ Do you have access to the performance information you need?
■ Do you have enough time to review the information thoroughly?
■ Does the data analysis (or the tools for analysis) enable you to look at root causes?
■ Does the performance review process enable you to judge the state of health of your organisation?
■ Have you created an environment where people will tell you what is wrong and you can hear bad news?

Communicate direction

Performance measurement can be an extremely effective way of communicating direction because it focuses people's attention on what is important and what must be achieved. In the review process, performance is normally considered against higher level measures, but to guide activity you need to translate these overarching measures into goals and local objectives. The process of talking about broad goals and objectives and the consistency of that debate is important because it stimulates wider discussion throughout the organisation.

Leaders have a choice about the approach they take to goals and measures. They need to decide at what point the overarching measures are broken down into lower-level goals and milestones and who is responsible for doing it. If you rely on the management team to work through what is required to deliver outcomes, you are signalling that you are more interested in the outcomes themselves rather than how they are delivered. This is beneficial in some ways because there is a clarity of focus and you are leaving the decision about how something is done to the people who are actually going to do it. It allows them freedom to act and demonstrates that you trust them. However, this approach concerns some leaders because it makes them feel as if they have relinquished control. If you, as a leader, specify milestones and measures of progress, you are telling the management team what you expect them to do down to a level of detail. Some would see this as giving leaders greater certainty and control of progress, others would see it as interfering in day-to-day operational delivery, something that they are not competent to do.

Another important issue is whether measures are up to date. They should reflect strategic direction, and if the strategy changes, measures must also change. If they don't align, the best you can expect is that people in your organisation will be confused; at worst the conflict between the measurement system and what leaders are saying will prevent the new strategy from being implemented. The adage: "What gets measured gets done" is true. If people's performance is measured against a set of goals, they will strive towards achieving them even if they don't lead towards fulfilling a new strategy.

There is another way of communicating direction and that is by setting boundary controls, which, in essence provide a framework within which people can operate. Take, for example, co-operation and collaboration between police forces. Boundary controls would set out how far the integration can go. Considerable time and resource can be saved if you know which approaches are never going to be considered and stop them being explored at the earliest stage.

Ask yourself:

■ What is the role measurement plays in guiding the organisation?
■ Are your measures aligned with strategic direction and up to date?
■ What are your boundaries, what are you not going to do?
■ From the top level KPIs, do you understand what the organisation is trying to achieve?
■ Do your local objectives and measures align local action with achieving the organisational goals?
■ Are there possible unintended consequences from using your local measures that you need to watch to ensure activity stays aligned with what should be achieved?

Influence behaviour

The act of measuring activities will influence people's behaviour. How you manage the measurement process will make even more difference. It is very important to deal sensitively with information about under-performance when you have your review meetings. We all know that attributing blame is counterproductive, but you can do it unintentionally, without even realising it, by the way a question is asked, or a remark is made. As we have said before, everyone needs to be able to hear bad news and the earlier you find out that something is going wrong the sooner you can do something about it. So, you need to create an atmosphere in which people feel able to have an open and honest discussion.

You also want to encourage and motivate individuals, so recognition and praise is important, too. Friendly competition can be a spur to better performance but when this spills over to undermine collaboration it can become a real problem. Many senior Civil Servants we have spoken to have talked about "prodding" the organisation into performing better by constantly talking about performance and what can be done better. When you talk about "prodding the organisation" you are of course talking about people and any "prodding" must be done skilfully so that people really work on improvements rather than playing a game of "how to look good to the boss."

Some of the highest performing organisations we know have a clear set of values that they reinforce constantly through the behaviour of their leaders and managers. In evaluating performance, they look at *how* something has been done as well as *what* has been done, to ensure values have been upheld in the process of meeting targets. There is a danger that behaviours change when an organisation comes under pressure or a crisis hits.

Performance measurement can move from being a guiding and learning mechanism to a stick to beat people with. Leaders can prevent this from happening if they are visible in their support and continue to demonstrate the values of the organisation. Leaders and managers need to know what acceptable behaviour is and what it isn't. Defining this through the organisation's values helps people know where they stand. It provides a guideline on what is acceptable and what isn't and it strengthens the culture of the organisation. This is particularly important because you need people to have trust in performance measurement processes. If they are seen as having a negative influence, it will be hard to persuade people to be honest and engage with them.

Sometimes, of course, there is persistent underperformance. So, how should you deal with it? Underperformance is not usually the fault of an individual. It's often caused by a problem in the system and/or the environment in which people operate. So, don't automatically assume it is someone's fault. The first step is to talk to people to ask for their ideas and to analyse processes and systems, which can be adapted and changed to improve performance. But if performance doesn't improve then you will need to look more closely at individual performance. Perhaps there is an issue with training or miscommunication. It may be that individuals are not in the right job. One of the leaders we spoke to told us one of his most important tasks was to "get the right people into the right seats."

Whatever the reason for underperformance you must deal with it, even if it means moving someone on. It is not the easiest issue to deal with and it helps if you have a structure and a set of guidelines that people can follow.

Ask yourself:

■ Do you run your performance review meetings in a way that encourages open discussion and collaboration?
■ Do leaders demonstrate the values of the organisation?
■ How do you deal with under-performance?

Stimulate action

Your measurement process must stimulate timely decision-making and appropriate action-taking. Ideally decisions should be taken based on data and evidence, but it is not always possible to have as much data as you would like, because it takes time to collect. There is a point at which waiting for more data and evidence actually causes more harm than good, because it is delaying action. At some stage leaders will have to exercise judgement. (If you have read through the book sequentially by chapter you will have seen the section on judgement in Chapter 3.) Bringing together a team to work through the information that is available before deciding on a course of action is very effective. As decision-making isn't confined to the upper echelons of the organisation, it is useful to have a formalised system setting out what discretion and authority individuals have – and when they need to refer a decision upwards. As long as the limits of authority are not too confined, this approach is liberating rather than repressive because the limits of authority are often higher than individuals think they are.

Ask yourself:

■ Does your organisation maintain a culture of reviewing evidence and data before making a decision?
■ Have you established appropriate levels of authority referral in decision-making?
■ Do actions result from these decisions? If not, why not?

Facilitate learning

The performance review process should provide a great opportunity to learn. With the right approach, review meetings should enable your team to develop their understanding of what the organisation is trying to achieve, how it is progressing, based on the data in front of them, and how actions to improve are working out in practice. Different perspectives and views will be brought to bear on problems and alternative solutions debated. Learning often occurs when things either go wrong or start to go wrong. Being able to learn from current or past mistakes is enormously important but this won't happen if people don't feel able to be open about what hasn't worked. We have already mentioned the aviation industry which is often upheld as an exemplar of learning because they have so many mechanisms for investigating accidents (Syed 2015). They have systems for exploring why near misses occur and for anonymously reporting issues and concerns. In another setting, healthcare has, rightly or wrongly, been accused of protecting its members and, as a result, not fully understanding what went wrong and thus, not learning from mistakes. So, leaders must create a climate for individual and organisational learning to take place.

Learning also comes from people challenging each other. Challenge can be seen as undermining a carefully developed plan, but it is a means of gaining the views of people from a variety of backgrounds, who have different knowledge and experience and therefore different perspectives. This broader view helps with learning. Of course, challenge also brings a level of scrutiny. But it can be overdone and must be handled in a positive manner.

Ask yourself:

■ Do you run performance review meetings in a way which encourages people to challenge and learn?
■ Is the culture of learning ingrained in your organisation?
■ What is the mechanism for learning from mistakes?

The pitfalls

We all know that performance measurement has a dark side; that is where measurement doesn't work or where it is manipulated for the purposes of meeting goals. We will cover this throughout the chapters, suggesting action you can take to avoid the worst problems, but here we will highlight some of the main traps so you can spot them. We feel sure you will have encountered some of them already.

Establish position

■ People choose inappropriate measures so that performance looks better than it is.
■ A silo mentality, where each part of the organisation performs well on paper in its own silo, but the performance of the whole is undermined by the silos all working separately.

Communicate direction

■ Having too many measures, resulting in confusion and people not being able to focus on what is important.
■ Having too few measures so that the organisation focuses on a very small set of goals to the detriment of its longer-term health.

Influence behaviour

■ Having a high blame culture where people focus on hiding poor performance or creating excuses rather than improving the situation.
■ Having a reward system that encourages people to set low targets so they can be met; this behaviour often means the level of real performance that could be achieved is disguised and rewards short circuit the learning that could have been gained.

Stimulate action

■ Tampering: interfering in a process for the sake of it, destabilising it and reducing performance

■ Asking for more information so issues are either ignored or not addressed at the appropriate time.

Facilitate learning

■ Focusing solely on learning, so that there is no accountability.

References

Syed, M. (2015) *Black box thinking, the surprising truth about success,* Hodder & Stoughton, London.

Chapter 11

Linking measurement to strategy

The performance framework provides a summary of what a performance measurement process can do and the role of leaders and managers in applying it successfully. In this chapter, we will set out in more detail the process of implementing it, looking at some useful tools that will help you to develop and implement measurement systems aligned to strategy in the context of your own organisation.

Before you begin to create a system to measure how well you are doing, you must have a good idea about the level of performance you need to reach to deliver your strategy. The first requirement then, is to have a strategy that is likely to be effective in achieving your purpose and one that is clearly understood throughout the organisation. Although this sounds reasonably straightforward, many organisations struggle to implement their strategies, so it is worth spending a few moments here to explain the reasons. There has been extensive research to explore why this happens and most of it concerns the private sector.

We find the six silent killers of strategy (Beer & Eisenstadt, 2000) a very useful framework for thinking about the reasons for implementation failure. The framework was developed from research conducted in the private sector in the United States, but when Mike was chairing an NHS conference a few years ago, one of the speakers presented the results of a study into failing NHS Trust Hospitals in the United Kingdom and she cited each of the six silent killers of strategy. We believe this framework holds for the public sector as well. The six silent killers of strategy are as follows:

Ineffective senior management team: the team must not only be capable but be seen to be capable; people so people have confidence in them. You can

DOI: 10.4324/9781003099895-14

probably all think of senior teams who can't work together and are often at each other's throats in public as well as in private.

Unclear strategy and conflicting priorities: when strategy is unclear or has conflicting priorities that haven't been resolved, this is a clear sign of an ineffective senior management team. In this case, efforts are dispersed too widely, and people are unclear about where they should concentrate their efforts and resources.

Top-down or laissez faire senior management style: too much dictatorial communication will lead people to feel they have no ownership, and they will lose interest as a result. On the other hand, if there is too little direction and input from senior managers people think they are just not interested. If the senior team isn't interested why should the rest of the organisation be interested?

Poor vertical communication: as a senior manager who is constantly reflecting on the strategy, it is easy to assume those further down the organisation will understand what is being done and why. This may not be the case. Creating channels of communication that enable easy flows of information down the organisation is essential. But you must remember that communication is two way.

Poor coordination across functions: this can lead to the development of the silo attitudes we discussed in the leadership chapter, where people guard their own territories. This is often driven by performance measures which are locally focused, and by a management style that requires people to meet their personal goals.

Inadequate leadership skills and development lower down the organisation: an organisation does not only rely on senior managers, important though they are, local leadership is critical for implementation. Local leadership can be easily destroyed by senior management action. This can happen when senior management change direction without thought for how this undermines local leadership. This can also happen when local leaders are not allowed to act, so have to ask for permission every time they want to change something.

Turning this framework from a negative – why does strategy execution fail? – to a positive – how do you improve your chances of successful policy implementation? – is a useful approach. Here is a way of thinking about it and a list of questions to ask yourself.

Firstly, you need clarity in your strategy. This is more than having a document, it is about looking at strategy in the round with its inherent conflicts and priorities and ensuring these are made explicit and are understood. Success mapping (see the section later in this chapter) is an effective process for clarifying strategic intent and for developing priorities. You can do success mapping with your senior management team, or any other team for that matter, and it will act as an aid to promoting a common understanding of what needs to be done. The process also creates commitment to actions that have been agreed.

Ask yourself – and others around you – whether the strategy is clear and whether conflicts and priorities are really understood.

Secondly, you need an effective senior management team. An effective senior management team is one which has arguments in private, but once policy is agreed, accepts "cabinet style" responsibility and gets behind the implementation regardless of whether individuals believe the solution is their preferred one or not. All teams need to discuss and debate decisions they are making, and it is important that alternative views are shared. Accept that arguments will happen, and this is usually not dysfunctional as long as agreement is reached and members of the team feel able to support decisions that have been made.

Ask yourself whether you have an effective senior management team that is able both to voice dissent and reach agreement.

Thirdly, walking the path between Command and Control and Laissez-Faire is not an easy one. Of course you need direction, but it is also true that people work better when they have some freedom to operate in the way they see fit and a choice in the actions they take. People lower down any hierarchy often have more detailed knowledge and are better placed to make these decisions. Tell people what you want them to deliver but leave how it should be delivered to them. Take a look at the framework in figure 5.1 on page 80.

Ask yourself whether you have clearly communicated the expected outcomes and given people the freedom to develop the path to achieving them.

Fourthly, communication is important. By communication, we don't simply mean top-down communication. Although this is important, bottom-up communication is important too. Top-down communication should be focused on the direction of travel; bottom-up communication should be focused on feedback around what is actually happening and whether it is having the right impact.

Ask yourself if you are receiving timely and truthful feedback.

Fifthly, the coordination of functions and departments across the organisation often provides a rich opportunity for improvement. Individual departments can run well – the call centre has been optimised or the maintenance team is very efficient – but the interfaces between them could be improved. Breaking down silos and enhancing communication will enable better coordination and effectiveness.

Ask yourself whether there are opportunities for better alignment between departments.

Sixthly, it is local leaders who implement strategy and policy. Support from top managers is important but local leaders deliver change. So, developing this group is exceptionally important. Alas it is often the case that once senior managers have developed a policy, they move on to the next big thing without providing ongoing guidance and support.

Ask yourself whether you have capable local leadership and how it can be strengthened.

There is another reason why strategy can fail particularly in the public sector. That reason is paying insufficient attention to stakeholders. In the public sector there is a wide variety of stakeholders, many of whom have conflicting wants and needs. You may find, for example, that members of the public want 24-hour access to a certain service, but employees do not want to work night shifts. How can you resolve this dilemma? Can you compromise and run the service until 10 pm, say? Or do you absolutely need 24-hour access to certain services? And what impact will such a decision have on groups of stakeholders and the costs of the service you are providing?

In the rest of this chapter, we will focus on making your strategy or policy actionable. To do this you will need to develop your plans so they can be simply communicated to the whole organisation. You will also need a mechanism whereby you can track progress against the implementation of those plans, stimulate debate about what is and isn't working, making decisions, and taking action. We will start will the performance measurement cycle.

The performance management cycle

Put simply, the strategy process looks like Figure 11.1. The plan, do, study, act cycle goes back to the 1920 and the work of Walter Shewhart. Most people know this from the later version promoted by Demming, plan, do, check, act, but we prefer the word "study" as this requires a much more detailed investigation of whether or not your actions are having the effect you want.

It is a continuous process of collecting internal and external information and data, examining your capabilities, deciding what you are aiming for, discussing what this means for your organisation and considering the implications. You should then do something as a result of this planning. Once your interventions have happened, you need to study the results. This will lead you to reconsidering your plans in the light of debate and creating a further plan of action which you implement. Then, ideally, you repeat the cycle making strategy and policy making integrated with implementation in a continuous cycle.

In the UK public sector, there is often a distinct divide between policy-making and implementation. Policy have the ideas, others implement. This division isn't helpful as you can see from both the six silent killers of strategy and the performance management cycle, that interaction between what you are trying to achieve and what

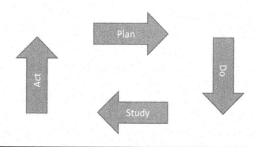

Figure 11.1 The performance management cycle.

works is critical to becoming effective. The division between policy and implementation is possibly the greatest barrier to effectiveness.

So how do you integrate policy/strategy and implementation? There are three tools which can be used to bridge the gap. The first is the Performance Prism (Neely et al., 2002) which will help you structure your thoughts about stakeholders, strategy, processes for delivery, resources, and capabilities you need. The second is success mapping, a tool that is highly effective in helping your team turn a policy or strategy into an implementable plan on a page. The third is the balanced scorecard, and in this section, we will focus on "balance" which is often forgotten.

Being clear about what you are trying to achieve and how you are going to achieve it will help you communicate better throughout the organisation. Clarity of purpose is essential, but as we heard from Javed Khan of Barnardo's, people need to believe it and not just understand it.

The performance prism

The **Performance Prism** (Neely et al., 2002) is a useful framework for analysing what groups of stakeholders want and need and how you may be able to accommodate them, if at all. It is a performance framework that brings to the fore the elements you need to track to deliver policy. The starting point is to identify who your stakeholders are. This may seem obvious but give it careful thought because people often overlook important groups and this leads to major problems in implementing policies. When you have identified who all your stakeholders are, consider what they want and need from you. "Needs" can be different from "wants" which are desirable but not essential. Having identified these, turn your thoughts to which specific needs you are going to meet and what they mean for your strategy. You then need to think about the processes required to deliver that strategy and the capability and resources you will have to build. Finally, you should think about what you need from your stakeholders. It's probably easier to see all that in the form of a diagram (Figure 11.2).

Let's look at that in more detail.

The starting point is stakeholder analysis because organisations don't exist to deliver a policy or implement a strategy, they exist to serve their stakeholders. Understanding these wants and needs is a first step, as is deciding what you can and can't satisfy.

The next stage is to make choices, and this forms the basis of your strategy. Some stakeholders' needs are primary needs, essentially what you have been tasked to do, so there is little choice but to do them. Other wants are secondary, and you must judge what can and can't be delivered. Some stakeholder needs (as you will have gathered from using the change tools) are not compatible with the requirements of your main stakeholder group. You will have to honest about this and explain and justify why some wants are not going to be satisfied. You may find yourself having

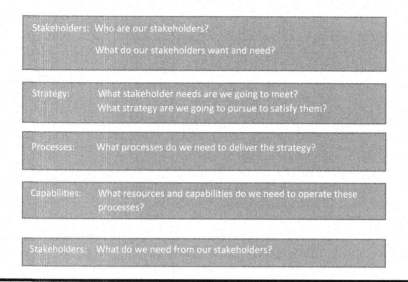

Stakeholders: Who are our stakeholders?

What do our stakeholders want and need?

Strategy: What stakeholder needs are we going to meet?
What strategy are we going to pursue to satisfy them?

Processes: What processes do we need to deliver the strategy?

Capabilities: What resources and capabilities do we need to operate these processes?

Stakeholders: What do we need from our stakeholders?

Figure 11.2 The performance prism.

Source: Adapted from Neely et al. (2002).

difficult conversations, but if you don't make these choices explicit at this early stage, you will only store up trouble for the future.

Once you have decided what the strategy is, you must, of course deliver it, and to do that you need effective processes and projects to carry through the implementation. You also need sufficient resources and capability. If you get processes, projects, resources and capability aligned it will stand you in good stead for the future.

Remember, the relationship with stakeholders is not only one-way. You need things back from them, whether that is resources, cooperation on design or just honest advice and feedback. The prism reminds you to track that you are getting back what you need from your stakeholders.

Success mapping

One very useful approach to creating clarity is success mapping. The result is a success map (sometimes called a strategy map). We prefer to talk about "success" rather than strategy as it is more inclusive. The statement "Other people do strategy" is true for most of the people working in your organisation, but it's likely everyone wants to be successful. We also want to use success mapping as a process, a journey you take to help you clarify what you are trying to achieve and how to achieve it.

A success map helps you to make explicit links between various actions and outcomes. Essentially you ask the question: "What do we need to achieve?" and beneath that another question: "How will we achieve it?" This is repeated several times. When you start you will have a messy picture of all the ways things can be done, but by working through the most important factors that need to be done, you will be able to refine your success map into something much simpler. You should also check your logic bottom up. The "what/how?" questioning should take you down the success map, but if you start at the bottom and ask "why?" you are doing something, the answer should be the objective above.

At the end of the process, you should have a concise picture which helps in communicating what is to be achieved, what actions are to be taken and why. Ideally you should end up with a picture on a page.

Here is a simplified example of a success map for improving the educational attainment level of a population (Figure 11.3). In practice, there would be more boxes, but the trick is to keep the map as uncluttered as possible. Resist the temptation to make it more sophisticated by filling in all actions. Include only the most important actions. By doing this you also clarify priorities.

This is not an individual task. It is a good idea to bring together the group of people running the organisation or that part of it, to produce the success map rather than doing it on your own. Each person will have their own idea of how the organisation works and it is only by working together that you can create and share a common group of objectives and actions. In the public sector we would strongly advise having both policy people and implementation people present. That way you bridge that policy – implementation gap. In addition, include line management and don't delegate this to a staff team. Line managers are more than capable of engaging in this process, whilst also pointing out what will and won't work in practice.

The process is quite straightforward. Taking the simple example from Figure 11.3, ask the question:

"What is the organisation trying to achieve?"

- A better qualified population

How is it going to achieve that?

- Increasing the participation in education, and
- Improving teaching standards

Now, what we are trying to do is

- Improve teaching standards

How are we going to do that?

- By making teaching attractive as a career and encouraging good people into the profession

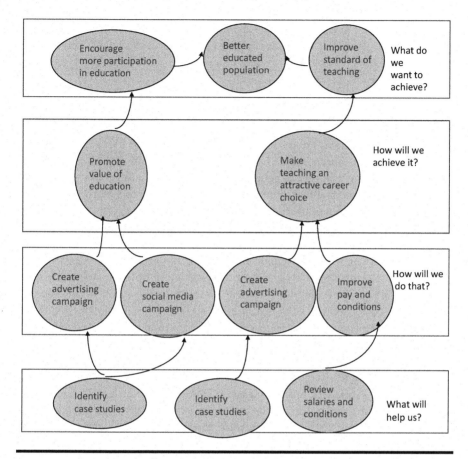

Figure 11.3 A simplified example of a success map.

A success map will work from the top down, but it should also work from the bottom up. So, using the example above, if I am asked to produce a case study about the experiences of a teacher, I can see through all the "whys" the direct link to the overall objective of improving the educational attainment of the population. I can understand how the work I am doing feeds in directly to the key objective and this will affect how I go about doing it.

Once you have a success map, you will have a list of key priorities and a picture of what you need to measure in your organisation. We will go on to talk about the measurement of these objectives in the next chapter.

Just a final comment on success mapping. One useful way of doing this – especially within the public sector - is to create a success map from the perspective of each of your key stakeholders. Starting from the stakeholder needs you can work through how they could be delivered. This will take some time, but the investment is well worth it because at the end of the exercise you will see alternative views of what you are trying to deliver. You will then have to make choices and create a final success map that captures the journey you plan to take. This then allows you to communicate precisely to the rest of the organisation how you will implement your plan.

Creating a balance

In your success map, you are recording only the key actions. Likewise, when you come to deciding on what to measure, you should measure only the most important activities. We cannot emphasise this enough. During the course of our interviews, several people told us how they were overwhelmed with the number of targets and priorities they faced. Some of these were even conflicting, making it necessary to navigate a route around them so that everyone was satisfied but wasting time and resources in the process, which is obviously neither efficient nor effective. Reflect on the words of Einstein which we quoted earlier and make your performance measurement and management system "as simple as possible but not simpler." Sometimes you do need a high level of sophistication and sometimes you don't. If the system is too complicated it can be easier to manipulate and there is a point at which the benefits of extra complexity are outweighed by the time it takes to produce and analyse and the fewer the people who will understand the results, anyway.

One way of looking at the design of your measurement process is to imagine the cockpit of a plane. The cockpit is packed full of displays providing data and gauges showing a variety of measurements. It is not possible to look at them all so the most important displays are in the pilot's line of sight. Now, you need to think what "most important" means, so let's take an example of an information panel with which most people will be more familiar – the instrument display in a car and how it is laid out. As you are driving along, what do you need to know? Well, of course, you need to know that you have enough fuel to reach your destination – or at least have an idea of when you will need to refuel or recharge. You will need to know that there is enough air in your tyres, enough water in the radiator and you will want an idea of how far you have travelled. But the on display right in front of you is the speedometer, because you will need to glance at that from time to time as you drive to ensure you are not exceeding the speed limit. The other gauges are less prominent because you don't need them all the time. In some cases, you just need to know when something is wrong – when tyre pressures are low, for example. The same is true of measures in an organisation. It is necessary to look at some of them on a regular basis, others less so. That doesn't mean to say you won't be measuring them if they are important, but it does mean they will be reviewed when it is appropriate.

There is another perspective to performance measurement and that is creating balance. Continuing with the driving example, you need to make sure everything is running well with your car in order to have a smooth journey and reach your destination safely. Without the correct tyre pressures, you will have a bumpy ride; if you don't have enough fuel your car will stop; if your satnav doesn't work you may lose your way. It's the same in an organisation. Everything you do has an impact on something else and that is why you must think about the consequences for other operations when you decide to make changes. Returning to the driving example, as I drive along, I must keep my eyes on the road ahead and I must watch my speed, but it is equally important that I notice if I am running out of fuel for my journey. In an organisation, if all I focus on is finance then nothing will happen. To be effective everything should be in balance and everything should work correctly.

One tool to help you build this balance into your measurement system is the Balanced Scorecard. It was developed in the 1980s, so the chances are you have already heard of it. The idea behind its development was the need to reduce reliance on financial measures. Bob Kaplan, one of those who championed its use, pointed out that by only using financial measures you may encourage undesirable behaviour. An example of this would be to delay capital expenditure to meet short term financial targets. By delaying expenditure, you are saving money this year so you will meet short term targets, but as a result you will be postponing benefits arising from improvements in efficiency and capability and that will adversely affect the performance of the organisation in the longer term. When targets have to be met, there is often pressure to cut expenditure on training and staff development, for example, because you cannot see an immediate return or tangible result. This is a pity because cutting the staff development budget can have repercussions beyond the obvious capability issues. It can also affect staff morale and result in higher turnover because employees feel their employers are not willing to invest in them.

The underlying principle of the Balanced Scorecard is that there is no single indicator of performance. You need to identify what the most important factors are for your organisation's success and measure key activities in those categories. Everything is linked. No factor stands alone, whatever the organisation.

The original balanced scorecard looked like Figure 11.4. As you see there are four boxes: **Finance** which is self-explanatory, **Customers** – these could be patients, clients, or whatever you call the people for whom you are supplying a service or product, **Internal Perspective** – the most important processes you need to be good at doing in order to deliver your services or products and **People and Learning** – this is important because if you do not consider your people you wouldn't be engaging their abilities and talents, and if you don't consider innovation and learning you will not be preparing for the future. These boxes work for most organisations with a little adaptation. In the figure, we have shown arrows which represent how performance in one perspective impacts on performance in other perspectives.

Thinking about what is important for performance in this way has a number of advantages. It provides information on the most important activities in a single picture. It also enables managers to consider all the key operating measures together and see how improvement in one area impacts on another. With the people and

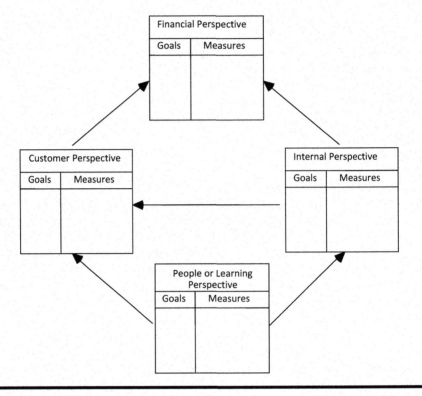

Figure 11.4 The original balance scorecard.

Source: Adapted from Schneiderman (1987) and Kaplan and Norton (1992).

learning category, it builds in consideration of the future. This is done alongside the more day-to-day and backward-looking (but still essential) factors such as finance. Perhaps most important advantage of all is that it encourages discussion about organisation-wide performance, helping to break down the dreaded silos.

People often think the Balanced Scorecard is only appropriate for the private sector, but it can be applied everywhere (you can even adapt it for your own personal development, by re-adjusting the labels on the boxes).

Here is an example of a hospital and the activities that may be in each box:

Finance: is probably quite clear as it will include items such as cost of services; income and grants, capital expenditure, and so on.

Customer Perspective: is likely to include patient satisfaction and satisfaction of commissioners of the hospital's services, and key factors that make the patient feel safer and more confident.

Internal Process Perspective: may include waiting times, success rate in operations, safety issues, staff turnover, and morale.

People and Learning: could be research into new treatments, staff training, and development, any projects to establish best practice from other hospitals, for example.

Let us look at what to measure from another perspective. Much has been written about efficiency and effectiveness of police forces. It is difficult to measure and to make comparisons and establish benchmarks between police forces across different areas, because each region faces different challenges. Not only do the types of crime vary, but the response of the public varies, too. If the population of a particular area does not have reasonable relationships with the police, they are less likely to report a crime and, if the crime isn't reported it cannot be investigated. Nevertheless, it is still a crime whether it is domestic abuse or the theft of a mobile phone.

During a training session with a group of senior police officers it became apparent that there was much emphasis on reducing the rate of crime overall. They struggled with the meaning of that because, on the face of it, catching a burglar had the same weight as catching a murderer. Identifying and arresting a small number of petty criminals who were responsible for a large number of small crimes would result meeting performance targets. Now, of course there is nothing wrong with that. The principal stakeholder for the police is the general public and being burgled or having your mobile phone stolen is highly unpleasant. During the training session, the police officers looked at what they should be focussing on, using the success map we described earlier. They put more weight on monitoring and taking action on root causes, such as domestic violence. By doing this, one force thought they could reduce the murder rate by 30%. Measuring activity relating to root causes may not have such an immediate effect on results recorded in performance measurement processes, but it will bear fruit in the longer term.

One of the people we spoke to, Tom Wheatley, Governor of Wakefield prison explained that many crimes, such as drug dealing, were committed by people who were essentially operating in a marketplace. If one of those people went to prison, someone else would come in to fill their place. The only way to make a real impact was to reduce demand.

Coming back to measures, then, it is important to measure the clear up rate of relatively minor crimes because they matter to stakeholders. If you happen to live in an area of the country that is plagued by antisocial behaviour, you will want the police to spend time catching the perpetrators. However, it is also important to measure progress towards dealing with root causes for crimes that have yet to occur, whether that is working with so-called problem families to reduce the likelihood of antisocial behaviour or acting on reports of domestic violence to reduce the likelihood of someone being murdered the future. You must understand what your stakeholders want to see, but also work on activities that may not yet be visible to stakeholders because they matter for the future.

Some people may respond to this by saying the police exist to clear up crime. That is rather like saying hospitals and GPs are there to treat patients. Where does the responsibility lie for taking preventative measures? We would argue that for a service to be effective – and sustainable – it must deal with both aspects in an integrated way, breaking down silos and working across agencies to reduce demand for their services in the future. Changing the way performance is measured to include progress towards tackling root causes can help by ensuring the longer-term goal is not forgotten in the midst of day-to-day activity.

So, what does balance mean to you? You don't need to take the original four perspectives developed for the private sector, but it is worth taking the time to consider balance. You should be thinking about the balance between

- The focus of your attention on what you are doing now with the results you wish to deliver,
- Delivery of your objectives with the building of capability for the future,
- Focussing internally and focussing externally, and
- Delivery and the wellbeing of your team.

You may also wish to think about the balance between your focus on efficiency and effectiveness.

References

Beer, M. & Eisenstadt, R. (2000) "The six silent killers of strategy," *Sloan Management Review*, Summer.

Kaplan, R. S. & Norton, D. P. (1992) "The balanced scorecard - measures that drive performance," *Harvard Business Review*, January/February, 71–79.

Neely, A., Adams, C. & Kennerley, M. (2002) *The performance prism*, FT Prentice Hall, London.

Schneiderman, A. (1987) *The first balanced scorecard*, Schneiderman.com

Chapter 12

How to measure performance

Both the Balanced Scorecard and the prism help you identify *what* is most important to measure. The next question is *how* to measure. As people focus on activities that are being measured, you not only need to be sure you are measuring the right ones, you need to know you are measuring them in the right way. Here are some questions to ask.

Is a measurement going to achieve what you want?

Be absolutely clear about why you are measuring something. What is the outcome you would like to see? Until you know that you won't know how to measure it.

Here is a true example of a measure that certainly didn't have the required outcome. An airline was concerned that it was taking too long for passengers to retrieve their luggage on arrival. To put this right, they added a new performance target for baggage handlers, which was "the time taken from the arrival of the plane at the gate to the point at which the first bag appeared on the luggage carrousel." What happened was that one or two bags arrived more quickly on the conveyor, but the remainder of the luggage took just as long to turn up. Nevertheless, the baggage handlers had met their target.

Another story (possibly apocryphal) that makes us laugh is that of the company producing nails in the former Soviet Union. Workers were given a target of producing x tonnes of nails in a given period. Apparently, it is easier and faster to make bigger nails than lots of small ones, so they produced one enormous nail of the weight required to make their target. It was probably useless, but they had hit their target. The adage, "Hitting the target, but missing the point" clearly applies here.

DOI: 10.4324/9781003099895-15

Some methods of measuring are, to quote another of our interviewees "just daft." One such measure was the number of new people taking part in a voluntary drug testing scheme. Initially the numbers would be high – everyone would be new to the scheme when it was first introduced so it would be easier to get larger numbers of individuals to agree, but as time goes on it would be harder to find new people and it would look as if no progress was being made. Also, enrolling on a scheme is one thing but staying with it is quite another and for the outcome to be effective people would need to stay with it. So, the measure may have had some validity at the start, to track the uptake, but once it was established it was meaningless and time-wasting.

Are there unintended consequences?

Measuring performance in the wrong way, too slavishly, can result in serious consequences. One of the people we spoke to went so far as to say that managing by targets resulted in corrupting standards of culture and values rather than serving the public. In that instance, he was talking about law and order, arresting someone to meet a target, for example, but the point is valid in other arenas, too. This problem is being recognised and in many organisations, where once there was an appraisal process measuring personal performance largely by the extent to which an individual had achieved their targets, there is now a system which also looks at *how* they achieved them. If someone achieves their targets by ignoring the values of the organisation, are they really achieving their purpose?

Examples of unintended consequences are numerous – waiting times at hospitals which, in the past, have resulted in people either being admitted or being kept in ambulances outside. We have already mentioned the idea of delaying training expenditure to meet a target (known as "gaming the system") or stretching a point and classifying something as something else in order to make the figures look good. So, it's worth thinking through very carefully what the implications of your chosen measurement are and whether people can find a way to make it look better without actually improving performance itself.

There is another aspect to the issue of unintended consequences and that is setting up expectations by measuring something. If you measure employee satisfaction, for example, then employees will expect you to take action to improve areas where they believe the organisation and its managers are failing.

Can you measure in a consistent way?

It may seem to be a good idea to measure something, but if you cannot measure it consistently then it is not worth measuring because you will not be able to establish trends. A one-off measurement is of little use and can lead you to draw misleading conclusions.

You also need to develop a universal understanding of definitions; everyone must understand exactly what you are measuring. Here is an example. Teams around the country were tasked with going out and visiting clients, and each team was given a target number of people to visit during the year. It became very clear at a quarterly review that some teams had done exceptionally better than others. This led to concerns about performance in some areas. If some people could do it, why were others so far behind? On closer inspection it was found that those teams had brought groups of people together and had included each individual as a visit, whereas others had visited people at their workplaces and in instances where they had brought people together, they had counted it as one visit.

Can you establish cause and effect?

Sometimes it is too hard, or even impossible, to measure a qualitative factor directly and accurately. That does not mean you should not try to measure it if you think it is important. It usually means you have to find indicators which you can use to signify a position. Just be as sure as you can of strong cause and effect and try not to make assumptions, both at the stage of designing measures and when you come to review them.

Let us take an example here of a widely used measure: employee satisfaction. This is usually established by means of a survey of employees conducted on an annual basis. People are asked to rate how they feel about a basket of factors such as physical working conditions, hours of work, availability of resources to do the job, and capability of management and leadership. You can make some assumptions, based on research, that these factors affect satisfaction, but the importance of each one of them may vary according to the organisation. We know of one workplace which included in the survey the question: how visible are senior managers? The results showed visibility was relatively low and you might conclude that employees were unhappy about that. However, on further inspection, it was found that employees were quite satisfied with the situation as it was. They were happy to be left to get on with their work and to know they could approach senior managers when they needed to. So, in this case there was no link between low visibility of senior managers and staff satisfaction. It would have been better to ask the question in a different way: "How satisfied are you with visibility of senior managers?"

Here is another example of how important it is to test your assumptions. An airline discovered to the amazement of many executives that customer satisfaction often went up when there was a slight delay to departure. This seemed completely counterintuitive, so they decided to investigate further. They found that when departure was delayed, the crew made special efforts to communicate with passengers. The captain would make an announcement explaining the reason for the delay (usually nothing to do with the airline) and would explain all the steps that were being taken to make up for lost time. The cabin crew would bring around extra drinks and would take time to talk to passengers because they knew that placating people at this stage would make for less hassle when they eventually took off. So, not surprisingly, delaying departure was not the answer to improving customer satisfaction, but improving communication with passengers and adding small touches to service was.

Can you create a useful measure without making it too complex?

We have seen some measures that are so elaborate and complicated that their value is far outweighed by the cost of producing them. There are occasions when a great deal of effort has been put into researching a formula and allocating weightings and complex calculations and, in the end the process has become more academic than useful. There was one measure we came across, in connection with litter, which defined how big a piece of paper would be to be classed as litter. (Yes, really!) Note, we are not saying here that you should not pay attention to the formula or to precise definitions, just that you should evaluate whether it is worthwhile to develop one that is complex.

The other problem with complicated measurements is that they become more and more removed from their original purpose. People forget why they were developed in the first place and measures become entities in their own right. In some cases, when something is too difficult and time-consuming to measure, some individuals are even tempted to fudge the results.

Who will be responsible?

Designing a measurement process is a waste of time if there is no action as a result. In order for there to be action you must ensure someone has responsibility for reviewing and acting upon individual measures and overall performance. You can have collective responsibility, but having a named individual removes any doubt and makes it more difficult for actions to slip through the cracks, where everybody thinks someone else is doing something and in reality, nothing is happening.

How often do you need to measure?

It takes longer for the results from some activities to appear than it does from others, so think carefully how often you need to measure something. If you measure an activity too frequently you may be reacting to a blip in the results rather than to what is actually happening. In essence you are responding to a problems which doesn't exist.

The performance measure record sheet

The performance record measure sheet provides a very simple way of recording each measure and, in the process, helps you to clarify your thinking and ensures everyone has a common understanding. We recommend that once you have a clear idea of your objectives from creating your success map, you use the record sheet to design appropriate measures to track progress against these objectives. As with other activities, we suggest you work with a small team on the design of each measure. This will bring together different perspectives and enable you to create better measures for your organisation. The framework for the Performance Measure Record Sheet is shown in Figure 12.1. The template is used widely within the NHS and over the years, thousands of managers in both the public and private sector have been trained in its use.

Let us give two examples of how you can use measures to create focus. Firstly, we will discuss an example of the key measure for a social policy and how the reshaping of this measure changed focus from the activity towards the outcome. Secondly, we will describe a cycle of changes to a measure, that reflected the growing maturity of the organisation. This too, moved the organisation from activity towards achieving the outcomes and benefits, but in this case the journey was an important part of making that transition.

We will begin with a policy example. The policy was to improve the wellbeing and life chances of indigenous Australians. This was to be achieved by encouraging greater economic activity. To achieve this the local government created various initiatives, but the one we are focusing on is the enterprise fund. The government

Measure	What should this measure be called?
Purpose	Why is this being measured?
Relates to	To which strategic objective does this relate?
Target	What level of performance is to be achieved and by when?
Formula	How is this measure calculated?
Frequency	How often will you measure and how often will you review?
Who measures	Who collects and reports on the data?
Source of data	Where is data collected from?
Who acts on results	Who is responsible for taking action?
What steps can they take	What action can be taken (outline possible steps which may be taken)?
Notes and comments	

Figure 12.1 The performance measure record sheet.

Source: Adapted from Neely et al. (1996, 1997).

decided that it would give grants to business start-ups being run by people from that community. The initial measure is presented in Figure 12.2

However, when we took the team responsible through the process of redesigning the measure, there was a long conversation about what the policy was there to achieve. Was the idea simply to distribute money to the community, or was the idea to create sustainable enterprises within that community? There was also some concern that people were taking the grants as they were available, but not creating sustainable businesses.

The team concluded that the real intent was to create sustainable enterprises, so the measure was restated as Figure 12.3. Now the focus isn't on the number of grants given, but on the percentage of enterprises still in business two years after the award of the grant.

By redesigning the measure in this way, the focus is being subtly shifted from the grant approval activity to creating sustainable enterprises. This is far harder to achieve, but the team believed that the new measure better reflected the policy intent.

The second example is something many organisations attempt to from time to time, the implementation of a suggestions scheme. Often when the suggestion scheme is implemented, the focus is on measuring the number of suggestions received. This may will stimulate some activity, but what you really need are good suggestions.

Measure	New enterprises for indigenous Australians (IA)
Purpose	To create new enterprises and improve wellbeing and life chances within this social group
Relates to	IA economic activity
Target	50 grants for be issued this financial year
Formula	Number of grants issued in this financial year
Frequency	Measure monthly, reviewed quarterly
Who measures	IA enterprise grants team
Source of data	Minutes of grant approach board meetings
Who acts on results	IA enterprise grants team
What steps can they take	Promote the scheme, encourage applications, review application, advise applicants on criteria and suitability, process applications
Notes and comments	

Figure 12.2 First measure example.

Measure	New sustainable IA enterprises
Purpose	To create new enterprises and improve wellbeing and life chances within this social group
Relates to	IA economic activity
Target	50 percent of enterprises trading after two years
Formula	Number of enterprises trading two years after grant issue X 100 Number of grants issued in base year
Frequency	Measure and review quarterly
Who measures	IA enterprise grants team
Source of data	Grants awarded and enterprise continuity review
Who acts on results	IA enterprise grants team
What steps can they take	Promote the scheme, encourage applications, review application, advise applicants on criteria and suitability, supporting business plans, creating an enterprise support network, review successes and failures, learn from experience
Notes and comments	

Figure 12.3 Second measure example.

To encourage good suggestions, you may well change the measure. The number of suggestions is now less important, so the measure could become the number of suggestions accepted for implementation. This puts a quality threshold in place. It will make the achievement of the measure harder, but it is more focused on what you are trying to achieve. But naturally, the journey doesn't finish there.

Ideally, acceptance of suggestions is just the start of the process, good suggestions should be implemented. You could then reflect this new need by changing the measure to the number of suggestions implemented.

The final step is of course when the suggestions are working and are having a positive impact on the organisation. To reflect this, you could update your measure to ensure it captured a signal that positive impacts – financial or nonfinancial – were resulting from the suggestions scheme.

For some, this is a long and tedious journey, but let us just review what is happening. Your initial emphasis is on encouraging suggestions, so you are measuring the whole organisation. You then focus on accepted suggestions, so besides the organisation, there is now a focus on the suggestions review team. As you move to measure implementation, the focus changes again, and finally you are reviewing whether all this activity is worth it or not.

We would argue that this journey is both necessary and useful if you are really hoping to put in place an effective suggestions scheme. Until you encourage individuals to put forward their suggestions, you won't have any suggestions to review. Until you review the suggestions that have been made, you won't know whether any of them are good ones that you can implement, and without implementing any suggestions you won't achieve any benefits. Each step in the journey is necessary as it encourages the behaviours you need for the process to work. If you started with the final measure – the benefits from the suggestion scheme – you would find this is too far removed from the day to day to create the change desired.

We have given these examples to make two important points. First, measures influence behaviour, so getting your measure correctly defined is really important. Second, measures usually need to develop over time. You should therefore review your measures appropriately and make sure they still align with whatever you are looking to achieve.

How to set targets

Research over many years has shown that targets are good for providing staff with clarity and purpose and for encouraging higher levels of performance. However, the setting of targets is often fraught with politics and heated debate, with people responsible for achieving them wanting them as low possible, so they can be reasonably sure of reaching them and those setting the targets wanting them to be as high as possible. We will talk about the process of setting targets a little later on but want first to discuss the different types of targets and the purposes they fulfil.

Stretch targets are those which are high but achievable and are designed to motivate people to reach higher levels of performance. If you set stretch targets, you will have to accept that some of them will not be met. Whilst stretch targets are good in terms of improving performance, setting stretch targets for every activity is likely to reduce motivation. Like a piece of elastic, if you stretch people too far and in too many different directions, performance will decrease on all fronts. So, save stretch targets for activities where extra performance will make a big difference. The Covid vaccination programme in the United Kingdom is a good example of a stretch target. The numbers of people to be vaccinated in a short period of time seemed astonishingly high, but there was great motivation get it done and people throughout the country were highly resourceful in their efforts to achieve targets. Is this sustainable over a very long period of time? Probably not, and you could not expect the same level of performance for every vaccination programme or health initiative.

Realistic targets are those that reflect the most likely outcomes with good use of resources and people performing their jobs well.

Minimum targets are base levels that should be achieved all the time. You can use these as a type of benchmark, with everything above them being acceptable and anything below unacceptable. Over time you may want to increase your minimum targets as, perhaps, technology improves, or people find better ways of doing things.

How do you decide what level of target to set? One critical factor is the requirement of stakeholders, both internal and external. If you use the Prism tool we described earlier you should have identified the wants and needs of your stakeholders and examined and resolved conflicts as far as possible. You will have a better understanding of the expectations of your stakeholders and their priorities.

However, expectations are one thing and fulfilling them quite another. So, the next step is to estimate what is reasonable now and what may be achieved in the future. Establishing current capability can be done by looking at data over a period of time and by talking to people, but do not be tempted to take too short a snapshot because you may be looking at a time period when something unusual happened to change the results. Once you understand current and past performance you will need to consider whether the past is a good predictor of the future. Is there anything on the horizon that is likely to have a big impact? Is the country likely to go into recession, for example?

If you are setting targets across a range of similar organisations – such as schools – you must also consider the context in which they are operating. Although the institutions themselves may have a similar purpose, the challenges in achieving a target may be far higher in some areas than in others.

When you set a target, you must also think about the impact the focus you are putting on that activity will have on other activities. Some people we spoke to felt there was too much "silo thinking" when it came to targets. The most obvious example is housebuilding, where a target for building *x* houses has implications for infrastructure, schools, GP practices, water usage and many other factors. The difficulty, of course is where you draw the line.

Another of the problems highlighted by interviewees was the frequent changes that came about either when there was a change of government or a change of minister. These changes filtered down to become changes in targets, so you would start to concentrate on improvements in one area, only to find the target had been changed and you needed to turn your focus to another area. This was occasionally useful, though, as one person said: "Sometimes there is the possibility of pushing targets well down the line because you know they will be changed by the next administration, anyway."

The final element in the target setting process is communication, discussion, and planning for how to achieve the required levels of performance. It is important to involve people in the setting of targets wherever possible, but in reality, that is hard to achieve, and individuals often have little say over the targets they are expected to meet. They can have some say over how they meet those targets, though. People actually doing the job often have an idea of how a task can be done better, or how a small injection of resource will make a significant difference to performance. So, involving people in the "how to do it" discussion helps in gaining their commitment.

Some common problems

The Centre for Business Performance at Cranfield conducted a study into problems associated with target setting (Franco-Santos et al., 2010).

These were:

- Targets that were always based on past performance encouraged people not to reach for very high standards because they would be expected to do the same the following year and they feared they were unlikely to achieve the same result.
- Targets that were allocated inappropriately resulted in some people being over-whelmed because they had too much to achieve, and others were perceived to have an easy time. This was particularly dangerous because it also undermined team performance.
- Sometimes targets were perceived either as being too high or too low, both of which resulted in people behaving in unexpected ways. If the targets are perceived as being too high, individuals may take one of two actions. One is to take risks in an attempt to hit the target, which they wouldn't normally do and the other is to become demotivated and not bother to hit the target at all. If the target is perceived as being too low, then individuals may play things very safely to ensure the targets are being met and not be motivated to achieve higher levels of performance.
- Targets based on the wrong performance measures meant performance was not related to what the organisation was trying to achieve. (This is a particularly nasty one.)
- Targets were not periodically reviewed to ensure they were still relevant. Sometimes major events occur, and you have to consider whether the target is still viable. You need to consider what level of change can be tolerated before you amend the target.
- Targets were given to people and there was no ownership so they didn't bother to aim for them.
- The interrelation between targets was not considered so achieving a good result in one area had an adverse impact in another.

Here is an example of the problems that can be caused inadvertently when you pay insufficient attention to the setting of targets and how you reward people for meeting them. Several years ago, Mike was working with a pharmaceutical company which had two main product ranges which we'll call the "old range" and the "new range." The old product range provided about 50% of the company's income and sales were generated and managed by one sales director supported by a personal assistant. The other half of the income was delivered through the new product ranges which were more complex. To deliver that half of the income there were two sales directors plus a sales and administration team of several hundred people. When Mike arrived at the offices for a meeting, there was a tense atmosphere as the sales director for the old product range was negotiating her target for the following year. In the year just completed, she had suggested to her boss (the vice president of sales and marketing) that she could increase sales by the ambitious amount of 50%. Unfortunately, she had only managed a 45% increase. That was still a very substantial increase but because she had only achieved 45% rather than 50% it meant she had not met the target she had agreed with her boss and as a consequence she would not receive any reward for all the extra effort she had made. Clearly, this was a disappointment. So, in negotiating the target for increase in sales for the coming year, the sales director was suggesting a much lower figure of 2.5% which she thought she could easily achieve. Her boss, on the other hand was pushing for a 10% increase, although he thought he might have to compromise somewhere between the two figures. The result of her boss having accepted the ambitious target for the previous year combined with the sales director's disappointment at not receiving any reward for the enormous effort she had made, led to a complete lack of trust between the two. The target setting process, far from being a discussion about realistic possibilities for increases in sales volumes had descended into a bonus negotiation.

The best recommendation we can give is to create a supportive organisation in which you encourage a certain amount of risk-taking, learning, and personal development. This culture promotes greater ownership of targets and willingness to achieve them as well as willingness to point out when they are unlikely to work.

References

Franco-Santos, M., Marcos, J. & Bourne, M. (2010) "The art and science of target setting," *IESE Insight*, Fourth Quarter, Issue 7.

Neely, A. D., Mills, J. F., Gregory, M. J., Richards, A. H., Platts, K. W., & Bourne, M.C.S. (1996) *Getting the measure of your business*, Findlay, London.

Neely, A. D., Richards, A. H., Mills, J. F., Platts, K. W. & Bourne, M. C. S. (1997) "Designing performance measures: a structured approach," *International Journal of Operations & Production Management*, Vol. 17, No. 11, 1131–1152.

Chapter 13

Reviewing performance

Creating interest

Let us be honest here. The thought of a performance review thrills no one, or very few people anyway, but how you review performance will make a great difference to the effectiveness of your organisation. So, the first challenge is to encourage people to engage with it. More often than not reviews involve long and boring meetings with piles of reports, packed with numbers or traffic lights, that have remained largely unread until just before the meeting. The traditional approach is to work through the reports methodically looking at KPIs and considering aspects of under-performance. This leads people focus on their own results, working out what they are going to say when the spotlight falls upon them, and looking at those where the red lights shine out from the page, grateful that the problem lies elsewhere. All this misses the point because the important signals lie in trends and sometimes in how results impact on each other. The numbers and results in themselves have little meaning, it is the conclusions drawn from them that matter.

How do you avoid this? At a very basic level you need to ensure the meeting is "comfortable." By that we mean you allow people enough time to read important material in advance, you pay attention to physical comfort and you respect people's limits of attention. Various figures have been cited for concentration span in meetings and some research has apparently shown that attention drops off after as little as 30 min. No one can concentrate for hours on end, but they will concentrate for longer if the meeting is interesting.

Start with the agenda. We suggest creating an agenda centred around a set of key performance questions which can be answered using the data and information provided by performance reports, combined with discussion. This helps bring together all the activities involved in producing an outcome, rather than looking at each one individually. Although individual scrutiny may be needed at a later stage, by

DOI: 10.4324/9781003099895-16

adopting this approach you are starting from a higher point and seeing a wider picture. Here is a simple and hypothetical example from a school. The head teacher has introduced a new policy prohibiting the use of mobile phones in class. Reports have been produced showing when and where the new rule has been violated and the consequences of the violation. Rather than immediately homing in on the figures that show many year 10s have broken the rule and only in certain teachers' classes, it would be better to start by reminding people why the new rule was imposed (to remove distractions and interruptions to learning), and asking whether those attending the meeting believed it was still the right thing to do and whether there was anything else that could be done in addition.

In our experience, it is always a good idea to start at a higher level and ideally with a reminder of purpose. Once you begin to discuss the detail, it is harder to move out of it and to see the broader picture. People seize on relatively small inconsistencies or inconsequential matters and prizing them away from lengthy discussion and analysis of those points can be very difficult, leaving less time to discuss really important issues.

The other problem is that homing in immediately on the figures with laser-like focus and picking out the bad ones creates an atmosphere in which people become defensive. Instead of thinking about the issue, they think about themselves and how they can justify or ameliorate a result. This will have resonance for many people thinking about the meetings they dread attending and the relief when it is all over for another three months. Review meetings should not be witch hunts. They must be conducted in a manner in which everyone feels able to contribute and problems are tackled as a group rather than with the chair of the meeting allocating blame. Of course, individuals must be held to account, but singling them out in a performance review meeting is not the way to do it.

The performance planning value chain

Depending on the size of your organisation and the resources at your disposal, another way of taking the discussion to a higher level and creating distance between the figures and individuals is to ask analysts to produce reports and to attend meetings. This happened to good effect in logistics and courier company DHL where analysts who collected data attended board meetings to present information and answer questions. Board members no longer felt the need to defend their function's performance but were able to look at performance more dispassionately.

The Performance Value Planning Chain provides a structure for reviewing performance and the outline of the approach is captured in Figure 13.1.

Asking a question enables you to focus on the data you need in order to answer it. So, if you ask the question: "We believed our automated appointment booking system would reduce the number of no-shows. Is that the case?" you can be clear about the information you need from the data you have.

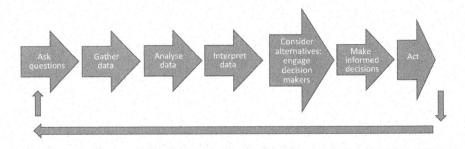

Figure 13.1 The performance planning value chain.

Source: Adapted from Bourne et al. (2004).

The second stage is gathering the data, which may come from your performance measurement process, your KPIs perhaps, but may also come from additional sources such as a survey. At this stage it is important to ask what accuracy of data you need. For some questions, an approximation will suffice, and you can avoid the time and cost of gathering detailed figures, but for others it will be important to have precise numbers. If you do not get the right type of data, you may have misleading input into your decision making.

Having gathered data, the next step is to carry out analysis. Look for trends, consider whether there are any obvious reasons for these trends. Keep asking the question "why?" There is a well-known Japanese approach to identifying root cases called the five whys. The argument is that if you ask why? five times and get the answer by the fifth you should have reached the real root cause.

Interpreting data is about putting the results in context, comparing with previous years, for example, or benchmarking against similar services. When seen on its own, a result can seem excellent. In January our score was 5 and now, in July, it's 15. We have increased our performance dramatically. However, if you compare your results with someone else's and you see they had 5 in January and are now at 25, your score doesn't seem quite so good. Using comparisons wherever possible gives a feel for performance from different perspectives.

The next stage is to consider what actions you will take based on your data analysis and the outcome you want to achieve. This involves discussing alternatives and the consequences of implementing them, looking at knock on effects and risks associated with each approach. In some cases, where you are likely to want to introduce a major change, it also involves considering the reactions of your stakeholders and deciding how you will communicate with them. Engaging senior level decision makers is clearly very important if you want action to result, so you will need to think how you are going to present your alternatives. It is similar to a marketing exercise, knowing what you want to achieve and considering how you will persuade different target audiences.

Of course, you do not necessarily need to take action. This is a trap into which some people fall because they always feel the need to act. Delaying action is a decision in itself and is not necessarily bad. You may feel you need more information or to give an initiative more time to bed down, and that is fine. You have thought about it and on balance believe that is the right decision. The danger comes when decisions are postponed because they are difficult and no one wants to face the consequences. A process-driven mentality sometimes leads to people to believe they have insufficient information on which to make a decision because not all the boxes have been ticked. However, they fail to see the risk posed by not acting. This tends to happen in organisations in which people feel they will be blamed if something goes wrong. If they decide not to act because they have insufficient information, they are, after all, only following the rules and are less likely to suffer the consequences if something does go wrong. So, taking action or not depends on the circumstances. The important factor is having a rationale for your decision.

Anticipating problems

You may have heard of Charles Handy's frog that sits in a pan of water that is gradually heating up until it is too late to jump out. It is not a pleasant image, but it encapsulates very well the idea of knowing something is wrong but not dealing with it until it is too late. You need to deal with problems before they become intractable, and the performance review meeting is a good place to do this. If you focus on an idea in a meeting, it will not suddenly disappear from your brain when the meeting finishes. You will, subconsciously be more aware of signals relating to that idea. So, in your review meetings it is worth taking time to look at trends and identify those which may cause problems in the future. You will be drawing attention to potential issues and when attendees leave the meeting, they will keep an eye open for any information that may help in making a decision in the future. In your meeting, you may want to agree a trigger point at which action should be taken. This helps ensure the issue remains on the agenda.

Learning from actions

Most people are au fait with the idea of learning from your actions. With a project, for example, there are reviews of what caused over- or under-spends, why it took longer to complete and how well new technology worked. All this information can be used to improve work on projects in the future. However, much less time is spent considering whether intended benefits actually resulted from doing the work. There are good reasons for this, which we highlighted in earlier chapters, such as difficulty in measuring qualitative outcomes, longer time scales involved and the need to produce concrete numbers for good news. So, when you conduct your performance reviews, don't forget to review outcomes as well as outputs. It's worth repeating the words of Andy Reed "Measuring outcomes seems tediously slow in a world of instant gratification. It's a long journey." But it is an important journey.

We've talked before about research into major government projects in the US where we found a wide variety of reasons why there was less measurement of outcomes. Some people considered the costs would outweigh the benefits. Others felt there was a political dimension. If the complexion of the government had changed during the progress of the project, the outcomes may not be seen in such a favourable light. And, as one person put it, "At what point do you use your measuring stick?" If you measure outcomes shortly after the completion of the project you may be missing benefits which arise later. All these views are valid, but we believe it is worth spending time to reflect on outcomes and to learn from what has and hasn't happened. How much time and resource you spend will depend on the circumstance, but if you don't see the results or your actions, only measure how well you did something, you will not learn about whether it was the right sort of thing to do in the first place.

How to look at data

You should always start with high-level questions about the most important aspects of performance. But you also need to know how to evaluate data, because it forms evidence for the discussion and that knowledge enables you to ask informed questions. So, we are going to spend a little time covering some of the key aspects. If you are a statistician or you know it already, just skip this section.

Sometimes you simply do not have sufficient data or information on which to base a decision, and sometimes you just have too much. If you do have it, you need to know what to look out for and what to use. Data is not information. Looking at individual figures is rarely of any use and even a years' worth of figures may not be all that helpful.

Have a look at the graph in Figure 13.2, which shows the number of days members of the public had to wait for a service. At a quick glance it looks as if something is going wrong. You would certainly think that if you only had figures for October to December.

Now look at the graph for the previous three years (see Figure 13.3). This puts a different light on the matter. You can now see a pattern. There is a seasonal element, with figures going up in the winter months which could bear investigation, but you can see that there has been an overall improvement over the four-year period. There is another basic point worth noting. Make sure you look carefully at how the data is presented because it can be shown in ways that are misleading, such as making some category sizes larger than others. An example of this would be when looking at data by age, when some age categories are larger than others

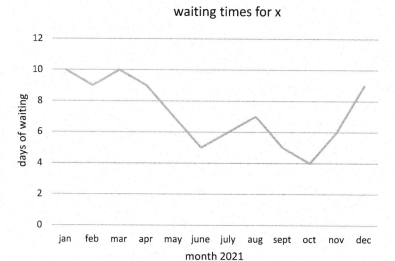

Figure 13.2 Waiting times graph.

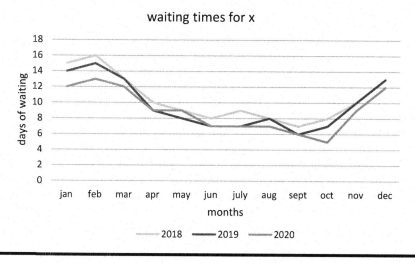

Figure 13.3 Waiting times graph with multiple years.

[31–40] [41–55] [56–69] [70+]. It may look obvious, but it does happen – perhaps for good reason sometimes – but be aware because it may be done so information paints a certain picture.

One of the reactions to be avoided is the knee-jerk reaction. You may be familiar with this. Something happens and everyone immediately jumps to conclusions and demands action to ensure it doesn't happen again. It is a gut reaction in response to a stimulus and is perhaps a survival mechanism. But knee-jerk reactions can seriously damage the effectiveness of an organisation because they usually result in change. Now some change is good, but if it becomes constant, and if changes are introduced in response to one event without considering impact on other activities, then there is a problem. Occasionally, of course, there are Political considerations. The public may expect to see a change in the law, for example, but it is essential to base decisions on evidence and fact where it can be established.

One tool for helping to identify whether an event is a one-off or something that needs to be looked at carefully is statistical process control (SPC) and there is software that will produce SPC charts for you. In every activity or process, there will be unexpected events. Say I commute to work by car and the journey normally takes 30 min. On a couple of days a week, I catch red lights and that adds 5 min to my journey so it takes 35 min. On Fridays, quite a few people work from home so there is less traffic and it takes me 25 min. As I don't want to be late, I normally set out 40 min before I am due to start work to allow time for a short delay, which means I don't have to worry about being late. However, once or twice a year, there may be an accident and my journey time takes an hour or more. I don't alter my schedule to set out an hour before my start time as a result of one or two accidents because I know they are the exceptions.

SPC charts use graphical representation to show natural variation in the data and separate *common* causes (such as the traffic lights) from *special* causes (such as the accidents). They also show when the whole process is beginning to shift. In my travel example, you would be able to see if my journey time is beginning to increase over time, perhaps because there is more traffic on the road.

Producing a chart is relatively simple, you plot the performance you are measuring on a graph in order of occurrence. When you have 10–12 points it is useful to calculate the average performance and plot this through the data. You can then calculate the upper and lower control limits which represent the upper and lower limits of normal variation that you would expect from the data you have collected. If in the future a data point falls outside the upper or lower limits, it is a special cause. SPS enables you to spend time examining the special cause events rather than looking at everything in detail. It also provides evidence of when something is, in fact part of a natural variation and when there is something out of the ordinary.

Here is an example showing the number of thefts reported in x district (Figure 13.4). All thefts will need to be investigated, but you may want to pay special attention to the month of September because it is touching the upper control limit (although not exceeding it).

A process will normally remain relatively stable if there is no intervention, but, of course the aim is always to improve things. You can use graphs and SPC charts to show how well a change has become embedded. Have a look at the example below in Figure 13. 5, which shows what happened when consultants came in to introduce new working practices in order to reduce waiting times.

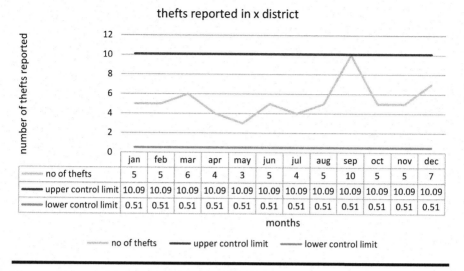

Figure 13.4 Graph of reported thefts for the year.

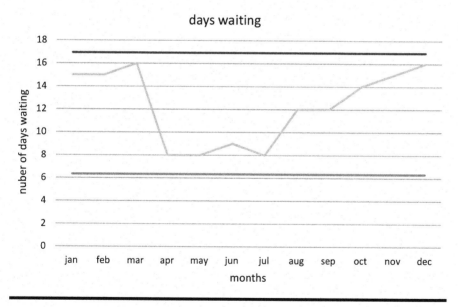

Figure 13.5 Graph of waiting times in days.

The new system was introduced in April and waiting time fell dramatically. However, they began to rise again when the consultants departed in August and people went back to their old ways of working.

Software will produce an SPC chart for you, but it is relatively easy to produce one for yourself. Here is a chart showing the number of trains late each month (Table 13.1).

Table 13.1 Table of late trains

Month	No. of late trains	Variance
Mar	15	
Apr	17	2
May	16	1
Jun	16	0
July	18	2
Aug	35	17
Sep	15	20
Oct	16	1
Nov	18	2
Dec	19	1
Total	185	46
Mean	18.5	5.1

List the number of late trains each month and then the variance between each month.

Calculate the mean from the number of late trains each month. In this case, it is 185/10 =18.5.

Calculate the mean for the variance 46/9 = 5.1.

Multiply the mean of the variance by 2.66 (2.66 is the constant used to calculate control limits (for statisticians the 3 sigma limit). In this case, it will be 5.1 × 2.66 = 13.6.

Calculate the upper control limit by adding 13.88 to the mean of late trains. In this case, 18.5 + 13.6 = 32.1.

Calculate the lower control limit by subtracting 13.88 from the mean. In this case, 18.5 – 13.6 = 4.9.

As you can see from Figure 13.6, there was just one month (August) in which there was an exceptional number of late trains.

SPC highlights anomalies which should be investigated. If you see something that looks strange in the data, it is always worth digging deeper as this lovely little anecdote shows. A supermarket manager was astonished to see an enormous number of chocolate eggs had been sold over a two-week period. It was beyond anything she had seen in her career. The temptation may have been to ask for additional stocks in order to keep up with the huge increase in demand, but before

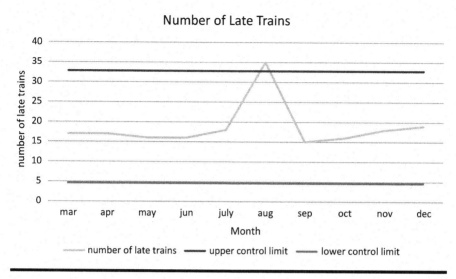

Figure 13.6 Graph of late trains.

doing this she decided to check out the chocolate egg phenomenon by talking to till operators. She discovered they regularly scanned the barcode on chocolate egg boxes when the barcode on another product was unreadable, which happened quite often.

Models and the use of models

Jocelyn Bell, the famous astrophysicist tells the story of how as a young researcher she made an impression. She noticed that eminent visiting speakers at the university always started their talks by stating their assumptions, before going on to talk about how these could be developed and then finishing with their enlightening conclusions. She made her mark by focusing on the assumptions on which the whole talk was based by asking what if these assumptions didn't hold. The answer of course was that the rest of the argument didn't hold either.

We tell this story because this is exactly how models work. They may be Black Boxes to all but the cognoscenti, but the predictions they deliver are based on a set of assumptions. If those assumptions are wrong, the model won't be very useful.

What is a model? A model is a way of projecting possible outcomes. The idea behind having a model is to help you better understand the world.

There are many different types of models. Some of the simplest are small replicas of the full-sized object. So, you will find architectural models – miniatures of the real building – that enable you to better visualise what the final structure will look like. However, more recent 3D goggles and digital technology have taken this type of modelling to a completely new level. At the simpler end you can now get a 3D picture of your new kitchen design, but at the more sophisticated end the software will allow you to walk around your new house before you build it. In both these examples the model allows you to see what the final product will look like so you can modify your design to ensure it meets your needs.

The ideas and components behind these architectural models are well understood as they are representations of a complicated but static reality. The models we develop and use in the public sector are fundamentally different. What you are trying to do with these models is to predict the future based on current information and trends. You may also want to model the interactions between independent actors represented in your model as this will help you to predict patterns of behaviours that cannot be foreseen by any other means. In essence you are taking information about what is happening today along with your best understanding of how people react to different stimuli and using this information through your model to predict what may happen in the future.

Here is an example of how this works in practice. Patrick Hoverstadt, our friend and Visiting Fellow at Cranfield, created a model of children's mental health provision for a local health authority. He turned this model into a simulation that could be used as a business game. The model has starting assumptions about how many children developed mental health issues and about the resourcing of the different mental health care providers. These health-care providers included different approaches from basic school pastoral support through counselling, psychiatric interventions to mental health hospital care. Further, he built into the model estimates of how successful each type of intervention was based on data from actual cases. This information also included best estimates of the consequences arising from timely interventions, delayed interventions, and the relative effectiveness of those interventions. At first sight, this may appear a relatively simple model but it allowed people to play with the relative resourcing between the different care channels and the results in a dynamic way.

Models can be very helpful in aiding decision-making and helping people to understand complex problems and, as a result, plan more effectively for the future, but they are not an answer in themselves. They are simply tools to be used. If you are the user of models, we suggest the following questions:

1. What are the main assumptions underpinning this model?
2. What are the main elements included in the model?
3. What are the key interactions between those elements?
4. What has been excluded from this model?
5. How confident are you in the interactions and assumptions being made?
6. How confident are you in the projections the model is predicting?

7. Given the predictions, in your judgement what is the model telling you and what actions are open as a result?
8. If the model assumptions are changed, can you simulate the effect of those actions?

By asking these questions you should be able to get a much clearer understanding of what the model is telling you and an idea of how helpful the model is to your decision-making process.

There appears to be a general belief that a model must be right. Models are never right or wrong. That is not the point of a model. They are just more or less useful, depending on the data available and the skill of those making the assumptions that go into them.

Asking questions

We have looked at statistical methods of establishing what the data mean, but nothing replaces the art of skilful questioning. This is not about asking questions for the sake of it. Many of us have been to meetings where we know one or two people will ask meaningless questions to show they have read a report or to make their own point. This is a mistake because insightful questions almost inevitably become lost amongst all the others or are never even asked. Insightful questions come from looking at the evidence (the data usually), evaluating where it came from, considering whether anything is missing and asking what the implications are. The question should be designed to check understanding or to move the discussion on. We have been emphasising the importance of working together, gaining consensus, looking for common ground, and building on that. However, it is important that questions come from independent thought.

Here is an example of what can happen when enthusiasm for initiatives and policies leads to lack of scrutiny of evidence on what is actually taking place.

Some time ago, in an attempt to widen participation in education, the UK government set up an Individual Learning Accounts scheme, where the costs of appropriate courses were subsidised. Most people liked the idea of the scheme and it was highly popular amongst politicians. Unfortunately, to quote the National Audit Office Report: "...the speed with which the Department implemented the scheme resulted in corners being cut." The Individual Learning Accounts scheme seemed, initially, to be successful and around 2.6 million accounts were opened with expenditure amounting to some £273 million against a budget of £199 million. But many of these blossoming numbers were the result of fraudulent claims. According to the National Audit Office, the Department "failed to monitor closely enough the escalating demand for accounts." Ultimately, the scheme had to be closed down but not before there was considerable loss of public money.

If an idea is a good one, it is easy to take good performance at face value, to be carried away with enthusiasm and not to look out for warning signs. Ensure you review real progress and not just activity.

What makes a performance measurement system successful?

Much of what we have described above relates to an individual organisation or initiative. You can easily adapt the processes and tools to suit your own school, prison, and job centre. However, you can adapt them equally well to work across several institutions. There are two factors which make for a successful measurement process. The first is how you implement it and the second is how you use it.

In terms of implementation, most organisations will already have some type of system in place, so you are probably talking about adjusting and improving what you already have. To be successful you need a clear purpose (one of those "what's it for" questions) and must make sure everyone, including your stakeholders, understand that purpose. Is the system in place as an aid to assessing the current level of performance, identifying and making improvements, and checking they are delivering benefits, or is it there to demonstrate good work, or even to show up bad results? Perhaps, it is there to provide information on which external stakeholders can make a decision? School league tables are an example of results of measurement that have the function of providing comparisons on which parents can make decisions about which school they want their child to go to, and also provide an element of competition as comparisons are open for all to see.

There is a difficulty in combining some of these purposes. It is well documented that some schools, for example, have tried to "off-roll" difficult or low achieving pupils so their exam results look better, "gaming" the system. In essence they are moving a problem somewhere else so, in the overall scheme of things, it may show the school in a better light but may not be effective for society as a whole. There are conflicting accounts of the usefulness of school league tables. Some show the motivation to do better that comes with seeing your results are lower than other schools' and that is important. But there are also reports of "gaming" we mentioned above, and of lack of motivation where teachers feel they can do little more because their catchment area is one of deprivation and their position in the league table will not easily be improved. Whilst measurement can be worked out with a formula, behaviour is not predictable, so it is important to consider whether the effect is likely to promote positive behaviour or cause desperation. Perhaps it would be better to focus on the level of achievement of pupils given the different environments in which schools are operating. In a sense that is measuring value added rather than absolute numbers.

You also need to be clear what you want people to concentrate their efforts on. Continuing with the education example, we heard one comment that teachers in one or two schools in an area could not understand why another school consistently had higher Ofsted results. They came to the conclusion that it was because the school examined in detail what Ofsted was looking for and focussed heavily on that. That may or may not have been appropriate, but it is an example of the importance of selecting very carefully what you are going to measure.

Here is another example, this time from Higher Education, of the difficulty of making comparisons. There have, from time to time, been discussions about creating league tables of universities based on the salaries of their alumni. League tables are based on factors that matter most and there is a question here about whether that means matter to society as a whole or to the individual and how these two interact. If you set salary level as the most important factor, what signal does that give about what society values? If a government invests tax payers' money in Higher Education it is important to see a return, but should that be entirely a financial return, or should it also include a measure of the contribution to society made by the alumni of that institution? Contribution to society is hard to measure, of course. How do you evaluate the contribution made by a CEO of a charity with that of a manufacturing director? We would argue that focussing on salary attainment is like focussing entirely on the finance box in the balanced scorecard and ignoring all the other boxes which are equally important. If finance were to be the only measure or even the predominant one, we may find a country full of investment bankers. Investment bankers are important, but no-one would argue that teachers, artists, musicians, and writers don't add something very important to the richness of our lives. What you need is a balance.

So, what is the answer? Needless to say there isn't a magic bullet, but there are some guidelines for how you set up and implement your system. The first is to understand what the purpose of your measurement system is. If it is multipurpose, think carefully whether those purposes can be aligned or whether they may cause negative outcomes. The second is to consider whether the factors you choose to measure are the most important (because that is where effort will be directed) and whether the way in which you measure them takes account of the contexts in which different organisations operate.

How you use your system should be aligned to its purpose. If you want to improve standards, then ensure the results are presented in a way that will motivate people to improve rather than dispirit them. That does not mean hiding figures, it means finding figures that show improvement, if there is any, rather than just showing someone is bottom of the class all the time. If you want to use results so individuals can make a decision, consider the factors that are important within that decision. For some parents, exam results will be highly important when deciding which school is best for their child, but for others, safety and pastoral care may be equally or more important. It should go without saying that results must be simple and clear. Those reading them should be able to understand what they are designed to show without being submerged in a welter of detail.

The final point to make here is that any measurement system must be up to date. It shouldn't change all the time, but it must reflect changes in strategy and also in the environment in which it functions, and the values prized by society. To take a simple example, many organisations now measure their sustainability and their equality and diversity credentials whereas a few years ago these factors would not have been on their radar.

Rewarding performance

It is much easier to understand and to design schemes for rewarding good performance in the private sector than it is for the public sector. Most private sector organisations have clear-cut goals which can be easily measured, whereas in the public sector, goals are less clear-cut, and harder to measure. Good performance is often rewarded at institutional level by allowing extra freedoms or more budget and bad performance is handled by removing budget or essentially "shaming" institutions by making public any deficits in performance.

One example of this was to be found in England where, some time ago, there was a scheme whereby hospitals were rated according to a star system, based on their performance against targets. Those which did not meet their targets were given zero stars and managers faced the threat of losing their jobs. Those meeting their targets were awarded three stars and given more autonomy. But you have to be careful what you choose to measure in order to award stars. If you were to choose slightly different factors you would be likely to get a very different result.

People will focus on factors against which they will be measured. Here is an example which illustrates the point well. Some time ago, a British Prime Minister was taken aback when a questioner commented that it was hard to get a GP appointment. He claimed it was because GPs had been set a target of 100% of patients to be offered appointments within two days. This led many GPs to refuse to book appointments more than two days in advance.

Some organisations in the private sector have used the tactic of shaming lower-performing individuals in public, although, thankfully, this is less common now. The theory was that making an example of lower performers would drive others to achieve better results. One illustration of this is companies who put up a list of salespeople, ranking them by value of contracts won, with those at the bottom of the list in red. Quite apart from generating unnecessary stress, this tactic did not necessarily have the desired effect. If a salesperson feared they were about to have a fallow month, they would spend their time chasing up smaller contracts where decisions would be made more quickly, rather than focussing on the longer and more profitable contracts which took more time to negotiate. They would also give more discounts which, again, led to a less profitable outcome.

Rewarding good practice or shaming bad practice in the way described above can have seriously adverse consequences. Far from encouraging institutions to be more effective it can encourage behaviours which make them less effective as people search for ways to avoid missing targets or even to meet targets that are inappropriate.

At an individual level there is little rewarding of good performance, although we understand from our interviews that many people fear repercussions when something goes wrong. This in effect is rewarding people for not taking risks and it leads to a culture where everyone tries to maintain the status quo. We will deal with that in more detail in the section below.

There is no easy answer to the question of how you reward good behaviour, but there are some factors that should be taken into account. The first point to consider is why people have chosen to work in the public sector. One key reason is that they want to make a difference to society. They want to be in a position where they have a purpose they believe in and can also earn a living. Contrary to common belief, money is not the greatest motivator once you have enough to live on. In an article in HBR, Dr Andrew Chamberlain (2019), Chief Economist from Glassdoor examines some of the driving forces behind job seekers' decisions and what matters to them at work. Interestingly pay does not come top of the list and that is true across all income levels. Culture and values of the organisation are at the top, followed by quality of senior leadership and career opportunities. We have already mentioned the research (Grant & Williams, 2019) showing public sector employees see a need for improvement in leadership capability, so here is both an opportunity and a threat. Improvements in management and leadership combined with the obvious public service element should make the public sector a very attractive option for careers, despite not offering the highest salaries and rewards. Being in an organisation where you feel you are doing good work which others appreciate and where you have the opportunity to develop and learn new things is rewarding in itself. Money does play a part – people must believe they are rewarded fairly for their work, otherwise they begin to feel exploited – but good leadership and values are also highly important.

Let us look at this from another perspective. You can view your work as a transaction, where you perform tasks and in return are paid for what you do. Alternatively, you can view your work as a partnership with your employer. In this case you are deeply involved in achieving a good end result and receive a fair rate of pay for doing that. The second, partnership view, is, in most cases, more satisfactory for both sides and has more intrinsic rewards. But to achieve it, the employer must regard employees as trusted partners in the organisation, and employees must take responsibility and act as if they are in partnership.

But how do you manage bad or average performance? There are well established approaches to dealing with bad performance, whether at an institutional or individual level, beginning by establishing what is and isn't working, identifying how improvements can be made, implementing those improvements, and providing support to make sure they happen. If Performance Improvement plans fail, then individuals either have to be moved to a more suitable role or managed out of the organisation.

Many approaches exist for dealing with average performance, such as providing training or mentoring where necessary. There are other ways, too. We know of an organisation where the manager of a department felt the performance of her team was reasonable but not quite at the right level. Things ticked along without too many problems but with no real improvement and no energy to look for new ideas. Reflecting on this and on what she might do, the manager realised many of the team had worked in the same type of job, if not the same organisation, for many years. They had become rather complacent and had no idea what the outside world looked like. To remedy this, she arranged for a group of staff to visit two completely different companies where there were similarities in roles. Following the visits, there was a great deal of discussion amongst staff about what was good and what was bad, about what they liked and what they didn't. Individuals could see for themselves what levels of performance were expected elsewhere and how other people tackled similar problems. This gave them a new perspective on their jobs and there were indeed improvements in performance.

Let us turn to the question of how you view risk-taking. What does good performance look like? Is it about keeping everything on track without any ripples or it is about taking calculated risks on occasions to create improvements? As it stands, from the people we have spoken to, it is the former. No-one wants to take any risks. So, it would be a step in the right direction to create a culture in which mistakes are seen as points of learning, providing of course, they don't happen all the time. Mike likes to say: "If you want success, you must be able to tolerate failure." As a leader you have to accept that if you want people to take risks, those risks won't always pay off.

The starting point for thinking about individual performance, motivation and reward is to create a picture showing what good performance looks like and ensuring everyone understands it. Start by making sure people understand the purpose of their work and the outcomes expected. You can then paint in some of the other factors – but not all because those doing the job are likely to know how to do it far it better than you. One factor you can paint in, however, is attitude to risk. In some cases, the risks may be so great it would be totally inappropriate to have much tolerance at all, but in others it will matter far less, and you can use the opportunity to develop and test out new ideas. If you are able to set some limits and allow people to operate within them, you will encourage new ideas as well as making the work more interesting.

Research shows that training and development is valued by employees and rewarding an individual by investing in their development is beneficial for both the employee and the employer. We know one or two organisations, mostly in the private sector, who reward people by sending them on a "one day jolly," but that has minimal lasting impact in terms of reward and motivation. Although one day courses can be very helpful for specific purposes, such as providing inputs of knowledge, you need to allocate more time to gain real benefit. The reward element starts when you pay attention to the individual, show them you value them by giving them your time, when you discuss their career ambitions and talk to them about what they feel they need in terms of development and what they would like to do.

One of the problems mentioned frequently during conversations with people working in the public sector (and particularly in the civil service) is that of staff turnover. This is a well-known issue. An individual does well in a job and then rapidly moves on to another role in another department or even to an outside organisation in order to get a pay rise or to increase their seniority. That means expertise is built up and then quickly lost to a department, and this is in addition to the upheaval of getting used to working with new people and, in some cases, the costs of recruiting. The Institute for Government explores the problem in some detail including the costs associated with it, in the report, *Moving on: the costs of high staff turnover in the Civil Service* (Sasse & Emma Norris, 2019). They propose reforms including pay progression linked to capability or performance and reward for building up depth of knowledge and experience. It is not the purpose of this book to propose policies for pay and promotion, but, for an organisation to be effective, employees must believe they are valued and rewarded reasonably for their work, their good performance and for their expertise. If talented individuals have to move to another role or even outside the organisation in order to get a pay rise it is neither efficient nor effective.

Whatever the detail of the reward system, there are some guiding principles. The first is to know what good performance looks like in different circumstances, because without this you cannot know what you should be rewarding. Do you need people to build deeper subject knowledge in a particular role? Do you need people who are willing to be more innovative, perhaps? The second is to ensure reward is congruent with the factors you are measuring in your performance measurement system and aligned to what is needed to achieve your overall purpose. The final point is to get to know people as individuals. Good leaders understand what motivates their key people.

Encouraging people to take risks

This sometimes feels like an intractable problem. On one hand leaders want to see new ideas, progress, and leaps in performance. On the other hand, individuals fear taking too much initiative or too much risk in case something goes wrong, and they have to take the blame. This fear is not unfounded. We live in an environment where we look for holes. We look for perfection where none is possible. Instead of celebrating a great achievement, we tend to look immediately at the details and point out what could have been done better. Of course, the truth is we need to do both. We need to celebrate the great achievement AND, at some stage, look at what could have been done better and learn from it. What matters is how the "hole picking" exercise is done. More about that later, first, let's construct a scenario.

The picture looks like this. The boss wants a solution to *x* problem but does not fully understand how complex that solution will have to be to achieve an effective outcome. However, those tasked with devising and implementing the solution do realise its complexity. In some cases, they look for a less-complicated answer to the problem that may suffice but may not fully rectify it, because that route is less risky. In other cases, they bring forward the ideal solution and point out complexities and inherent risks. The boss must now choose which approach to take. One answer is not ideal because it only partially solves the problem, the other may solve the problem in its entirety but things may go wrong. There is an initial assessment of benefits and risks which should make the decision easier. However, if the ideal solution still looks possible, there are other risks to be taken into account – the risks to personal reputation and career progression if all does not go according to plan. If the individuals in the scenario above work in an environment which is confrontational, in which blame is allocated and new ideas subject to minute scrutiny, the less risky solution will seem more attractive. If, on the other hand they work in an environment where people recognise that mistakes can happen and certainty rarely exists, where the atmosphere is supportive rather than adversarial then the more risky but better solution is more likely to be seen as the better option.

So, if you want people to try out new ideas and take risks then you must create the type of environment in which the downsides are not so great. An organisation in which there is no change or improvement is a stagnant one. Many people will be familiar with the type of organisation where there is plenty of activity but little progress because no one wants to make a decision. Meetings and consultations abound, there are amendments to the original idea, delays whilst more data and evidence is gathered and in the end, what was once potentially a good idea fizzles out in a welter of bureaucracy.

How can you learn from what went wrong without appearing to hole-pick? Much of what we said in the section about performance reviews applies here. The first step is to ensure the review is unbiased and impersonal and that everyone feels free to speak without being defensive. Think "discussion and collective responsibility" rather than "interrogation and sentence." If you concentrate on answering a question (e.g. What can we learn from the factors leading to low take-up of…? rather than, Why was the take up for … so low?)) before launching into the detail or apportioning blame, you focus minds on the learning aspects and in such an environment, it becomes possible to ask some challenging questions without making people clam up.

References

Bourne, M. (2004) "The performance planning value chain," Chapter D8, in *The hand book of performance measurement* (Mike Bourne editor), Gee Publishing, London, UK.

Chamberlain, A. (2017) "What matters more to your workforce than money," *Harvard Business Review*, January.

Grant, K. & Williams, R. (2019) "Leadership in the UK public sector: a renewed call to action," *Reflections on Leadership and People Practice Series*, 1, No. 2, December, https://www.napier.ac.uk/~/media/worktribe/output-2376960/leadership-in-the-public-sector-a-renewed-call-to-action.pdf

Sasse, T. & Emma Norris, E. (2019) *Moving on: the high cost of staff turnover in the civil service*, Institute for Government, London, IfG_staff_turnover_WEB.pdf (instituteforgovernment.org.uk)

Chapter 14

Governance

Governance provides the framework, the systems, and processes for how an organisation is run. It sets out who has the authority to make decisions and who is accountable and is, in essence, about the way the organisation is directed and controlled. It has been referred to as being *"....about the relationships between the board, management and shareholders to set company objectives and monitor performance"* Kelly (2010). Another definition is that *"Governance provides the structure through which objectives are set and performance monitored"* Kelly (2010).

But governance is not always organisation-wide, it is also about governing projects or even controlling change initiatives. The Association for Project Management defined governance in their 2019 Body of Knowledge as follows: "Governance refers to the set of policies, regulations, functions, processes, procedures and responsibilities that define the establishment, management and control of projects, programmes and portfolios."

Governance is an all-encompassing concept which has a significant impact on how effectively the organisation operates and on what can and cannot be done. Without good governance, an organisation lays itself open to risk and lack of transparency. It can also lead to people being uncertain about where their responsibilities lie, which in turn can result in delays in decisions being taken. A good governance structure is there to provide guidance and clarity. It is not there to generate bureaucracy and build hoops for people to jump through or build delays into everyday working. Governance processes must be carefully constructed to allow people freedom to operate without the chaos that results when everyone moves in different directions and nothing is achieved.

The public sector is responsible for some of the very biggest changes to the way people live and the biggest projects, so at the start of this chapter, we will focus on governance in the context of change initiatives and projects, with the intention of

DOI: 10.4324/9781003099895-17

teasing out how to structure objective setting and control when trying to deliver effective outcomes. Later in the chapter, we will discuss governance in the context of everyday operations. Let us start with some background.

Background to governance of change and projects

We will look at three aspects of a change initiative: delivery, implementation, and the ensuing results. These may seem a little artificial, but it is important to distinguish between these stages when talking about governance.

Delivery is about creating the outputs of the change. These outputs could be a new computer system, a new piece of infrastructure, such as a road, or a new operating procedure. Basically, they are the tangible elements that the change team creates.

Implementation is about how the change initiative modifies what people are doing or how they are doing it. So, using the examples above, implementation in those cases would be about how the new computer system is operated and used; how the infrastructure is used and how it changes the environment in which people live, and how the new operating procedure changes workflows and how people take actions.

Results are the outcomes and benefits achieved. Here we are defining outcomes as all the ultimate changes that occur as a result of the initiative (including both positive and the negative aspects), whilst benefits are the value added by undertaking the change initiative.

You can also talk about the efficiency and the effectiveness of a change. In the language of projects, efficiency is delivering the project scope within the time and cost set at the outset. These three elements are often called the "iron triangle," a terminology that strongly suggests that the three constraints should not be broken. Whereas, effectiveness, focuses on whether or not the project delivered the outcomes and benefits envisaged. In the world of public-sector projects, this idea of effectiveness is further complicated by the fact there are multiple stakeholders all with slightly different requirements in terms of the outcomes they anticipate being delivered. As the old adage says: "Beauty is in the eye of the beholder."

Phases of change

In Chapter 9 when discussing theories of change, we discussed Lewin's (1951) three phases, unfreezing, moving, and refreezing. In this chapter on governance, we want to be more focused on the process of change, from planning, through making the change itself, to embedding new ways of working into business as usual. We will look in a little more detail at each of these three phases.

The planning phase usually refers to the period of time between the idea for the change and the formal business case approval. Approval of the business case is the point at which funding and resources are agreed and the change initiative is given the go-ahead. There can be a difficulty right at the start, because ideas often emerge well before formal policy discussions. An idea may have its roots in a party manifesto. As a consequence, it can be fairly well developed before anyone has thought about how that idea and the change that accompanies it can be delivered in practice. As you can see, an idea can have travelled a long way before it is formally captured by the governance process. This can create a problem as a political party new to government will, understandably, be keen to put their ideas into practice. The governance process on the other hand, will be requiring them to step back and reconsider the whole idea from the perspective of how the change is to be implemented and whether, indeed, it is viable.

Even within the planning phase there are subphases that need to be worked through. These should include:

1. Policy alignment – does the intended change align well with the policy agenda and how does it support or hinder other policy objectives being considered? In central government, other policy objectives will naturally include those in the department sponsoring the change, but it should also include related initiatives right across government. In local government the questions are slightly different. The interface between the different departments should be considered, as well as how the policy aligns with partnerships (such as working with the police or health bodies for example) and how it aligns with the aims of central government.

2. Feasibility – is the idea deliverable at all? What are the initial estimates of time, costs, and benefits? At this early stage, the best way of calculating these items is often not to work them out from the bottom up, but to look at completed projects and change initiatives that have attempted to do similar things. These can frequently provide the best guide.

3. Initial appraisal – once feasibility has been established, this is the subphase where the initial costs, time scales, and benefits are calculated at some level of detail. If these estimates differ significantly from the figures suggested by the feasibility subphase, it is important to understand the causes of these differences and to analyse them carefully. It is not unusual for change initiatives to be subject to "optimism bias" in the early stages which is why the total costs of previously completed projects are often a good guide. At the outset of a new initiative, most people are keen for the ideas to go ahead and succeed and those enthusiastically producing bottom-up calculations may underestimate the complexity of what has to be delivered.

4. Alternatives – there are alternative ways of delivering nearly every change initiative. This is the subphase where these alternatives are identified and compared. People often get fixated on one approach, so it is important that alternatives are properly considered and reviewed. A project plan that doesn't contain a review of alternatives should be rejected.

5. Business case – having identified and considered alternatives, this is the point at which the formal business case should be created in order that the decision to proceed or not can be made. The level of planning here needs to be appropriate for the type of change being envisaged. It should be at a level of detail that allows a judgement to be made. How likely it is it that the change will be successful in delivering the outcomes envisaged? It should clearly state the level of confidence in the estimates provided and an assessment of the outstanding risks.

The second of Lewin's three phases is *moving*, which in this context is execution of the project. This is the phase between the approval of the business case and the handover of the project or change initiative to those who are going to operate with it in the new environment. Whilst this is frequently where most project management effort is expended; it is also the stage at which many of the critical decisions will already have been made. In a sense, the course has been set and, if there is no flexibility built into the process, the fate of the change will already have been determined.

The third of Lewin's three phases of change is *refreezing*. This is the operating phase after the handover from the project or change team to those who are responsible for business as usual. It is in this last phase that the benefits are accrued, so it is essential that those responsible for overseeing the change continue to follow what is happening. It is all too easy in some types of change to slip back into old ways of working because these are comfortable. It is rather like eschewing your smart new pair of shoes for the old comfortable pair that have become moulded to the shape of your feet. Hence Lewin's idea of *refreezing*.

Types of project

In Chapter 7, we discussed different types of change. In particular, we discussed the known knowns, the known unknowns and the unknown unknowns. We also presented Obeng's framework which differentiated between simple projects, sometimes called Painting by Numbers and News Bulletins, and more complex projects, sometimes referred to as Going on a Quest or Walking in Fog. In this chapter, on governance we are going to simplify these assumptions slightly using the two categories proposed by Bourne and Parr (2019). They suggested differentiating between fixed goal and moving goal changes.

In the fixed goal case, the goal the change is designed to deliver is well understood and it is not expected to alter significantly over the course of the initiative. In terms of Obeng's framework, Painting by Numbers and News Bulletin projects typically fall into this category because you know what you know, and you know what you don't know.

In the moving goal case, everything is far less certain. The ultimate goal of the change may be vaguely defined or may not even be fully understood. In moving goal situations, it is also likely that the ultimate goal will alter as the change progresses. It may only begin to emerge as broader understanding and consensus develops.

The reason we are highlighting these differences here, is that these two types of changes should be governed differently. Trying to govern a *moving goal* change using a *fixed goal* framework will result in frustration, as each time something emerges or becomes better understood, the governance framework will require a new set of plans and a recalibration of the initiative. On the other hand, trying to manage *fixed goal* changes using a *moving goal* governance framework will result in waste, because it will allow people delivering the project to explore alternatives when the plan has already been agreed and the delivery path clearly identified.

In the next section, we will combine the three different phases of a change, as outlined by Lewin, with the two different types of change (fixed goal and moving goal) to create a governance framework across the change lifecycle. We have set out a list of questions you should ask at each phase to help ensure good governance of your processes. The material we are presenting here has been drawn from research sponsored by the APM (Association for Project Management) and published in 2019 (Bourne & Parr, 2019).

Governance focus

Planning – from concept to business case approval

This phase of a project covers feasibility, initial appraisal, selection of an approach, and definition of timescales, costs, and benefits.

The governance questions we suggest you ask are as follows:

■ Are appropriate leadership and oversight practices in place?

■ How good a fit is the proposed project approach and outcomes with government and departmental policy?

■ Has the feasibility study been completed to an appropriate level of detail and has it been informed by individuals with the requisite expertise?

■ Has a soft analysis (that is asking qualitative questions rather than just asking about the numbers) been undertaken and informed by individuals with the requisite expertise?

■ Has a determination been made on whether the project should be classified as having fixed or moving goals and was that determination informed by individuals with the requisite expertise?

■ Has the identification of risks been done satisfactorily and has this work been informed by individuals with the appropriate expertise?

- Have alternative delivery approaches been suitably identified and evaluated and has this work been informed by individuals with the appropriate expertise?
- Has the identification of the preferred approach been justified satisfactorily and has this work been informed by individuals with the appropriate expertise?
- Have stakeholder benefits been identified and have stakeholders been appropriately consulted over the approach and the expected benefits?
- Is the business case complete and, if so, is it appropriate for the type of project being proposed?

If the change project progresses through the sub-phases outlined above, you should ask the following questions at each of those subphases:

- Is this particular change project still relevant and is it really needed?
- Can the project still be justified in terms of the latest assessment of timescales, costs, and benefits?
- Is this the right time to progress the project given competing priorities for resources and availability of high-level oversight and attention?
- Are the resources available and in place to proceed?

An appropriate business case is one that matches the type of project being considered. Therefore, you would expect that fixed goal projects would have different business cases from moving goal projects. With fixed goal change projects, the focus should be on:

- Producing detailed business plans with scheduling and costing,
- Identifying risks and how they can be mitigated,
- Unearthing any uncertainties and providing range estimates of the likelihood of them occurring, and
- Defining what the future state will look like when the project has been completed and setting out clear measures of success.

For moving goal change projects, the focus should be on:

- Producing a broad business plan with ranges of timescales and costings,
- Identifying risks with potential risk mitigation strategies where appropriate,
- Unearthing uncertainties with range estimates,
- Setting out possible unknowns; identifying the activities needed to find out what they are and then teasing out possible solutions and testing them out,
- Agreeing predefined criteria for halting the change project and initiating independent review before continuation or abandonment,
- Describing phased delivery paths, possibly with intermediate deliverables and review points, and
- Describing the intended future state with indicators of success.

Change execution – from approval to operation

The phase that stretches between the approval of the business case and operations is the main execution or delivery phase of a change project. Traditionally, the emphasis here is on project delivery, issues such as ensuring cost control and managing timescales, but it is a mistake not to include the broader issues, too, keeping the end in mind. These are the activities required to ensure the implementation is successful and, very importantly, that you achieve the outcomes and benefits you expect. During this phase, we suggest you ask some broad governance questions for both types of change, asking whether the appropriate leadership and oversight practices are in place for:

- Project delivery,
- Project implementation, and
- Delivering outcomes and benefits.

Looking at the requirements for fixed goal projects, the focus of the questions should be along the following lines:

- Are the risks being identified and managed appropriately?
- Are the uncertainties being reduced?
- Is the project being delivered (being carried out) efficiently?
- Is the project implementation being delivered effectively?
- Are the intermediate deliverables being implemented and used effectively and are they resulting in the benefits you expected?
- Can you still deliver the outcomes and benefits you planned originally?

However, for a moving goal change project, the requirements are different, and you should focus on the following questions:

- Does the change project still have clarity of purpose?
- Are people still keeping the outcomes and benefits in mind?
- Are the intermediate deliverables being implemented and are they used effectively; are they resulting in the benefits you expected?
- Do you have effective activities in place to identify what you don't know and to test and review possible solutions?
- Are the risks being identified and managed appropriately?
- Are the uncertainties being reduced?
- Is the change project implementation being delivered effectively?
- Is the change project delivery being managed well?

Operate

The operate phase occurs after the change project has been handed over to the operating department. In this phase, the focus is on encouraging use of the new product or service and ensuring it is used as intended. It is essentially about gaining benefit from the change that has taken place. At this stage, you should also consider how to evaluate the outcomes and benefits, understanding how they were achieved as well as learning lessons from the change journey. If you do this and you record what you have discovered, everyone will be better informed when you undertake any similar change project.

- Are the appropriate leadership and oversight practices in place for operation?
- Are the project outputs delivered in line with expectations?
- Was the handover conducted appropriately?
- Was the operating department prepared in advance for the project handover?
- Did the operating department embrace the project and aspire to realise the outcomes and benefits?
- Does the operating department have mechanisms in place to guide and track the continued delivery of benefits from this project?
- What was learnt during the delivery of the project?
- What was learnt during the implementation of the project?
- What were the unintended consequences arising from the project?
- What was learnt about the delivery of outcomes and benefits?
- With hindsight, was the project worthwhile, and if not, what should be learnt for the future?

There are more questions in the Theory of Change Chapter (Chapter 9) which you may find appropriate, depending on the type of project you are undertaking.

When undertaking a major project which, by its nature, is about change, it is easy to be single minded and ignore other peoples' opinions in order to make progress. Driving progress is essential and no-one wants to be bogged down in endless meetings and discussions, but it is important to recognise that there is more than one party involved in making any change successful. If you are to realise the outcomes and benefits you envisage, you need to ensure you have as much buy-in from your stakeholders as you can muster. We cannot stress this enough. So, the evaluation should consider not only the role of the change team, but also the role of the receiving operating unit and the reaction and influence of any other key stakeholders. You cannot deliver change without an effective change team and you will not be able to realise benefits without co-operation and support from users and key stakeholders. That partnership and handover is critical.

Success is only success when it is sustained. You want to ensure new services, products, or ways of working continue to be used or followed long after the change team has left. In cases where the project team hands over responsibility to users without also handing over a set of expected benefits which can be tracked, there is more likelihood that people will go back to their old ways. We recommend that governance and assurance mechanisms continue after the handover so the focus on outcomes and benefits is not lost.

Drawing again from the APM report (Bourne & Parr, 2019), we advise that fixed goal projects are reviewed differently to moving goal projects.

- Fixed goal projects should be evaluated on the delivery of benefits and also the efficiency of delivery.
- Moving goal projects should be evaluated on delivery and a final evaluation of outcomes for the costs incurred and efficiency noted.

For all change projects, the primary criterion for success is the delivery of benefits. If these are not delivered, the time, effort, and resource expended has been wasted. This should be blindingly obvious, but we still hear complaints from Project Directors that the Senior Responsible Owners of UK government projects are only interested in progress and not in the ultimate benefits. From our earlier project research, we understand this is true in other countries, too. Perhaps that is understandable because the benefits are often hard to measure, certainly harder to measure than progress and tangible factors such as cost and time, and they appear over a longer time period. For some projects, full benefits may not be realised for ten or more years and in that time most of those involved with the project will have moved on and there is no real will to go back and review outcomes. However, the fact remains: projects and change are undertaken to deliver benefits so you need a mechanism to provide assurance that those benefits are indeed being realised.

Fixed goal change projects are simpler to deliver than moving goal change projects. It should be easier to run these projects efficiently as there are fewer unknowns. If change projects have moving goals, then the solutions have to emerge or be discovered as work progresses. Under these circumstances the concept of efficiency is different. There will be some work that is carried out on discovering solutions that will end in a blind alley which is, of course, not efficient. Whilst you will not want to encounter too many blind alleys, if you do not encounter any, it may be because you have not searched well enough for the best solution. One senior project manager in the United States told us that if everything went strictly according to plan, that probably meant there was not enough stretch to achieve the best result. If efficiency is paramount in this type of project, then you are immediately imposing a straitjacket on those tasked with delivering benefits. We argue that efficiency should be noted, but the focus should be on whether money was wasted or not. When you carry out the evaluation, you should view the answer to this question not only with the benefit of hindsight, but also from the perspective of those running the project at the time they were making the decisions they took. Evaluating results with the benefit of hindsight is useful for future projects, but you shouldn't use hindsight to judge the performance of the project director and team. They could only work with the information and knowledge they had at the time.

A word about evaluating success

As we all know, very little in the world is clearly defined. There is little that is black and white and much that is grey. The same is true when evaluating success of projects, so it is worth taking a few moments to explore what it takes to adopt a mature perspective on the extent to which a change project has succeeded and what the implications are of taking a black and white approach to judging success.

Whilst there must always be the intention of realising benefits and creating value, not all projects will deliver benefits. In research and development for example, if all projects were to deliver results, it may reflect insufficient risk-taking in deciding which projects to pursue, thus restricting innovation and the advancement of knowledge.

With certain projects, it is impossible to determine whether the outcome was the result of the project itself. Take the example of defence: how can you tell whether the presence of a particular weapon or asset prevented a conflict? You can assume it may have played a part by deterring the enemy, but you cannot always know that absolutely. It is a judgement call, but that does not mean to say you should not go ahead. If your aircraft carrier is never tested in conflict, is that a good or a bad thing?

The other point to note when evaluating benefits is that in complex projects and change initiatives there are many variables and the extent to which benefits have been realised will depend on when you measure. Events such as recession or political change may affect the results significantly. Let's take a hypothetical example of building toll roads, where the decision to build was made on the basis of a particular set of economic conditions. Once the roads were built, the economy was hit by recession and fewer vehicles than expected used the roads which resulted in a lower income than had been predicted. That does not mean the project was a failure. Over time, when the economy improves, there are likely to be more vehicles and more income. With some projects, such as major IT systems, the rate at which users adapt to change is a major influence on when benefits will result. It is not always possible to know how long that will take.

It is, of course, very important to be honest about the outcomes because you need to be able to learn from them. To do that you need an evaluation team that understands the entire process, rather than relying on analysts who may only be able to compare results against the original criteria and context.

There is another dimension to this. Several interviewees (not in the United Kingdom) told us about the impact of the Political perspective on evaluating benefits. One person put it very clearly: "People always want to find something positive to say because they want to be associated with good news. If significant sums of money have been spent it, is important to demonstrate that value has been added." That is as may be, but it is essential not to confuse real outcomes with political "spin."

Governance of business as usual

We are going to illustrate governance of business as usual through two case studies. The first is a private sector energy distribution company located in the United Kingdom. The example is based on work conducted by Dr Veronica Martinez and Dr Michael Kennerley (2005) when they both worked in the Centre for Business Performance at Cranfield. The second example is from a division of a UK police force.

In many countries, energy distribution companies are in public ownership, but in the United Kingdom, this particular company is in the private sector, operating in a regulated market. The company had been created through the acquisition of three separate operating companies over a five-year period and at the time, employed some 11,000 people.

We are presenting this case for the following reasons. First, the company had a unique way of cascading their intent from divisional executive level right down to front line employees. Second, people in the organisation had a very clear understanding of what their roles were and how this differed by level of management. This informed the performance review meetings that created a highly effective way of communicating back up the organisation.

We will start by explaining how the company cascaded their direction of travel. The company's structure was fairly conventional, with a divisional board that oversaw three business units. These business units had functions, which oversaw the local operational teams. The process started with the divisional board, who created a plan for the next period. This plan was in the form of a success map with associated measures of success. Once the board had created and agreed their success map, they passed the map and measures down to the three business unit management teams. Those teams undertook the same process. Their plans were designed to support the wider goals of the organisation but also to reflect local priorities. Once completed, the business unit success maps and associated measures were cascaded again to the business functions. This process was repeated and the functional management created and passed on their success maps and measures to the operational teams. The final stage was the creation of the operational team success map and associated measures, which was used to manage local delivery.

What did this mean for both the organisation and those involved? It meant that at each level of the organisation there was a simple plan with associated success measures. These plans were created locally, so management at each level (and even front-line workers at the level of the operational teams) were all involved in the planning process. Their plans were guided by the success maps cascaded to them, but they had the opportunity to create their own plan and decide how they were going to support the objectives set by the level above. As we have said previously, this approach creates debate around how the plan is to be achieved, understanding of the plan and its priorities, and commitment to its implementation.

In practice, this meant the chief executive didn't have oversight of all the performance measures by business unit, function, or team across the organisation, because these measures of success were agreed at each level in light of the success maps. However, what it did mean was that if he walked into a local depot anywhere in the business, he could expect to see a success map on the wall and be able to have a conversation with anyone in the depot about what that success map meant and how the team was performing in relation to delivering the goals within that local success map. As one executive who was responsible for the division's performance and risk management put it: "Instead of getting agreement for 100% of my measures of success and '10% enthusiasm to implement them, I now have agreement for 90% of my measures of success with 100% enthusiasm to implement them."

You may think this generated a great deal of work, cascading the success map and measures from the most senior level to front-line operations in an organisation that employed 11,000 people. In fact, this process was done twice a year with the support of three and a half facilitators and over the years the company had been adopting this approach, the involvement had created a real understanding and capability to manage in this way.

Now let us turn to understanding the different roles at each level of the organisation, looking at how the emphasis changed at the different management levels. At the top level there were four simple points of focus and these were:

1. Focusing managers' attention on key objectives set by shareholders and regulators,
2. Empowering a culture of continuous improvement,
3. Creating a new set of firm's behaviours, including a positive attitude to failure and sharing best practices, and
4. Strengthening the firm's values including integrity, social responsibility, and excellent performance.

What we are seeing here is how the most senior managers are focusing on creating the environment in which others are enabled to perform. There is a focus on key objectives, but the other aspects are around creating a supportive culture, developing positive behaviour, and strengthening the values.

At the three business units, the focus changed to:

1. Supporting the achievement of key strategic objectives,
2. Encouraging friendly competition between business units,
3. Increasing directors' support and investment to implement operational changes and action plans,
4. Tracking the achievement of the regional unit strategies,
5. Feeding the firm's strategy, and
6. Celebrating success.

At this level we start to have a focus on performance, but the main emphasis is still on supporting others to play their part.

At the functional level, there is another change of emphasis. Here the focus is on:

1. Making people meet and discuss performance,
2. Improving analytical thinking skills together with expertise needed for generating and selecting improvement action plans,
3. Improving collaboration between functions,
4. Improving teamwork across functions,
5. Encouraging operational improvements, and
6. Improving process integration.

The emphasis is now on the management of performance though people and practices. The approach is through dialogue, development of analytical, and implementation skills whilst focusing on ensuring collaboration between the different functions delivering the business.

In many of the organisations we know, the performance management and governance process stops here. But in this company, the approach continues to the next level and so engages all the company's employees. Team performance briefing concentrates on:

1. Focusing people's attention on what is important to the company,
2. Improving employee knowledge and understanding of operations,
3. Building consensus for the development of new initiatives,
4. Creating an environment to support employees' acceptance of new projects,
5. Improving productivity,
6. Increasing a sense of achievement,
7. Improving problem solving capability,
8. Encouraging sharing of best practice,
9. Improving communication of performance across the business,
10. Supporting and feeding the business strategy,
11. Increasing employees' understanding of how their actions impact on the overall performance of the business,
12. Ensuring managers keep employees informed so they understand where the firm is going, and
13. Motivating employees by engaging them through taking part in decision making around new projects and action plans.

It is at this level in the organisation that the operational activities take place. The company engages all employees, not only in delivering services, but in the continuing development and improvement of these services. People at the operational level were supported by individual coaching to help them develop their sense of accountability whilst improving their skills and capabilities. Often individual coaching is only available to employees at managerial levels.

The development of this system of governance and performance management did not happen overnight, it took some time to develop the local leadership necessary for the approach to be successful. A collaborative approach to leadership created strong employee engagement both in delivery and decision-making. This is based on a belief that performance is better when people are engaged in the purpose of the organisation and have a say in their own future. But it also needs strong commitment from managers. Managers need to be vigilant to ensure the practices and principles are adhered to and there is no slipping of standards or loss of intensity of engagement.

Public sector example

Creating a governance structure that is effective requires a real understanding of how the organisation operates and how performance is delivered. One size doesn't fit all, you need to tailor your approach. Below we will give an example of an approach developed in policing, but we will start by describing the background and how the senior officers, led by Mick Stamper, envisioned what they wanted to achieve.

There is a wonderful phrase often used in the public sector and policing in particular; "getting a grip." Usually, it refers delivering the numbers because people think you have a grip if you know your numbers. However, Mick Stamper sees policing differently. As he sees it, the numbers are important, but you don't improve your numbers by focusing on them; performance is improved through appropriate activity. So, he started with the question, how do we ensure that our activities reduce crime and keep the public safe? To do this, he built a team of like-minded middle ranking officers and then set to work on being more responsive, providing clarity about how to operate and in engaging the hearts and minds of their whole team.

To be more responsive, they needed to delegate. Teams on the ground had to be able to respond 24 hours a day so decisions needed to be made as things happened and not as part of a scheduled meeting. This meant resources were directly controlled by the inspectors who would make decisions about deployment without having to refer that decision to a senior colleague. The result was that decisions were made faster and at the level where the leaders were close enough to the situation to make the right judgement calls. Empowering inspectors in this way certainly made them feel involved.

Clarity came from a different perspective on how performance improves. Nearly all police performance figures are backward looking; the number of crimes committed (yesterday, last week, in the previous month or over the year to date) or the number of arrests made (yesterday, last week and so on). You can't do anything about what has happened, you need to focus on what you can do now to stop it happening again. The approach taken was not to hold people to account for the numbers, but to hold them to account for their activity. What were they going to do to prevent crime, detect crime and keep the public safe? There was also the "all for one and one for all" rule. That meant you couldn't look good on your own. You wouldn't be recognised for performing well on your own patch if your neighbour wasn't and needed your help; the overall performance of the borough mattered more that individual performance.

Engagement was seen as the real driver of performance. How do we encourage the right behaviour? Mick Stamper talks about "Belly, Brain and Heart."

The belly is about fear, people are encouraged to do something, or often not to do something, because they fear the consequences. Fear is an extremely strong motivator, but rarely encourages the right response. People react instinctively, rather than taking a measured view of a situation. But control through "fear" is present in the public sector, either intentionally or unintentionally. Good leaders should work to root out fear.

The brain is about logic, it is about the rationale for doing something. We have talked a lot in this book about ensuring that people understand why they are doing what they are doing. Previous research from the Centre for Business Performance has linked the extent to which individuals understand their contribution to the organisation to the ultimate success of that organisation, (Bourne et al., 2007), but Mick Stamper's argument is that logic isn't enough.

The heart is about commitment, doing something because you want to, and you believe that this is the right thing to do. He argues that this is important for effective policing. There are really no formal ways of assessing whether an individual is performing to the best of their abilities or not. Every day, police constables exercise judgement: is something suspicious, or should they walk by? If you engage their heart and they want to do a good job for the force and the community they serve, that will guide their judgement and lead to better outcomes.

Fear is removed by creating clarity around what you expect police offers to do and then supporting them in doing it. If they work within the guidance and rules, they know they will have the support of their senior officers. If they go outside the guidance and rules, then they will still have support if that was the right thing to do based on the information they had at the time. Clearly, if they did something wrong, that would be dealt with, but clarity reduces fear. It took time to build a culture where that was understood and to develop a management style that ensured that happen, but the message did get through.

The logic was always to focus on ensuring activities were directed towards reducing crime and keeping the public safe. That was communicated widely and the question constantly asked, "what are you doing today to prevent crime, detect crime and keep the public safe?" This kind of interaction focuses effort and encourages debate at every level about what people are doing and the effect it is having.

Engagement was built on creating local ownership, getting officers to take ownership of their own patch and what happens on it. That comes from celebrating success. It comes from accepting things go wrong and crimes will be committed, but with the focus on stopping this continuing. The most important thing was officers needed to feel that they made a difference and that they did this by doing their best at what they were good at every day. That meant treating officers as individuals with individual strengths and skills and getting the team to use these strengths and skills to best advantage. It also meant not measuring everyone against a single standard. One final piece of engagement was capturing and exploiting ideas. John Spence's philosophy that "senior people aren't necessarily the brightest people in the organisation" held here too. Ideas can come from anywhere, and good ones need to be used. So, when the shift pattern was causing an issue, the response was to pass the problem to a team led by a couple of sergeants close to the problem to look at and suggest a better way of working. When the suggestions were implemented, this reinforced the belief that everyone can contribute.

Clearly, you need to trust your team and the leadership of that team, but occasionally you need to verify. Mick Stamper talked about being invisibly intrusive; he knew what the figures were even if he didn't expect the local leadership to know every detail, so he could use insights from the figures to keep an eye on things and then support when needed. Seeing the figures is useful, but if performance is delivered through activity, you need to verify that your intended culture is supported by the management style. To do this Mick Stamper and Mark Evans, Mick's senior colleague, would regularly do a shift on the front line. As Mick Stamper put it, "If you are in a car together for eight hours people can't help but talk," and officers remembered that Mark Evans did the Christmas Eve nightshift in the centre of town, possibly the worst shift of the year. These activities engage front line officers whilst giving first-hand insights into how things are and what is and isn't working.

Taking the hierarchical format we had for the electrical distribution company case above, the different responsibilities can be captured as follows.

Superintendent level responsibilities and focus

- Create the culture
- Develop and nurture the management style
- Translate Chief Officers' intent to local context
- Set direction
- Report performance

Chief Inspector level responsibilities and focus

- Reinforce the culture
- Promote the management style
- Translate direction into priorities
- Oversee use of resources, reflect, and respond
- Oversee management of discipline
- Oversee performance

Inspector-level responsibilities and focus

- Focus on local priorities
- Coordinate use of resources between and across the divisions, sense, and respond
- Manage discipline
- Empower the teams
- Reflect on past performance, learn, and respond

Sergeants level responsibilities and focus

- Manage local activity
- Communicate priorities
- Motivate team

Constable-level responsibilities and focus

- Act to prevent crime, detect crime, and keep the public safe

This approach to governance, setting direction, delegating responsibility, and focusing on activity, was supported by a culture of trust and an engaging management style. The result was a significant reduction in crime, but importantly, this was at a time when the force satisfaction survey showed its highest score. The engagement piece was working too. You may recognise many elements in this example that relate to mission command, and we believe this is a good practical example of how mission command was operationalised to good effect.

Freedom vs chaos

There is a dilemma for leaders and managers in the current working environment, where customers and clients expect fast turn-around of action and where situations can change rapidly. Where once, as a driver, I may have been happy to send my query by post to the Driver and Vehicle Licensing Agency and wait for a few days or even weeks for a reply, I now expect an answer to my question almost immediately. As a result, we expect employees to act quickly. We want them to be flexible and adapt to situations as they occur so they can provide the service customers and clients expect. On the other hand, we do not want corners to be cut, we want people to follow correct processes and we expect the rules of good governance to be maintained. There is a tension between governance, control and setting standards and allowing employees the freedom to do what they see fit in the circumstances. This tension exists in many organisations whatever the size or sector. In larger organisations there can be pockets of what we will call the straitjacket culture, where no one wants to risk using their own initiative for fear of being blamed when something goes wrong, and pockets of laissez-faire culture where anything goes and there is little control or enforcing of standards. It depends to some extent on the individual leader. Some leaders believe they must exercise discipline or lose control. Others believe they can leave everything to their teams without oversight. The balance lies in between. There is much research to show that performance is better when people have control over their work and when they have freedom to make decisions and act in the interests of getting the right things done. But this is easy to say and more difficult to do. Managers are often too nervous to allow autonomy and to delegate decisions, preferring to rely on themselves rather than on others to do a good job. Employees are often nervous to use their own initiative for fear of getting something wrong.

In Chapter 2, we discussed how leaders can create an environment in which individuals feel able to exercise common sense and take responsibility for achieving an effective outcome. In this section we will look at the issue of freedom v chaos from an organisational standpoint.

The first requirement is to create an organisation-wide framework in which each employee understands their role and the contribution they make. The energy provider we cited in the case study earlier provides a good example of one mechanism for doing this. The process of creating success maps and measures, enabled each person to understand what the organisation's goals were, what their goals were and what success would look like. So, everyone understood *what* needed to be done, the purpose of doing it, and to what level it needed to be done.

Alongside this there should be a set of guidelines on *how* it should be done. The "*how*" should be encapsulated in the values of the organisation. Sometimes values are described as a code of conduct for employees, but they should be more than that. Values should be ingrained into the way each person works, rather than being set out in a rule book that everyone is asked to refer to when necessary. As you would expect, values will include factors such as impartiality, objectivity, honesty, and so on as set out in the UK's Civil Service code, but each person needs to understand what these values mean for them in the context of their own situation. The organisation's values should throw a light on the way individuals are expected to behave and conduct their work.

When the *what* and the *how* are clearly established they must be communicated so key stakeholders understand what the organisation is about, what it is there for and the values governing its operation. This is important because *how* stakeholders understand your organisation will affect *what* they expect of it. Let us take an example from outside the public sector. On its website, The John Lewis partnership includes a statement about how its partners (all those working in the company) will operate:

Do Right: we act with integrity and use our judgement to do the right thing.

All or nothing: we put everything we have into everything we do.

Give more than you take: we put more in, so everyone gets more out.

Be yourself. Always: we're quirky, proud, and at our best when we are free to be ourselves.

We not me: when we work together anything is possible.

Whilst some of these statements may not sit well with public sector organisations (members of the public may worry if those working in prisons set out to be quirky), they do create a picture of how people working in John Lewis conduct themselves. As a customer, when I see these statements, I have certain expectations of how I will be treated. Let us take a hypothetical example. If someone on the customer help line were to tell me that "the computer would not allow them to do *x* to solve my issue," I would expect that person to find a way around the problem. If enough customers have the same expectation, then staff on the helpline should know very well what they are expected to do. What we are saying here is that when you set out values for how work will be conducted and when you communicate them to stakeholders, you build expectations amongst people using the services you provide and that in turn reinforces values to staff. It is inside out: you should be discussing the values with your staff and what that means for the way they do their jobs and outside in: if you do communicate then people outside the organisation will treat you accordingly. There are two points to note here: if you communicate values to stakeholders you need to ensure that your staff adhere to them.

So, the pillars of your framework are ensuring all employees know what their goals and roles are and those of the organisation as a whole; ensuring everyone knows *how* work should be conducted and enabling key stakeholders to understand what your organisation is there to do and what they can expect from you (and what they can't).

In his HBR article, "Structure that's not Stifling," Professor Ranjay Gulati (2018) gives the example of Alaska Airlines to show how a coherent framework for enabling independent decision-making can support and enrich freedom despite an organisation operating in a regulated environment.

Alaska Airlines was a small company that differentiated itself from competitors by providing excellent customer service. Employees were told to do "whatever it takes" to maintain a happy and loyal customer base. The problem was that this policy was so customer focussed there were no boundaries and some employees believed they had carte blanche to do anything to make passengers happy. Alas in January 2000, there was an accident killing 88 people aboard. The ethos of caring for customers came to the fore when employees did everything they could to support families of the victims. However, after this accident, the culture began to change. Quite understandably, safety became paramount, and more maintenance workers were recruited. In the wake of the 2011 terrorist attacks, security also became an issue. As the world became ever more uncertain, more discipline was enforced, as often happens in such situations, and this removed employees' autonomy on decision-making. They became unwilling to exercise any judgement in case they got it wrong. Standards of customer service slipped as frontline workers were using less discretion to solve problems and turned their focus, instead to ensuring on-time performance was maintained. Competitors started to gain ground. When feedback from front-line workers showed that bureaucracy was "tying their hands and creating frustration," the airline decided something should be done to remedy the situation. They devised a process

206 ■ *Approaches for making it happen*

by which employees could make independent decisions but, this time, within certain limits. Taking their cue from the Disney Institute's Four Keys, they defined four standards of service: safety, caring, delivery, and presentation. Each standard was ranked by priority with safety being the most important and within each standard there were guidelines for attitudes and behaviours. So, for example, it was no longer acceptable to allow a passenger to delay a flight so they could return to the terminal to collect a forgotten item and then provide other passengers with gifts to make up for the delay. On the other hand, staff could use their discretion about waiving a fee, if, for example, a passenger had to rearrange a flight as a result of injury. An extensive training programme was devised to support staff and help them feel more comfortable in exercising judgement, and managers were given guidance on how to handle the situation if employees were a little too generous. It was important that no-one would feel they were being punished for their decisions, otherwise staff would slip back into not wanting to take responsibility in case they got it wrong. So far this appears to have worked and customer service standards rose with the airline gaining J.D. Power's highest customer service ranking among traditional airlines.

Creating a framework and providing training is not the end of the story, though. It is important that any framework is maintained and kept uppermost in peoples' minds. There must be constant reinforcement of the ideas and of the types of behaviour you want to see, and any new recruits must be immersed in the values of the organisation and its purpose and goals. This is not a one-way process as creating an effective organisation is a joint enterprise between everyone in that organisation, so consulting and listening to employees on how ways of working are going is also an integral part of the process.

References

Bourne, M., Franco-Santos, M., Andrey Pavlov, P. & Lucianetti, L. (2007) *The impact of the investors in people standard on people management practices and firm performance*, Cranfield School of Management report, Cranfield, UK.

Bourne, M. & Parr, M. (2019) Developing the practice of governance, Association for Project Management Risborogh, Bucks, UK. developing-the-practice-of-governance-report_web1.pdf (apm.org.uk)

Gulati, R. (2018) "Structure that is not stifling," *Harvard Business Review*, May–June.

Kelly, É. V. (2010) *Governance rules! The principles of effective project governance*. https://www.pmi.org/learning/library/project-governance-principles-corporate-perspective-6528

Lewin, K., (1951) *Field theory in social science*, Harper, New York.

Martinez, V. and Kennerley, M. (2005) "Impact of performance management reviews: evidence from an energy supplier," *Conference Proceedings EUROMA, operations and global competitiveness*, Budapest, Hungry, June 19–22.

Part 3

Bringing it all together

In Part 1, we talked about creating the environment which is conducive for change and discussed the challenges and leadership aspects of being effective. In Part 2, we focussed on approaches to making this happen, discussing structures and tangible tolls to help you work through planning and managing change, measuring and managing performance, and creating a governance structure. In this final section, we are going to bring this together and reflect on what we have learnt from the people we interviewed in the process of writing this book.

DOI: 10.4324/9781003099895-18

Chapter 15

Four pillars of effectiveness

In the first section, we set out the reasons why we believe effectiveness is so important and highlighted the pressures that make it so hard to achieve. A large part of the solution lies in managing expectations away from the focus on short term results and the measuring of outputs and towards the realisation of outcomes and the longer-term benefits. This requires a major change in how people think and work and also in how they perceive and measure success. We then moved on to look at how you create an environment for change, concentrating on leadership, communication and thinking effectively, using intuition and evidence.

In the second section, we explained approaches for making it happen. Some of these are, in a sense, structural. Expanding your capacity through partnerships, for example, enables your organisation to become more effective by linking with others which have complementary expertise. Other approaches, such as stakeholder analysis and creating the capability for change are more about how you relate and work smoothly with others to progress new ideas. We have devoted a large part of the "making it happen" section to measuring performance because this contributes towards effectiveness in several ways – through motivating people, communicating direction, creating clarity, and providing information from which to learn, to name just a few. On the other hand, if you measure and reward performance in the wrong way you can do a great deal of harm, so it is very important to get it right. We then moved on to discuss governance, how you create a framework, and set of processes for how the organisation is run; a framework that is robust but flexible enough to avoid the mire of bureaucracy. Finally, we touched on the thorny issue of how you allow people freedom to act without causing chaos.

In this section we want to bring these ideas together, combining them into what we will call pillars that support the effectiveness of your organisation (see Figure 15.1). Bringing together factors for success into pillars provides a picture of what you need to create in order to build and maintain effectiveness. You must ensure you have strength

DOI: 10.4324/9781003099895-19

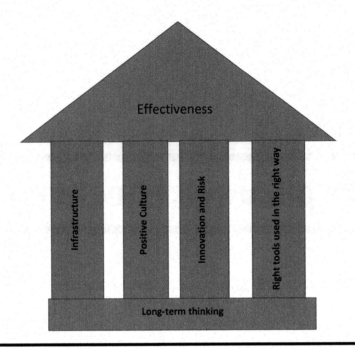

Figure 15.1 The four pillars of effectiveness.

in each of these pillars. You may have good IT systems, but they won't help you solve all your problems. Having a positive culture is excellent but is not sufficient in itself to make an organisation effective. If you have a weak infrastructure, for example, your positive culture will help paper over the cracks for a short time, but it will be unsustainable in the longer term. You also need to ensure that your pillars have a firm foundation. We've called the foundation long term thinking.

Let us have a look at what is contained in each of the pillars.

Pillar one: infrastructure

In this context, the infrastructure of the organisation is its fabric, the tangible assets such as people, IT and information systems, processes, and also capability and structures that add value such as partnerships. We have said on a number of occasions that you must have sufficient resources to be effective, but it is not only the quality and quantity of those resources, it is also a matter of having the right resources in the right place at the right time and ensuring they work well together.

It is not unusual for resources to be made available only when there is a crisis or to change processes immediately in response to an adverse event. Neither situation is a good one because there is insufficient time to consider what you really need and you can end up with infrastructure (whether that is people, processes, or partnerships) that tides you over a difficult period but does not fit well with lon-ger term plans. Whilst there will always be unexpected events that necessitate rapid changes to processes or resources, it is better to plan and to look well ahead so you can plot a path to your destination. If you are able to do that, it gives you time to see how your plans are working and make adjustments as you go along.

How can you enable that to happen? The first step is to encourage everyone to think about infrastructure as a whole – not just IT requirements which sometimes happens. Nothing exists in isolation. If you change a system or a process, like a chain reaction, it will have a knock-on effect somewhere else. If you decide not to replace staff in one department, then the effects may spill over into another area. So, it is important to think across functions and across the organisation as a whole.

The second point is to focus on future requirements and to keep the future in mind when making decisions about resources, even if it may at first not appear to be the most efficient approach. When Adnams, producers of beers and spirits, devel-oped their new distribution centre back in 2008, they did not take the less expensive traditional approach. The company decided this was an opportunity to put into practice its values of making great products without costing the earth, so they chose to create a sedum roof. Sedum is a thick and fleshy plant which not only looks good but also has a number of environmental benefits as it keeps the building warm in winter and cool in summer, reducing the need for power. It also helps to filter out pollutants from the air. Adnams decided to go further, and they harvest the excess rainwater from the roof and use it to wash their lorries. It was not only the roof that was special and different. The company decided to construct the walls from locally grown hemp, lime, and chalk. Bricks made from those materials are more energy-efficient to manufacture and help to regulate internal temperature, but they hadn't been produced on such a large scale before, so Adnams had to invest in machinery to make enough of them for their building. At the time, the decision to have a sedum roof and use hemp, lime, and chalk blocks for walls was a brave one, and many a finance director would presumably have vetoed an idea that appeared rather quirky and was likely to be more expensive at the outset. However, looking to the future it was clear that energy costs would be rising and that there would be ever-increasing pressures for companies to reduce their reliance on fossil fuels. That knowledge com-bined with the fact the approach fitted well with the company's sustainability cre-dentials gave them confidence to go ahead. The decision paid off (literally) as energy costs rose substantially in the following years. This was not the only benefit. The company received recognition and awards for their sustainable approach, and this raised their profile and their credentials as an attractive employer.

Resourcing for the future is not only about the structural assets such as build-ings, it is also about people. In the section about Changing the Thinking we talked about the importance of following through a line of questioning to a point where you have enough answers on which to base your actions. If you have decided you will include the introduction of a new automated service as part of your strategy for the next five years, you will, no doubt, think about the technology you will need to make it happen. You will also think about the people needed to operate and maintain that technology and the training that will be required for those whose work will be changed by the automated system. But it is worth broadening out that thinking. Will it be possible for some of those people to work from home? What will be the effect on the people using the new automated system? Are there likely to be any unforeseen consequences? Can the system be used or adapted for anything else? How confident are you in your estimations? What we are saying here is, think about the resources you will need to be effective in the future, do it in a logical and focussed way but not in such a narrow and linear way that you miss an issue or consequence lurking on the perimeter that will affect your successful outcome – or indeed an opportunity that could boost the chances of success. Joe Badaracco, the John Shad Professor of Business Ethics at Harvard Business School quotes the mantra: "Work the problem as a manager and resolve it as a human being."

Have you ever been faced with the situation where you know you need additional – or perhaps different – resources to achieve an aim but also know that the process of acquiring those resources will be very protracted and time consuming? Faced with that situation many people are deterred from seeking what they really need and instead, find a way around that will achieve a result but not the best or most sustainable result. The process of acquiring new resources must be robust. It is important that there is value for money (and we mean by that value over the lifetime of the resource, not the lowest cost). There must also be good evidence that an asset is actually needed. However, if the process is too rigid and too bureaucratic it will hinder rather than help. There must, of course, be a transparent evaluation of whether a resource is needed and that should include consideration of how it fits with future plans; but if those looking for resources are always met with the answer: "no, unless you can make a superhuman argument to the contrary," they will be unwilling to put forward cases that may in fact be good ones. When people come to ask for additional resource or propose changes to existing resources, they should at least have a fair hearing,

We are not making the argument that you should always accede to requests for additional resources but there is a balance between focussing peoples' minds on what they really need and starving them of resources. In organisations where you can have whatever you want there is often less resourcefulness, people are not forced to find innovative ways of getting things done. We have seen organisations where more and more people are recruited, adding so many layers of hierarchy that the real purpose of certain roles is unclear. On the other hand, there are other organisations where adding a relatively small amount of resource would make a huge difference to their success. There is a third type of organisation in which some parts are over-resourced, usually because the leaders in that area are very vocal and powerful, whereas other parts need more. The answer is that you need a truly objective way of evaluating what is needed without that process being over-bureaucratic.

Resource is not only about volume, you also need the right type of resource. There are various ways of bringing in the right type of resource. We have already discussed partnerships in Chapter 5, where linking with other organisations who have complementary experience and skills expands your capability, but it's important also to consider the balance between using internal and external resources. Using external contractors and consultants can help to tide you over a short-term problem. They can also bring in specialist expertise that is needed for a specific task and, because they are not from within the organisation they should, in theory at least, be independent and free from any baggage. The downside is that they may not fully understand the values of the organisation or what "makes it tick" and if they are overused, you may be undermining your permanent workforce and failing to build capacity and therefore, longer term resilience.

Effective organisations tend to be those that are agile. They are able to be proactive, to see what is likely to be coming their way and to respond quickly. This is just as important in the public sector as it is elsewhere. Public-sector organisations must respond to changes in society and to changing values. They must be able to respond to advances in science and technology and to changes in the environment in which their citizens live. But agile does not mean without firm foundation. Having a cadre of highly capable staff forms part of that foundation. One of the key factors that differentiates an agile organisation is the ability of those people to work well together across functional divides, and the ability of leaders to create a picture of what needs to be done whilst allowing people freedom to do it in the way they see fit. We have already described ways of doing this. Sometimes people associate agile with being tight on resources, lean and mean, but this is not the case. To be agile you must have enough time away from the day-to-day operations to be able to look to the future. You must also have spare resource to enable change to happen. A great deal of focus in the public sector is on efficiency which is about resource being fully used all the time but that is not conducive to being able to see what is coming and adapt accordingly.

There is one last point we would like to make here and that is you must review your resources regularly. You need to know that what you have in place is still fit for purpose and able to be adapted for what is yet to come.

Pillar two: culture

Culture permeates throughout an organisation, affecting every part of it, from the people who are selected to work in it, to the decisions that are made and the way in which people relate to each other. With the right culture there is less friction enabling work to progress more smoothly, there are free flows of communication and there is enthusiasm and motivation for everyone to do their best. Of course, things will go wrong because they always do, but with the right culture the organisation will be more resilient and able to cope with setbacks and not only that, it will also be an attractive place to work. It is important then that you encourage a positive culture and one that reflects the type of organisation you want to create.

We tend to talk about culture as if it is a solid and tangible object and in a sense it is tangible. When you walk into an organisation you can get a feel for how things are. We recently visited a building site and observed that all the materials were tidily stacked, the floors were frequently being swept to keep the building clean and the builders all smiled when you met them. They were focussing on what they were doing and talking to each other about their work. They were not working on anything grand like a smart new office block or conference centre, they were in the process of renovating an old house, but they gave every indication of being interested in what they were doing, and they appeared to be enjoying their work. So, culture is tangible, but it is not one solid lump, it is made up of many small elements.

Those who study organisational culture point to a small number of key elements that are present in organisations which have a positive culture. They are:

Vision: this means a clear picture of purpose and destination, where everyone inside the organisation and key outside stakeholders understand what the organisation is there to do and what their role is.

Values: these are the guidelines for how work is conducted. Some people think of the values as the moral compass of the organisation. Values will, for example, set expectations on how you will be treated as an employee or customer or supplier. Some values, such as honesty, will be common to all organisations (one would hope) but there will be differences according to the nature of the work.

Effective teamwork: this comes partly as a result of the vision and values – people motivated to work together to achieve a common aim.

Good communication flows: if there is a free flow of communication where everyone feels able to express their opinion without fear of being judged, you will create an environment where more ideas will be shared, and you will also ensure that grievances and little annoyances come to the surface and can be dealt with before they become too serious.

Practice: it is all well and good stating what your vision and values are but unless they are seen to be practised, no one will take any notice. If senior managers belittle people when they bring forward ideas that are, perhaps, a little flaky, other people will not feel able to bring forward better proposals and good ideas will be lost.

As we said in Chapter 2, culture does not suddenly appear, it takes a long time to develop and as it grows it is constantly being reinforced by peoples' actions and behaviour. Once bad habits develop (such as failing to share information, for example), more and more people see that it is all right to behave in that way and over time it becomes the norm. Culture is not changed by changing the structure of an organisation, but it can be changed with good, strong leadership and with the implementation of systems and processes that align with the culture.

We won't repeat what we said in the leadership chapter. Suffice it to say that if leaders are perceived to be trustworthy and capable and working in the interests of employees and stakeholders then the chances of success in effecting culture change are reasonable. We would go further than this. Perception is important, but leaders must actually be trustworthy, capable, and working in the interests of employees and stakeholders. Words are not enough. They may work at the beginning to rouse and enthuse the troops, but people will eventually see what is really happening if actions are not consistent with words. Leaders must exemplify the behaviour they want to see in their organisations.

The second element concerns developing and implementing systems and processes that align with the culture. Processes are sometimes not changed when the environment in which they operate changes, and such "legacy" processes can act like blockages. To take an example of this: under an earlier management system, individuals may have had to get approval for a certain course of action. With the advent of new technology those individuals now have more information at their disposal, making the decision about that type of action a much easier one. However, if the old regime of seeking approval is still in place, it will cause an unnecessary delay and will detract from a culture in which people are trusted to do their jobs. In fact, just this one small glitch will make some people less likely to use their initiative on other matters, too, because they perceive they are not trusted to make what is now a relatively small decision.

Introducing new working practices can reinforce culture and values. Bringing people in different parts of the organisation together so they understand how others work is often effective in diminishing the silo mentality. Creating cross-functional teams to come up with solutions for specific problems is another way of helping to cement relationships and promoting the idea of teamwork. But, to be accepted, these working practices must not be seen as a burden to individuals. We know of one organisation where individuals were urged very strongly to become involved in voluntary work and were allowed time off work to undertake their chosen activities and then report back in the corporate newsletter on what they had done. At first sight this may seem to be an excellent initiative that reinforced the company's values of supporting the community. In some parts of the organisation it did, indeed, go down well. In others it caused discontent. The difference was that some parts of the organisation were better resourced than others and individuals had more time to spare. In other departments, there was too much pressure of work and people who had a couple of days away to support a local charity returned to a mountain of work. In this particular case there was dissonance between the values of supporting the community and caring for the individual employee.

Performance measurement systems are directly linked to organisational culture. They can either be seen as positive or negative because, as we frequently hear, "what gets measured gets done."

If you focus only on the achievement of goals without paying attention to how those goals were reached you may be undermining your organisation's values and culture. It is a tricky balance. In the earlier chapters, we discussed the pressure people face to set goals and publish whether they have been reached or not. It appears to be a black and white situation: if the goals have been reached all is well, if they have not been reached, all is wrong. In reality there is no (or very little) black and white, only shades of grey. In achieving your goals, you may, to use another oft repeated phrase: "Hit the target but miss the point." Goals and targets are important in motivating people and in putting a spotlight on areas which need resource, but they must be treated with care. The problem is, how do you persuade stakeholders that not achieving a goal may actually still reflect a good performance?

There is no instant fix to this problem because many stakeholders are used to seeing hard and fast targets. It is a matter of influencing people and demonstrating to them that it is safe to take a pragmatic approach. Influencing senior people to see that focussing on achieving a target may actually be drawing attention away from overall long-term effectiveness is a first step. Suddenly removing all targets is unlikely to work, but gradually changing the focus so that targets are seen as indicators rather than ends in themselves will set the course for changing expectations.

Culture is formed by interactions between people, so recruiting appropriate people is essential. Rather like "legacy" processes, recruiters sometimes get into the habit of recruiting the same types of people. If you want the organisation to move on, to be more innovative and less risk averse, for example, always recruiting people who are safe and process driven, will not work. You have to be careful though because suddenly catapulting people who are very different into the workforce can be counterproductive. There should be some type of fit with the organisation, at least a sharing of the organisation's values, or the new people will leave or cause too much disruption making it harder to effect any change in the future. The ideal is to encourage diversity of views but a sharing of values.

In articles about culture change there is often mention of the importance of "place", that is physical setting. Trying to promote a culture of openness and approachability in an ancient office building that has long corridors flanked by closed doors is not easy, but neither is finding the resources to move or adapt your office building. However, if you are aware of the effect of the working environment on people's behaviour you can take steps to mitigate the negative effects. In the example above you could encourage office-sharing and keeping the doors open. You could create open areas for meeting up and sharing of ideas over a cup of coffee.

Physical symbols do matter, though. In an earlier chapter, we highlighted the example of an organisation where new, smart uniforms signalled the beginning of a new era where each person was given more responsibility and expected to act in a more professional way.

So, culture change is not an exact science but there are guidelines for achieving it. Firstly, you need to understand what the prevailing culture is. That understanding comes not from written documents but from listening and talking to people over a period of time and from observing what is actually happening. You will need to determine what must change. Where are you moving to? What will look different? How will people behave differently? How will you know change is taking place? The next step is to look at systems and processes and determine to what extent they should be changed or adapted. Do they support new ways of working or will they present barriers? Perhaps the most difficult step is to persuade people – stakeholders and employees – that change is required. You will need to ensure you have some strong supporters and sponsors of your case for change and we have suggested various approaches and tools to help you think through how this can be done. Like any change, culture change is a journey, and you must be able to bring the majority of people along with you and if some key people are proving to be too resistant or disruptive then you must find ways of moving them elsewhere. Once you reach your destination, which may take some time, you need to ensure the changes stick and that people do not fall back into their old ways of working.

How do you know when things are not right? Sir Bernard Jenkin gave us a very insightful description of a failing organisation as one in which:

■ Most people know something is wrong but they won't say,
■ Lots of meetings are taking place and agreement is reached but people come out of the meeting saying something else, and
■ People at the top are the last to know something is wrong.

If you detect any of these indicators, it is time to act.

Pillar three: innovation and risk

Innovation is the way you improve things. To innovate you need to change what you are doing or what you are creating, or possibly both. So, innovation is not having the idea, it is implementing it. We are making this point because most people think that those who come up with the ideas are the innovators. We argue that the real innovators are those who implement the change. Under this pillar, we will start by describing the different types of innovation before going on to discuss the different levels of risk associate with each type. We will close this section by suggesting ways you should think about the innovations you are making and the risks involved.

Types of innovation

There are two typologies often used to classify types of innovation. The first typology classifies innovation by the focus of the change. The three types are often referred to as product innovation, process innovation and business model innovation. The second typology classifies innovation by the type of change. These two types are often referred to as incremental innovation and radical innovation.

In everyday life we see product innovation all around us. There are new smart phones, new car models, new fashions in clothing and even new pre-prepared meals. The public sector does product innovation as well. It could be argued that putting vehicle licencing on-line was a product innovation. But, the public sector isn't really a producer, so in the main, the focus is on process innovation and business model innovation.

Process innovations are often not visible to the customer. Changing the order processing system may make the delivery of orders easier, but if the customer is dealing with a call centre, this process innovation may be invisible. However, process innovation often improves the service to the customer. Implementing a new GPs consultation scheduling system may improve the use of GPs' time; putting the booking system on-line so patients can access it directly will be seen by many as a service improvement.

Business model innovation is sometimes referred to as the way organisations create and capture value and this definition works well for the private sector. In the public sector, business model innovation happens too and this occurs when the whole way things are delivered changes. To illustrate this we will start by giving you two private sector examples. Ryanair's entry into the short haul aviation market was a real business model innovation. The previous model was that passengers paid to get from A to B. Ryanair's innovation was getting the local destination to cover some of these costs, so instead of the passenger paying for everything, Ryanair was supported by local authorities in bringing in passengers to a destination which boosted the local economy. Mike remembers attending a presentation by Block Buster Movies who talked about their business model innovation. This was based on their analytics of what customers hiring their videos wanted and they didn't want to write about this innovation at the time – they saw it as a competitive advantage. But it wasn't long before a more significant business model innovation occurred with films being downloaded from the web thus changing the whole way movies were delivered to customers. Now, let us turn to how the public sector does business model innovation. The privatisation of energy in the United Kingdom was a fundamental change to the business model. So was the privatisation of the railways (although this business model may well be about to change again). The more recent NHS funding reforms, putting senior doctors in charge of local budgets, is business model innovation too. These innovations fundamentally change how products and services are funded, forcing change to the way the products and services are delivered.

Now let us consider incremental and radical innovation. Incremental innovation is the gradual but continuous development of the way things are done and delivered. This type of innovation starts with the existing product or service and looks at ways this can be improved. In the private sector, Japanese car makers have been seen as being very good at this. They take a car and continuously improve it to make it more reliable and take out cost. In the public sector, organisations should be doing this too. Improving library services to move from lending books to acting as gateways to accessing knowledge would also be an incremental innovation. We will take another example, public housing. Here is an example of incremental innovation in the way the maintenance is delivered. Initially there would have been a maintenance person for every job. However, analysis revealed that this was wasteful as the person sent did not have the right skills to fix every problem. To remedy this issue, the work was split between initial assessment and the ensuing repair using different people for each activity. This improved efficiency in terms of the use of peoples' time, but could delay the repair as the assessor would have to report back and get approval before the work could be scheduled. A further incremental improvement was introduced by giving the assessor an Ipad and using this to communicate with head office whilst on site, speeding up approval for the repairs. The device could also be used to capture the specific requirements before the assessor left the premises. The next incremental change involved automatic scheduling of the maintenance visit once the systems were sufficiently integrated. These examples highlight the key elements of incremental innovation; starting with the existing process, thinking about improvements, implementing them and then going round this cycle again.

Radical innovation is very different. Radical innovation doesn't start from the existing process, it starts from the problem to be solved or the service outcome to be delivered. Improvements in film processing for many years was driven by incremental innovation. Digital photography was a radical innovation. Japanese improvements in car design and manufacture were in the main incremental innovations, whereas electric cars are a radical innovation. The public sector does radical innovation too. Moving paper-based tax returns on-line was a radical innovation. More recently putting other public services on line such as vehicle tax and passport renewal are radical innovations. One could argue that Universal Credit is a radical innovation too.

Innovation and risk

In the last section, we discussed the different types of innovation. Let us now turn our attention to the risks associated with each type of innovation.

Taking our first typology, product and process innovations are lower risk than business model innovation. This is typically the case as product and process innovations are more tightly bounded, whereas business model innovation usually requires innovation across all three typologies.

Taking our second typology, incremental innovation has the lower risk. In each change, you are taking part of an existing process and improving it. This is based on existing knowledge and if carefully managed has very little associated risk. In reality, if the change does go wrong, you can simply reverse it. So incremental innovation may move you forward, but because this is done in a step-by-step manner, it is a relatively slow way of improvement.

Radical innovation is a far higher risk, because you have to create a completely new process. This could be using existing technology, which will contain aspects of risk, but this may involve using a new technology, or using an existing technology in a different way. Radical innovation often changes the way you interact with your customer; this too increases the risks as, until the change is implemented, you wouldn't be certain how your customer would react.

We are making these points here because in selecting how you improve something, you should not only be considering the outcomes and benefits you want to achieve, but the time it will take to deliver them and the risks involved. It is very important to engage with your stakeholders so they understand both the approach you are taking and the risks involved. Flesh out the alternative approaches to innovation and present them in terms of timescale, certainty of outcome along with potential advantages and disadvantages. This will help you to establish the risk appetite of your stakeholders and will help you to manage expectations.

Ask yourself the following questions before you make a decision:

- What is the real outcome and benefit I am trying to achieve?
- How quickly does this need to be delivered?
- Does this lead me towards incremental or radical innovation?
- What are my options for implementing the change?
- What are the risks associated with each option?
- How can I reduce these risks?
- What risks remain?

Risk increases as you move from:

- Product or service innovation to business model innovation,
- Incremental innovation to radical innovation,
- Local or small change to national or large-scale change,
- Using existing technology to using existing technology in a new setting,
- Using existing technology to using a new but tried-and-tested technology,
- Using existing technology to using a new but untried technology, or
- Simple change (few stakeholders) to complex change (multiple and dispersed stakeholders).

When you assess your change, if you are tending to the right-hand side of the list above, it should give you pause for thought.

Whose risk is it anyway?

An innovation versus risk discussion isn't easy. This is true of both the public and private sectors. Politicians and senior staff often want certainty and it rarely exists. Just because this discussion doesn't happen, it doesn't mean the risks aren't there. The question is "who is left holding the can at the end of the day?"

Politicians and senior staff are always in the firing line. They are responsible and will often be held to account if a change doesn't deliver the expected benefits. Junior staff may be complicit as they may not have brought all the risks to the attention of senior sponsors. They are much closer to what is going on and often more knowledgeable.

There have been several attempts to pass the risk to the private sector too. Sometimes, they can be blamed and used as a scapegoat. But this is all about managing perceptions rather than about being effective. The private sector will charge you for taking on this risk and Figure 15.2 shows how risk sharing and cost relate. So you will need to ask yourself, what is the most effective way to share risk? Should you pass this across, but pay for the private sector to take on the risk? Or can you find alternative mechanisms where you (the public sector) shoulder far more of the risk allowing your suppliers to be able to make clearer evaluations and so offer keener prices?

One last set of comments on "whose risk is it?" Government and other parts of the public sector have to partner with the private sector to implement many of the innovations, changes, and improvements they need to make. We are emphasising the word "partnership" here as it is government delivery policy to work in partnership. When things become impossible, the private sector partner may have the option of handing the contract back, or in extreme circumstance, go out of business. So, the public sector always takes the ultimate risk. However the contract is constructed, this is the reality of the situation.

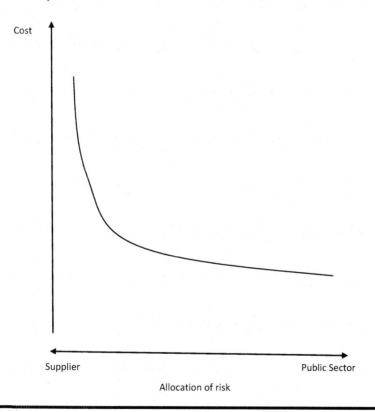

Figure 15.2 Allocation of risks between parties and the associated costs.

When Mike was introduced as the Director of The Government's Project Leadership programme to Sir John Manzoni (who was Chief Executive of the Civil Service at the time), the first question John Manzoni asked was "does this contract work for you too?" If you are working in partnership, this is probably the most important question to ask.

Conclusion

To be truly effective you will need to understand not only what you are trying to deliver, but the risks involved too. You need to have a reasoned conversation about these risks because they exist whether you like it or not. Being wise after the event can often be avoided if you can be honest and open about what you are doing.

Some tactics you should think about using:

■ Be open about the uncertainty and risk you face – don't minimise them.
■ Talk about ranges of delivery dates not absolutes.
■ Talk about ranges of costs in the same way.
■ Talk about ranges of benefits too.
■ Don't let politicians, senior staff, or journalists deflect you from taking this approach.

Finally, if you find someone responding to you by using the tactics we have outlined above, then perhaps you need to engage with them rather than pushing them to be more certain than they are. You may just be starting a genuine conversation about innovation and risk and it will be in both your interests to do that.

Pillar four: right tools used in the right way

It may seem like a side issue to include a pillar that focusses on using the right tools in a book about effectiveness that discusses major overarching concepts. However, tools are critical because they guide your thinking. Your thinking (and therefore the end result) will depend on which tools you have used. There is a very apt quotation from psychologist Abraham Maslow, which he adapted from philosopher, Abraham Kaplan, "To the man who only has a hammer, anything he encounters begins to look like a nail." If you use a very strict and formal approach to setting targets, for example, you will drive certain behaviours, and outcomes will be different from those which you would achieve by using a different approach. The tools you choose to use and the information you gain from using them form the basis for planning and decision-making and ultimately affect the way in which the organisation is directed. So, it is important you select the right tools, deploy them at the right time and in the right way.

In Part 2, we focused discussion on two sets of tools, firstly, those used for planning and managing change and secondly, tools for measuring and managing performance. In this section we are going to help you think more broadly about all the tools and approaches you use, but with particular reference to performance and change.

Change tools

We will start with the change tools. The tools you select will guide your analysis and this analysis will strongly influence your decision making. When thinking about a change, identify the influencers and the people who will be affected by your change, both inside and outside the organisation. Reflect on the change journey and your capacity to deliver it in light of everything else that is going on. You should also think about dependences and priorities. If you do a thorough stakeholder analysis, it will help you understand both your external and your internal stakeholders. You then need to consider how these stakeholders are positioned with respect to your planned change and how you are going to engage them. Think of change as a journey and use the tools we have described to think about people who are embarking on that journey. Think about the destination and who will be involved in ensuring travellers reach that destination and consider how those taking the journey and those enabling it to happen, may react. In that way, you should be better placed to anticipate and understand peoples' reactions to what you are doing. You should also think about capacity to change, both in terms of the change team's capacity and capability to deliver, and also the recipients' ability to absorb the change you are implementing. Finally, if you understand how your intended change fits into wider priorities and any other initiatives it depends on, you should have some comfort that you are doing the right thing at the right time. Of course, this reflection may also reveal that this is not the right time because other initiatives and priorities don't align and if that is the case you must be prepared to put your ideas on hold until a better time, or to adapt them to the circumstances.

Tools can be used at different times and for different reasons. Major change initiatives tend to fall into four stages: upfront planning, business case approval, management review, and evaluation.

By upfront planning, we mean the early idea stage. This is usually a time when there is much excitement about a new idea and sometimes this enthusiasm needs to be tempered with a dose of realism, but not to the extent that you smother innovation and motivation. Stakeholder analysis tools, such as force field analysis help you to identify important issues at this stage.

Business case approval is a big step in any change initiative as it is the point at which significant resources are committed. Your use of tools should help you develop and present that business case and head off unfair or ill-considered challenges to your thinking. If you are in the position of the person approving the business case, you will want to see a thorough stakeholder analysis and a strong argument showing how the proposal will deliver the required outcomes. Theory of Change is a good tool to enable you to do this.

Management reviews are important, especially during longer projects. In practice, they often focus on project delivery and progress; issues such as how much money has been spent, adherence to schedule and technical aspects of delivery. But new issues can emerge at any stage of the change journey. After business case approval, these changes may be so significant that you must re-valuate. You evaluate primarily to ensure that you believe the time, effort, and resources being expended are still justified by the outcomes and benefits you expect to be delivered. If there is a significant change, for example, in circumstance, in political priorities, or even in resourcing or support, you may well find it beneficial to re-evaluate. This will confirm whether you should be continuing, pausing, and redirecting or even stopping the change. It is in no one's interest to continue with a change that is no longer needed or has minimal chance of delivering benefit.

Evaluation should be done at the end of each change initiative to enable you to reflect on what has happened and to learn from successes and mistakes. You often learn a great deal more from mistakes than from successful change initiatives, but to be able to do this you must create an environment in which people feel able to discuss freely what has taken place.

This brings us to discussion of using change tools in the right way. Who should you involve in thinking about your change? Who should be directly involved in using the change tools? We strongly recommend "workshopping" – if that is a real word. This means bringing together appropriate people to discuss and share information, using the tools, in a workshop environment. Ensure you create a cross disciplinary group because the different backgrounds will enable you to develop different insights. You should also involve line managers, senior sponsors, and key decision makers wherever possible. Senior people often claim that they are too busy to be involved, but in our experience, the more involved they are the more successful your change initiative will be. Workshops dilute power with expertise. We don't want to be too unkind but perhaps this is sometimes the real reason why many senior people don't want to become involved. They don't want to face the real decisions that need to be made.

One final point, the use of tools for decision-making in a workshop must be real. Mike can remember one organisation which ran a series of "world cafes" and other such events designed to engage relevant key stakeholders in discussion of future directions and changes. Nothing that came out of these discussions ever changed the direction of travel, or even influenced the implementation of changes, and it soon became obvious that this activity was nothing more than window dressing and was, in effect, wasting everyone's time. Those who had been involved were reluctant to become engaged in any activity of this type in the future. But there are other examples of explosive moments, when the depth of debate in the workshop brought discussion to an end and people had to take time out to reflect and think what they were really trying to do before resuming.

Performance tools

In many respects, the performance tools we discussed in Part 2 are similar in nature to the change tools. They fall into two distinct categories. These are performance design tools and performance review tools.

Performance design tools help you decide what the goals are and how they should be measured. These have many similarities with change tools as they take the form of frameworks to help you think and make design decisions. Performance review tools are present all the time, guiding, and influencing behaviour.

There are three key tools that support the design of measurement systems. The first is the balanced scorecard, with the emphasis on "balance." Balancing the different aspects of your organisational performance is important and you should think through what "balance" means for you, rather than accepting the four dimensions of a standard balanced scorecard. The second tool is the success mapping tool which helps you create a linked set of objectives and actions. It helps to highlight the resources needed to deliver the level of performance you require. The result of your success mapping exercise should be a plan on a page that will enable you to communicate effectively with the wider organisation. The third tool is the performance measure design template which allows you to capture the information you need to implement your measures or KPIs.

Performance review tools include those associated with the performance planning value chain. They help you organise information, so you are prepared and supported in your decision-making. Think about the questions you want to ask, the analytical tools you could use including Statistical Process Control and tools for root cause analysis. You should also consider how you will interpret this information and create meaning to guide your action.

Your design of goals, measures, and targets should be timed to reflect changes in what you are trying to deliver. If you are about to embark on a change initiative or are introducing a new policy or strategy, the changing of goals, measures, and targets communicates very clearly that there is a change of direction. It is important to make sure they do change, though, if they remain the same your organisation will be guided by an outdated control system.

Designing the measurement system to align with policy and strategy initiatives is important, but you also need to have a regular heartbeat of a performance review process. The pace of the heartbeat should differ for different levels in the organisation. For the front-line team, this may focus on weekly tasks and performance. For middle managers, a monthly review may be appropriate. For senior staff, it may be a quarterly oversight. The pace of the heartbeat needs to reflect the speed of your decision making. But it must be done in such a way that you can see the results of your interventions before you take further action. Hence our suggestions for different timings of the reviews at different levels of the organisation.

It is important how you use the performance reviews. A good success map and set of KPIs can be rendered virtually unusable if the review process is managed in the wrong way. Chapter 10 on the performance framework addresses this in detail but we will give a quick summary here. With the design tools (the balanced scorecard, the success map, and the performance measure design template) your focus should be on engaging effectively with the right people.

With the review tools (performance value planning chain, statistical process control, and root cause analytics) the focus should be on:

- Outcomes; everything else should be subordinate to that,
- The big picture, whilst understanding how everything else delivers the big picture,
- What matters not what is easy to measure,
- The longer term rather than focusing too much on the short term, fast moving indicators,
- The future, and what the measures tell you about the future, not the past,
- What needs to be achieved, rather than what makes people look good,
- Trends rather than RAG (red, amber, green) ratings,
- Trends rather than two-point data comparisons,
- What the data suggest is happening and the judgement calls you need to make,
- Whether the changes you planned have been completed, and
- Whether the changes that have been completed are having the effect you expected.

Using the performance tools to create a review that develops an engaged conversation and debate will help you move from data to considered action. Supposed "good news" travels fast, but what you really need your performance measurement system to do is to pick up bad news early. If you can do that you will have more time to react and recover. A blame culture and politics can get in the way of this happening, so you should be constantly reviewing the culture surrounding your measurement and management system.

They are only ever tools, people are in charge.

The foundation: changing the thinking

Each of the pillars described above is underpinned by thinking about the longer term, whether that is considering the future when you are acquiring and allocating resources, instilling a focus on achieving outcomes into your culture, looking ahead for innovations, and being prepared to accept some risk in the process because there is uncertainty, or looking at longer term results when measuring performance.

To be effective try to think long term although political processes do tend to militate against this. If you are a politician who wants to change things for the better (and most do) you must engage in longer term thinking.

You cannot get to the long term in one leap. So if you are only there for a while, try to set the direction and create foundations from which others can build in the future. Break down the project or initiative you are working on into smaller units so there are deliverables along the way but keep the focus on the longer-term outcomes. In that way, anything you do in your period of office or tenure will not be lost and will be available for others.

Wherever you are working, think about the future and what could happen politically, economically, technologically, and socially that could affect what you are trying to do. If you take those factors into account as you work towards the future you may be able to build platforms that are useful for multiple scenarios, not just for the plan you have in mind.

It takes a long time to wean people away from the security of poring over short-term results and making knee-jerk reactions in response, but it is necessary. It can only be done through an education process of all stakeholders, including the media. Soundbites always make better headlines than long-term success stories and it is difficult to communicate uncertainty without seeming to be too vague. But, when you are talking to stakeholders don't make things more certain than they really are. (In our experience, if you think something is certain it isn't!)

Chapter 16

Reflections

In this final chapter, we want to reflect on some of the key messages that emerged from our interviews and informal chats.

Starting on a positive note, all the people we spoke to were committed and enthusiastic about what they were doing and what they wanted to achieve, and this was true of politicians and employees.

Culture and associated systems and processes hold people back

People want to do a good job, but many of them feel they are hindered by hierarchical structures and a command-and-control culture and the systems and processes that are associated with them. In some areas, the concern that blame will be forthcoming if something goes wrong leads to the introduction of layers and layers of checks which can be time consuming and which add to bureaucracy. This is not the only problem. Concern about being blamed also means people are reluctant to take risks and this leads to frustration and inertia and a feeling that you have to look over your shoulder all the time.

Some of the people we spoke to felt vulnerable in pursuing people-centred approaches. One person put it like this: "It's so at odds with our cultural norms and all the messages that surround us...... And yet those companies that get it, and embrace it, like Apple, etc. are hailed as the ultimate businesses. Bizarre contradiction in my view." Others felt that the Covid crisis had enabled a loosening of some of the rules and that it gave a real impetus for cross-sector working and cutting through some of the hitherto restrictive bonds. The real test would be whether this new way of working would remain after the end of the crisis and several people reflected on

DOI: 10.4324/9781003099895-20

the need to learn from what had happened and to retain some of the new working practices.

Training and professional development is essential

We heard from and about good leaders, but also heard about the need for training and professional development and especially leadership development. This was true for MPs and elected representatives as well as for employees. No one can be expected to be fully competent in their role if they have insufficient induction and little training.

Individuals need to be able to gain experience. If people are never allowed to make a decision themselves, they never gain experience of how to do it and when they eventually have to make decisions, they lack the capability. People learn from their mistakes. If we either don't allow situations where mistakes can be made, or if they are covered up the learning doesn't happen.

The practice of moving people on too quickly is also unhelpful because individuals then do not see a change or initiative through to the final delivery. Expertise and experience should be valued and people should not always have to move for promotion or increases in pay.

Willingness to take advice and trust and respect others

One of the key attributes of a good leader is to know when to take advice and where to find it. This raises several points. There is a need, sometimes, to look outside the organisation to observe what works well. Some people noted how much they appreciated the sharing of best practice within local government, but others felt there was a need to cast the net wider. Linked to this is requirement to balance the type of people who work within an organisation. You need people who have technical training and those who are exceptionally bright (not that these two are mutually exclusive). You need people who are good leaders and you need people who understand processes and procedures. It is important to respect individuals for their particular knowledge and talents. An organisation can only be effective if it works as a whole unit from the most senior leaders to people working on the front line.

Policy makers and those who implement policy must work well together

Any divide between policy making and policy implementation is a fundamental barrier to effectiveness. There should be open discussion about the feasibility of implementation and individuals must feel free express their concerns. If an initiative is not working and shows no sign of being implementable then it should be stopped. An unimplementable policy is a waste of time.

Decentralise where you can and allow people to get on with it

The question of decentralising came out strongly in our discussions. There was a feeling (from central and local government) that there should be direction from the centre but freedom to act locally, because those closest to the issues were best placed to deal with them. This applied not only to local/central government but also within departments. The role of the leader is to set direction and guidelines and to ensure resources are in place. Beyond that, the leader should trust those doing the work to do it in the way they feel best.

Remove structures and processes that force short-term thinking and action

There are many examples of structures that force short-term action, from the way performance is measured (which we have described at length) to the way funding streams are structured. Whilst there are reasons for this – the pressures described in the first chapter – these structures and processes can detract from effectiveness. There should be more consideration of the consequences – and in particular the type of behaviour such processes and systems will encourage.

Encourage cross-departmental and cross-sector working

This was already beginning to happen and was widely welcomed. The focus should be on the job that has to be done and on the outcome rather than on the individual players, potential competition between them and how their performance is measured.

These ideas aren't new but by shining a spotlight on them and by providing some practical insights and tools, we hope to contribute in a small way to putting greater focus on effectiveness.